Flourishing Foodscapes
Designing City–Region Food Systems

DESIGNING CITY-REGION FOOD SYSTEMS

Johannes S.C. Wiskerke
& Saline Verhoeven

With contributions by
Jacques Abelman
Laura Bracalenti
Claire Callander
Joy Carey
Chloé Charreton
Maxim Cloarec
Nevin Cohen
Lola Domínguez García
Marielle Dubbeling
Anna Maria Fink
Antoine Fourrier
Pepijn Godefroy
Paul de Graaf
Floris Grondman
Karen de Groot
David Habets
Daniel Keech
Niké van Keulen
Kim Kool
Tim Kort
Jerryt Krombeen
Madeleine Maaskant
Minke Mulder
Ruut van Paridon
Matthew Reed
Cecilia Rocha
Lara Sibbing
Paul Swagemakers
Marieke Timmermans
Louise E.M. Vet
Mark van Vilsteren
Marc C.A. Wegerif

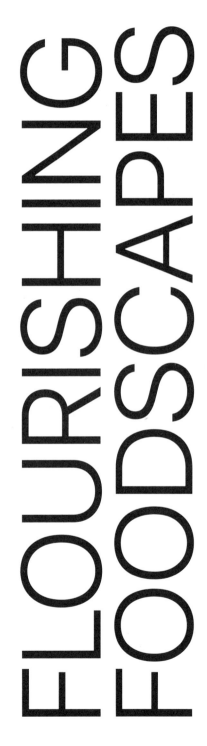

FLOURISHING FOODSCAPES

Academy of Architecture, Amsterdam
Valiz, Amsterdam

My family used to have a vegetable patch in an allotment garden in Amsterdam-Noord. The Dutch word for this type of vegetable garden is *moestuin*. We would grow lettuce, carrots, courgettes, and strawberries. Right next to the allotment was a McDonald's. The fast-food chain's logo, that big yellow M, towered above the surrounding buildings. For years, my children were under the illusion that it was the M of *Moestuin*. Each time we passed one of these poles while on holiday the children would cheer from the backseat of the car: look, a *moestuin*!

This memory came back to me when I saw the results of the Foodscapes research group, on which this book is based and which it elaborates. Headed by Han Wiskerke, the research group did its work at the Academy of Architecture Amsterdam from 2013 to 2016. Wiskerke and his researchers emphasized three themes in the research groups programme: the spatial changes in cities and the countryside and how these changes influenced each other, the social and economic relations within city regions, and the possibilities to develop more sustainable foodscapes at the regional level through design.

The book *Flourishing Foodscapes* reflects the outcome of this research programme. The researchers identified five design principles for foodscapes, dedicating a part to each one. Together, these parts constitute the core of this publication. In addition, a large number of case studies are presented (from Ede to Dar es Salaam and from Cairo to San Francisco) to which students of the Academy of Architecture have also contributed.

The major changes of today increasingly demand social involvement and an innovative attitude from designers in their role as analysts and advisers. More complex issues require designers who are capable of flexible thinking. Therefore, the Academy of Architecture decided to integrate research in its educational programme. Research-by-design is more and more becoming an essential step in looking for answers to the big questions, of which food provisioning most certainly is one. It is a method for developing perspectives for a world of growing complexity.

Flourishing Foodscapes demonstrates that food provisioning not only concerns the countryside but the city just as much. Many urban governments have come to realize this. In Amsterdam the number of initiatives in city gardening—from restaurants growing their own herbs to companies experimenting with hydroponic micro farming—can no longer be counted on the fingers of one hand. But this is only the beginning. What a wonderful world it would be when the McDonald's poles would no longer mark a fast food outlet, but a place where vegetables grow.

Madeleine Maaskant
Director Amsterdam Academy of Architecture

Johannes S.C. Wiskerke & Saline Verhoeven

INTRO-DUCTION

Farm shop De Buytenhof in Rhoon (NL), photo: Dirk Roep

From January 2013 to June 2016, we coordinated the Foodscapes research group at the Academy of Architecture of the Amsterdam University of the Arts. The Academy of Architecture funds and hosts temporary research groups to involve design students in research activities, to incorporate research findings in different teaching activities, and to focus on topical themes for spatial design. As the name of the research group suggests, our topical theme is food, and more specifically how our everyday social and physical environments (or landscapes) are shaped by food and at the same time shape food provisioning practices (i.e. food production, processing, distribution, retail, cooking, and eating). This book is the result of a variety of research and design activities that we carried out with students, spatial designers, and researchers, complemented with relevant contributions from other colleagues with whom we have collaborated during the years we coordinated the Foodscapes research group.

Why Food?

Food is an important theme for a number of reasons. The obvious one is of course that food is one of the basic necessities of life: we need to eat to survive. Furthermore, food plays an important part in our daily lives. We dedicate time to eating (alone or with others), to preparing our meals, and to buying food. In addition, many people are producing food for their own consumption; for some this is mainly a hobby, for others it is an additional supply to the food they buy, and for yet aother group it is the main source of nutrition. Also, many people are professionally involved in the production, processing, distribution, marketing, sales, cooking, and/or serving of food: e.g. farmers, cheesemakers, truck drivers, shopkeepers, cooks, and waiters.

There is, however, much more to food than the range of food provisioning activities from farm to fork. Food is also linked to many of the world's contemporary challenges, such as population growth, urbanization, climate change, health, energy, biodiversity, waste, and social inequality. Or as Carolyn Steel writes in the introduction of her book *Hungry City: How Food Shapes Our Lives*: 'Feeding cities takes a gargantuan effort; one that arguably has a greater social and physical impact on our lives and planet than anything else we do.' One example of this is the share of food in a population's ecological footprint. The latter refers to 'the total area of productive land and water required continuously to produce all the resources consumed and to assimilate all the wastes produced, by a defined population, wherever on Earth that land is located'.[1] The share of food varies roughly between 35 and 55%.[2] In the next chapter we will elaborate on the relation between food and contemporary global challenges.

Why Approach Food from a Combined Social Science and Spatial Design Perspective?

Exploring, analyzing, imagining and designing food practices, food systems and food environments can be done from different disciplinary perspectives and professional domains. For this book we have chosen to approach this by combining sociological research and spatial design. While the sociologist can explore, analyze and write about the social relations of food provisioning and about the places and people that are linked to one another through food provisioning practices, the spatial designer can, in addition to exploring and analyzing these relations spatially, also visualize them. Furthermore, the designer can also visualize other possible food practices and food environments by setting specific priorities and making explicit what the spatial consequences of different options are. An important one being spatial quality, something that seems to be largely missing in debates about the future of food.

As editors of this book and authors of this chapter (and several other ones) we represent these two disciplinary fields (rural sociology and landscape architecture) and professional domains (academic research and design) and we have both experienced the added value of this collaboration and interaction based on a shared interest in food and shared concern about contemporary and future food systems (see also next two pages).

1   W. Rees and M. Wackernagel, 'Urban Ecological Footprints: Why Cities Cannot be Sustainable—and Why They are a Key to Sustainability', *Environmental Impact Assessment Review* 16, no. 4 (1996), pp. 223–248.

2   T. Lang, 'Crisis? What crisis? The Normality of the Current Food Crisis', *Journal of Agrarian Change* 10, no. 1 (2010): pp. 87–97; R. Madlener and Y. Sunak, 'Impacts of Urbanization on Urban Structures and Energy Demand: What Can We Learn for Urban Energy Planning and Urbanization Management?', *Sustainable Cities and Society* 1, no. 1 (2011), pp. 45–53.

As for many people in the West food for me wasn't something that I thought about a lot. But learning from art projects, noticing all kinds of entrepreneurs opening food-related businesses, and travelling to Japan where I saw people take care of food as if it were a precious jewel, I realized that food and the production of it can touch people emotionally. Food can be beautiful. I wanted to learn how.

My father grew up on a small farm. We would often visit my grandfather and great-grandfather there, who were still running it. I loved picking the various berries and eating the tasteful cherries. But what I remember most is my great-grandfather in the hallway with a blue plastic can. Fresh milk straight from the cow, supposedly very healthy and us children had to drink it. It did not taste very nice, actually it was pretty awful, but the thought of it brings back good memories. Food can leave unforgettable impressions.

Travelling to the coast of East-Timor later in life, we were looking to buy some fish, but a market was nowhere to be found. When we asked around in the village, people invited us over. They went out onto the sea to catch some fish, fried it, and joined us for dinner. Meanwhile we enjoyed their garden with coffee plants and fruit trees. It looked like they grew just what they needed and had planted it in such a way that it provided shade and looked beautiful.

Being with a Dutch agricultural engineer who was teaching people about efficiency and intensifying yields I wondered, can we combine the two approaches? As a landscape architect I deal with the public realm all the time. What are people's motives to invest time, money, or energy in what the space looks like? How does culture influence our foodscape and what we eat? Although they lived close to the sea, still fish was hardly part of the regular diet of the people of East-Timor. How come?

I learned that we should use design skills to create sustainable, fair, and beautiful food systems, when months after I gave a talk in Japan about smart agriculture I was contacted by Murata Electronics—a multinational company and innovator in electronics—to provide input on new business opportunities in agriculture by provising sensoring and WiFi solutions. They work with big agricultural companies such as John Deere and talked to horticulture and glasshouse experts in the Netherlands. But when I got feedback afterwards they told me that especially my information and advice was valuable to them because it was something the other companies could not tell them. You think differently, is what they told me later.

It taught me that it is important not to talk about agriculture, but about food, people, and environment. Not just focus on yields, technology, and economics, but look at the whole picture. Use data and research to understand people's decisions based on personal opinions, cultural background, or business motivations to act. I hope this book will inspire people to do so.

Han's (Johannes') Interest in Food and Spatial Design

My interest in food and in the role of spatial design has been shaped by two episodes in my life. The first one was a childhood experience, the other one was in my academic career, about a decade ago.

From 1978 to 1982 I lived in Yemen, where my father was involved in setting up a seed potato project. I spent many hours with Yemeni farmers in their fields and we were often invited for lunch by one of the farmers. Used to Dutch lunches, which usually consisted of one or two sandwiches and a glass of milk and lasted less than half an hour, we found that Yemini lunches were a different experience. Warm meals, with lots of different dishes and lasting an hour or more, quite often followed by a two-hour khat chewing session. Eating, drinking tea, and chewing khat had an important social function. During those hours business deals were made, community disputes were discussed (and sometimes settled) and political issues were debated. The social aspect of eating together with larger groups of people, which until then was linked to special festivities (such as the birthdays of my grandparents and Christmas dinners), was clearly part of the routine of everyday (rural) life in Yemen. However, my time in Yemen was also the first time I was confronted with hunger and malnutrition. Later on in life I travelled to various countries in the Middle East and Eastern Africa and saw many cases of hunger and malnutrition. These experiences have had a profound and ever-lasting impact on me and made me aware of the enormous socioeconomic inequalities that exist between and within countries with regard to access to and affordability of nutritious food.

Since my appointment as Professor of Rural Sociology I have been involved in a large number of international (mainly EU-funded) research projects about food provisioning. Initially, these projects focused on the dynamics of farmer-driven new food networks and short food supply chains as means for them to improve their livelihood. An invitation by the Peri-Urban Regions Platform Europe (PURPLE) in 2008 to give a keynote lecture about food and food policy in the era of urbanization, triggered me to think about the future of food provisioning from an urban rather than a rural perspective. On the one hand this resulted in several new research proposals, of which some were funded, and on the other hand in attending and participating in several events about food in the urban realm. One was a workshop by Carolyn Steel organized by Stroom The Hague (an independent arts and design centre) as part of their Foodprint programme. After that workshop I had many conversations with Carolyn and we were both captured by the fact that despite our very different disciplinary backgrounds (architecture vs. rural sociology) and starting points (the city vs. agriculture) our analyses of the food system and its problems and challenges were virtually the same. Moreover, we saw many complementarities and potential synergies between spatial design and social science in addressing these challenges. Another event—a meeting with a group of architects —added to that, in particular a remark by one of the architects: 'Good spatial designers are able to change people's everyday physical environment in such a way that new practices and routines emerge without people actually realizing that they are doing things differently.' All of a sudden everything fell into place: the relationships between production and consumption practices and production and consumption environments as well as the reciprocal links between agricultural landscapes and urban food environments. And how and why spatial design and social sciences have something to offer to one another.

When in 2012 I was asked by the Amsterdam Academy of Architecture to become 'lector' (professor of applied sciences) for a period of four years it felt like a dream come true: being able to further explore and improve the link and interaction between scientific research and spatial design with a focus on the topic of foodscapes. I have enjoyed every minute of it and hope this book reflects that joy.

This book is about the present and future of food provisioning practices and their social and physical environments and how these practices and environments shape each other. This introduction is followed by a chapter in which we discuss how food provisioning has changed over the last centuries, including its spatial dimension, what the implications of these changes have been, what the contemporary and future food challenges are and why there is an urgent need to do food differently. One way of doing that, we argue in this book, is to adhere to a set of principles for designing and redesigning foodscapes. We have identified five socio-spatial design principles, and these constitute the five core parts of the book. Each part begins with a chapter to introduce the background and importance of that particular principle. This is followed by four chapters, each dedicated to a specific case that serves as an illustration of that particular principle. Several cases are examples of accomplished projects, policies, and/or spatial interventions, some are examples of socio-spatial transformations in progress, and the others are spatial designs and imaginations of future possibilities. Through this set-up and the combination of social sciences and spatial design, and of theory and practice, we anticipate that in addition to providing new perspectives on and approaches to foodscapes studies and design, this book also contributes to the debate about the future role of designers.

Johannes S.C. Wiskerke
& Saline Verhoeven

Ranching
and Livestock

Grains and
Field Crops

Forests

Dairy
Farming

URBAN CENTRE ⟶ MARKET
GARDENING ⟵ MARKET

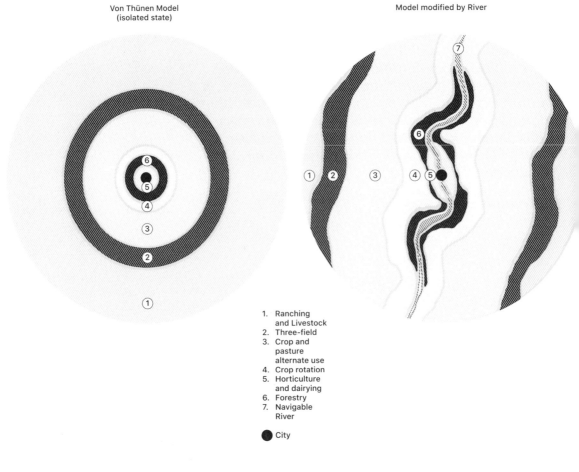

Von Thünen Model
(isolated state)

Model modified by River

1. Ranching
   and Livestock
2. Three-field
3. Crop and
   pasture
   alternate use
4. Crop rotation
5. Horticulture
   and dairying
6. Forestry
7. Navigable
   River

● City

Johannes S.C. Wiskerke & Saline Verhoeven

THE SPATIALITY OF FOOD PROVI- SIONING

For many centuries the location, size, and growth rate of cities was largely determined by the amount of food and energy that their rural hinterland could produce.[1] The German landowner and geographer Johann Heinrich von Thünen was one of the first authors to analyze the spatial relationship between a city and its productive rural hinterland.[2] In his book, originally published in 1827 and entitled *Der isolierte Staat* [The Isolated State] he envisioned a single market town surrounded by agricultural land and nature. Central to this Von Thünen model—based on the assumption that the land surrounding market towns is completely flat and has no rivers or mountains and that soil quality is the same everywhere—is that four concentric rings of agricultural productivity surround the market town:

1. Dairy farming and fruit and vegetable production close to the market town, as these products were perishable and had to be brought to the market quickly. Also, these are products with higher added value and thereby a means to cover the higher rents for land close to the market town.
2. Forest providing timber and firewood for fuel and building materials. As wood is heavy and difficult to transport it has to be produced not too far from the market town.
3. Extensive field crops such as cereals, which are less perishable than dairy and vegetables and much lighter than wood, so they could be grown further away from the market town.
4. Grazing is located in the outermost ring, because a) it requires the most space and b) animals can walk to the market town, where they are slaughtered and the meat is sold.

Beyond this last ring is wilderness, which is too great of a distance from the market town for any agricultural product to be profitable.

This spatial dependency between cities and surrounding countryside only partially held true for cities that were located close to the sea or along a navigable river. Therefore, Von Thünen's model has been modified to incorporate cities and market towns located along a navigable river. The concentric circles then become stretched-out ovals with agricultural production zones on either side of the river, as transporting food, fuel, and building materials over sea is much cheaper than over land.[3]

The spatial proximity relations between specific foods (e.g., vegetables, milk, cereals, meat) and city as well as the relation between location, size, and growth rate of a city and the productive capacity of its rural hinterland began to fundamentally change with the introduction of the railway system.[4] For the first time in history it was possible to transport food over land over long distances at low costs. It also meant that perishable products, such as milk, could be produced farther away from towns and cities as they could be transported over longer distances in relatively short time.

Following the introduction of railroads, spatial proximity relations between cities and agricultural production rapidly became weaker with the introduction of new technologies, such as airplanes, refrigerated and frozen transport and storage, and processing and packaging of food.[5] This has considerably increased the shelf life of food products[6] and global sourcing of 'fresh' food has become a common practice[7]. The advent of railways and subsequent technologies 'emancipated cities from geography, making it possible for the first time to build them any size, shape, and place, but 'as cities sprawled, food systems industrialized, and the two began to grow apart'.[8]

1 C. Steel, *Hungry City: How Food Shapes Our Lives* (London: Random House, 2008).

2 C. Clark, 'Von Thünen's Isolated State', *Oxford Economic Papers (New Series)* 19 (1967), pp. 370–377.

3 N. Morley, *Metropolis and Hinterland: The City of Rome and the Italian Economy, 200 BC–AD 200* (Cambridge: University Press, 1996).

4 Steel, *Hungry City.*

5 J.P. Johnston, *A Hundred Years Eating: Food, Drink and the Daily Diet in Britain since the late Nineteenth Century* (Montreal: McGill-Queen's University Press, 1977); Steel, *Hungry City.*

6 D. Kilcast and P. Subramaniam, *The Stability and Shelf-Life of Food* (Cambridge: CRC Press, 2000).

7 A. Bonnano et al., *From Columbus to ConAgra: The Globalization of Agriculture and Food* (Lawrence: University Press of Kansas, 1994).

8 Steel, *Hungry City*, p. 38.

The growing apart of cities and their food systems has changed their relationship in multiple ways. Following Eriksen, we can distinguish three spheres of changing relations:[9]

1. *Spatial.* For many food items, in particular in industrialized economies, the physical distance between the site of production and the site of consumption has increased. According to a study commissioned by Rabobank Amsterdam the ingredients of an average Amsterdam diner collectively travel 33,000 kilometres.[10] In November 1992 in Food File, a British Channel 4 TV magazine programme, Tim Lang coined the term 'food miles' to 'help consumers engage with an important aspect of the struggle over the future of food—where their food comes from, and how'.[11] Two years later, the Food Miles report was published, in which the causes and impacts of long-distance food transport were thoroughly explained and discussed.[12] This report—and the many studies that have been published since— show that long-distance transportation of food is economically viable because of cheap non-renewable fossil fuel energy while externalizing all other costs, such as the effects of climate change, to which today's global industrial food system is a main contributor.

2. *Social.* The increased physical distance has also changed the social relations between actors involved in different food provisioning practices, such as the consumption, cooking, trade, distribution, processing, and production of food. Many farmers have no idea where and by whom their products are eaten. Similarly, most consumers have no clue where their food comes from and who produced it.[13] To a large extent this has to do with the changing nature of agricultural production: from growing food to growing ingredients for the food processing industry. Concomitantly, the importance of the supermarket as main food outlet has increased enormously in the 20th century.[14] Transnational food processing

9 S.N. Eriksen, 'Defining Local Food: Constructing a New Taxonomy: Three Domains of Proximity', *Acta Agriculturae Scandinavica, Section B: Soil & Plant Science* 63 (2013) (sup1), pp. 47–55.

10 S. de Boer, P. Bos, and J.W. van der Schans, 'Voedsel verbindt Amsterdam: Ontwikkelopgave voor een duurzame voedselvoorziening van de metropoolregio Amsterdam' (Amsterdam: Rabobank, 2011), www.groenegastvrijegordel.nl/pdf/rabobank.pdf (accessed 12-10-2017).

11 T. Lang, *Local/Global (Food Miles)* (Bra: Slow Food Foundation, 2006), pp. 94–97, www.city.ac.uk/__data/assets/pdf_file/0007/167893/Slow-Food-fd-miles-final-16-02-06.pdf (accessed 12-10-2017).

12 A. Paxton, *The Food Miles Report: The Dangers of Long-distance Food Transport* (United Kingdom: Sustainable Agriculture, Food and Environment [SAFE] Alliance, 1994).

13 T. Cammelbeeck and I. Smit, *Traceerbaarheid en transparantie in de voedselketen* (Den Haag: Consumentenbond, 2014).

14 J. Kirwan et al., *Macro-level Analysis of Food Supply Chain Dynamics and Diversity in Europe* (SUS-CHAIN report no. 10), 2004, www.sus-chain.org.

industries and retailers have become powerful players in contemporary food systems as the key intermediaries between farmers and consumers. Consequently, relations between producers and consumers become more and more anonymous.[15] And this creeping anonymity in relationships is accompanied by an increasing level of formalization in relationships through detailed production regulations and quality control systems to compensate for the lack of direct contact and personal trust.[16]

3. *Values.* With the growing share of processed foods, the global sourcing of food, the year-round availability of food products, and the growing importance of supermarkets as food outlets, there has also been a change in the values that actors attribute to food and in the conventions (i.e. exchange rules and agreements) that shape the interactions and relations between actors in food systems. Global industrial food systems in particular are organized around commercial and industrial conventions.[17] 'Commercial' refers to the importance of price, or more precisely, low prices in shaping food production and consumption practices. 'Industrial' refers to the growing significance of standards and quality assurance schemes in food systems. A more recent change is the increasing importance of civil conventions, which refers to collective principles such as animal welfare, fair trade, and environmental protection. These civil values are, however, usually incorporated in quality assurance schemes and thus inextricably linked to industrial conventions.

Although these changes are generally seen as representing the prevailing trend in food system dynamics, it is important to note that alternatives to this mainstream globalized industrial food system are emerging and growing. Albeit very diverse, these alternatives do have certain characteristics in common: reducing the spatial distance between production and consumption, (re-)establishing social relations between producers and consumers, and emphasis on domestic conventions such as attachment to place and tradition (frequently re-

15 L. Philips, 'Food and Globalization', *Annual Review of Anthropology* 35 (2006), pp. 37–57.

16 J.S.C. Wiskerke, 'On Places Lost and Places Regained: Reflections on the Alternative Food Geography and Sustainable Regional Development', *International Planning Studies* 14 (2009), pp. 369–387.

17 K. Morgan, T. Marsden, and J. Murdoch, *Worlds of Food: Place, Power and Provenance in the Food Chain* (Oxford: Oxford University Press, 2006).

ferred to as *terroir*). Examples are farmer's markets, community supported agriculture, origin-labelled food products, and solidarity purchasing groups. We will discuss the differences between the globalized industrial food system and alternatives to this mainstream system in more detail, as for the purpose of this book it is important to be aware of differential socio-spatial food system dynamics. Finally, it is also important to mention that in some countries industrial food systems are still in their infancy and may remain relatively insignificant.[18] Hence, the mainstream in those countries exhibits many characteristics of the alternative in industrialized economies.

Contemporary Food System Challenges

Cities become disconnected from their food provisioning systems and at the same time globalized and industrialized food systems are on the rise. This has not only changed the spatial distance, social relations, and values among producers, consumers, and other food system actors, but has also brought about a set of food system challenges that need to be urgently addressed. In this section we will briefly outline these challenges, most of which are also central to the cases depicted in this book as these challenges are (or have been) the starting point(s) for proposed or implemented socio-spatial transformations.

Resource Depletion and Scarcity

Food provisioning depends on the availability, affordability, and quality of a variety of natural and human resources, such as energy, nutrients, seeds, water, land, and labour. How resources are used and how much of them are needed to produce food differs between modes of food provisioning. Some of the crucial resources are being depleted at a rate that is likely to make them scarce. Changes in resources—i.e. in type and volume, but also in how they are used—are therefore inevitable if we are to safeguard food provisioning in the long term. The most important resource constraints for food provisioning are:

18 M.C.A. Wegerif, *Feeding Dar es Salaam: A Symbiotic Food System Perspective*, PhD thesis (Wageningen: Wageningen University, 2017).

1. *Fossil fuel.* Food production, processing, transportation, and storage have become heavily dependent on fossil fuels. As a result, the food system contributes significantly to greenhouse gas (GHG) emissions and hence to climate change.[19] Life cycle analyses of Western diets indicate that it takes on average seven calories of fossil fuel energy to produce one calorie of food energy.[20] The 'heavy fossil fuel users' are pesticides and chemical fertilizer, food processing and packaging, and cooling (during transport, storage and in shops).[21] Regarding the type of food product, animal proteins require more fossil energy to be produced than crops.

2. *Water.* Most of the world's surface water and groundwater is used for the production of food. Approximately 65% of our daily water consumption is water embedded in food, i.e. the amount of water needed to produce food. This is also referred to as virtual water. For the production of animal protein (meat, dairy, and eggs) the water footprint is much higher. Beef cattle have the highest contribution to the global water footprint, followed by dairy cattle, pigs, and chickens. Industrial forms of livestock husbandry have a higher water footprint than grazing systems. We can therefore conclude that 'from a freshwater resource perspective, it is more efficient to obtain calories, protein and fat through crop products than through animal products'.[22]

A similar conclusion was already drawn for the use of fossil fuels. This means that dietary changes will have a significant impact on resource needs if nothing changes in the way food is being produced. We will come back to this in part 5 of the book, where we will discuss the relation between diet and agricultural surface area needed to feed the metropolitan region of Amsterdam.

19 A. Carlsson-Kanyama and A.D. González, 'Potential Contributions of Food Consumption Patterns to Climate Change', *American Journal of Clinical Nutrition* 89 (2009), 1704S-1709S.

20 M.C. Heller and G.A. Keoleian, *Life Cycle-based Sustainability Indicators for Assessment of the U.S. Food system* (Ann Arbor: Center for Sustainable Systems, University of Michigan, 2000).

21 D. Pimentel et al., 'Reducing Energy Inputs in the US Food System', *Human Ecology* 36 (2008), pp. 459–471.

22 M.M. Mekkonen and A.Y. Hoekstra, 'A Global Assessment of the Water Footprint of Farm Animal Products', *Ecosystems* 15, no. 3 (2012), pp. 401–415.

Environmental Degradation

Many farming practices and systems are increasingly perceived as degenerative, as they deplete natural resources and are energy- and chemical-intensive. Such farming systems contribute to environmental pollution, such as the emission of nitrate to groundwater, of ammonia to the air, phosphate saturation of soils, and emission of pesticide residues to the air and to ground and surface water.[23] Soil degradation is another effect of modern agriculture. Being a vital resource for the production of food, feed, and fodder and maintaining or improving the productive capacity of the soil requires good management. However, across the globe much soil is not managed well and this may have negative impacts on food security. A simulation of the effect of soil degradation on long-term food security in China predicts that

> ... food crops may experience a 9% loss in productivity by 2030 if the soil continues to be degraded at the current rate... Productivity losses will increase to the unbearable level of 30% by 2050 should the soil be degraded at twice the present rate.[24]

Agro-ecological methods of production, although sometimes questioned for their lower productive capacity, have proven to be very successful in stopping and even reversing soil degradation.[25] Intensification of production and a prevailing focus on high-yielding varieties in plant breeding has also resulted in a massive genetic erosion and disappearance of many crop populations adapted to local circumstances.[26] Furthermore, the modernization of farms and the countryside has also resulted in the loss of non-agricultural biodiversity. In many European countries land reconsolidation measures that were implemented to make the countryside suitable for modern farming, have led to the destruction of natural habitats and historico-cultural landscapes. Similarly, large parts of the Amazon are deforested each year due to the growing need for agricultural land for the production of soy or biofuels.[27]

23 M.M. van Eerdt en P.K.N. Fong, 'The Monitoring of Nitrogen Surpluses from Agriculture', Environmental Pollution 102 (1998), Supplement 1, pp. 227–233.

24 L. Ye and E. van Ranst, 'Production Scenarios and the Effect of Soil Degradation on Long-term Food Security in China', Global Environmental Change 19, no. 4 (2009), pp. 464–481.

25 P. Tittonell et al., 'Agroecology-based Aggradation-conservation Agriculture (ABACO): Targeting Innovations to Combat Soil Degradation and Food Insecurity in Semi-arid Africa', Field Crops Research 132 (2012), pp. 168–174.

26 B. Visser, 'Effects of Biotechnology on Agro-biodiversity', Biotechnology and Development Monitor 35 (1998), pp. 2–7.

27 E.F. Lambin and P. Meyfroidt, 'Global Land Use Change, Economic Globalization, and the Looming Land Scarcity', Proceedings of the National Academy of Sciences of the USA 108 (2011), pp. 3465–3472.

Climate change has and will continue to have a tremendous impact on the productive capacity of agriculture worldwide.[28] Some regions are expected to benefit from global warming as this will create a more productive environment (longer growing season, sufficient rainfall), while many other regions are likely to suffer due to severe droughts and floods. In particular sub-Saharan Africa, currently one of the most food-insecure parts of the world, but also the region with the highest population growth and urbanization rates, is expected to face significant declines in agricultural production. In particular the frequency and severity of extreme climate events will have the highest negative consequences for food production as well as for food distribution.[29] This will negatively affect food availability, food accessibility, food utilization and hence food security (FAO, 2008). The relation between food and climate change is a dualistic one. On the one hand, agricultural production is largely negatively affected by climate change but, on the other hand, it also contributes to climate change by emitting GHG. As indicated in the previous section, the production of animal proteins as well as the use of chemical inputs, food processing and packaging and cold transportation and storage are important GHG emitting food provisioning practices. This dualistic role also implies that agriculture can mitigate climate change through reducing GHG emissions by changing food provisioning practices. This also includes efforts to reduce food waste, including packaging.

Waste (Food and Packaging)

At the global level, enough food calories are currently produced to feed 10 billion people, yet approximately 40% of the food produced is not consumed due to harvest losses on the farm and post-harvest losses further up the food chain, including post-consumer waste. Reducing harvest and post-harvest losses can therefore contribute both to alleviating food insecurity[30] and to mitigating climate change. In industrialized economies food losses primarily occur in the latter stages of the food chain: in supermarkets and restaurants,

28 T. Garnett, *Cooking up a Storm: Food, Greenhouse Gas Emissions and Our Changing Climate* (UK: Food Climate Research Network, Centre for Environmental Strategy, University of Surrey, 2008).

29 W.E. Easterling et al., 'Food, Fibre and Forest Products', in *Climate Change 2007: Impacts, Adaptation and Vulnerability: Contribution of Working Group II to the Fourth Assessment Report of the Intergovernmental Panel on Climate Change*, eds. M.K. Parry et al. (Cambridge and New York: Cambridge University Press, 2007.

30 H. Herren, 'Agriculture at a Crossroads', Lecture for the All Party Parliamentary Group on Agroecology, Tuesday March 15th 2011, London: House of Commons.

and at home.[31] For many developing countries food waste primarily occurs in the first stages of the food chain, during harvest, storage, and transport.[32] Especially for perishable products such as fruits and vegetables, harvest and post-harvest losses are high. Poor transport infrastructure between city and countryside, together with a lack of cool storage are the main causes of these food losses.[33] Hence, improving rural-urban distribution connections and creating and preserving space for urban and peri-urban production of fruits and vegetables are key means to reduce food waste and thus enhance urban food security.[34] In addition to the food waste challenge there is also the challenge of food packaging waste. Over the last decades this has increased, due to the combined effects of population growth, increased levels of consumption, and a growing share of processed food in people's diets.[35]

Social Inequalities

Cities developed in places that had a natural advantage in resource supply or transport. Hence, cities provided opportunities for social and economic development: 'Cities have always been focal points for economic growth, innovation and employment.'[36] For a long time and in most parts of the world urbanization has gone hand in hand with economic development. However, in recent years the accelerated pace of urbanization has made cities socioeconomically more diverse. Typical for many cities, in particular in developing countries, is the significant difference between the upper- and middle-income class, and the low-income class when it comes to access to clean drinking water and electricity and presence of adequate sewage and solid waste disposal facilities.[37] The reproduction, or perhaps even acceleration, of urban inequalities is often attributed to poor urban governance, i.e. municipal authorities unable to keep up with the speed of urban growth and/or with the increasing complexity of urban governance as a result of decentralization of policies, but also to neo-liberal reforms of urban services, which tend to exclude the urban poor from access to these services.[38] Socioeconomic inequalities translate directly into differences in access to and affordability of food.

31 T. Lang, 'Crisis? What Crisis? The Normality of the Current Food Crisis', Journal of Agrarian Change 10, no. 1 (2010), pp. 87–97.

32 J. Aulakh and A. Regmi, 'Post-Harvest Food Losses Estimation-Development of Consistent Methodology', Agricultural & Applied Economics Associations, 2013, pp. 4–6.

33 J. Gustavsson et al., Global Food Losses and Food Waste (Rome: FAO, 2011), pp. 1–38.

34 H. Renting and M. Dubbeling, Innovative Experiences with (Peri-)Urban Agriculture and Urban Food Provisioning: Lessons to Be Learned from the Global South, SUPURB-FOOD deliverable 3.5 (Leusden: RUAF Foundation, 2013).

35 J. Thøgersen, 'A Critical Review of the Literature', Environment and Behavior 28 (1996), pp. 536–558; J.-C. Moubarac et al., 'Processed and Ultra-processed Food Products: Consumption Trends in Canada from 1938 to 2011', Canadian Journal of Dietetic Practice and Research 75, no. 1 (2014), pp. 15–21; Food Consumption in the Netherlands and its Determinants: Background Report to 'What is on our plate? Safe, healthy and sustainable diets in the Netherlands' (RIVM Report 2016-0195) (Bilthoven: National Institute for Public Health and the Environment, Ministry of Health, Welfare and Sport, 2017

36 B. Cohen, 'Urbanization in Developing Countries: Current Trends, Future Projections, and Key Challenges for Sustainability', Techology in Society 28 (2006), pp. 63–80.

37 Ibid.

Of the 7 billion people on the planet today, more than 2 billion suffer from diet-related ill health: obesity, malnutrition, and hunger.[39] Especially the rapidly rising prevalence of overweight children is alarming. Simultaneously, malnutrition is also a growing health concern, which, like obesity, is more prevalent among the socioeconomically disadvantaged segments of the urban population. In Europe and North America there is a high incidence of malnutrition among elderly people.[40] Child malnutrition is a major concern in many developing countries. Although the overall percentage of child malnutrition is going down worldwide, the prevalence of stunted growth among young children remains high in Africa and South-Central Asia. Particularly in western and eastern Africa the slow decline in the percentage of malnourished children combined with the rapid population growth leads to an increase in the numbers of stunted children: from 44.9 million stunted pre-school children in 1990 to an expected 64.1 million in 2020.[41] Globally, hunger in its most extreme form has decreased from over 1 billion people in 1990–1992 (18.9% of the world's population) to 842 million in 2011–2013 (12% of the world's population). According to the former United Nations Special Rapporteur on the Right to Food these figures are an underestimation of the global hunger problem as

> ... these figures do not capture short-term undernourishment, because of their focus on year-long averages; they neglect inequalities in intra-household distribution of food; and the calculations are based on a low threshold of daily energy requirements that assume a sedentary lifestyle, whereas many of the poor perform physically demanding activities.[42]

In addition to diet-related ill health, the food system also has an impact on environmental health. Food transport—whether food delivery to outlets by trucks or transporting food by cars from supermarkets to home—contributes to GHG emissions and air pollution. Urban air pollution becomes worse due to the disappearance of the urban green;[43]

38 V. Broto, A. Allen, and E. Rapoport, 'Interdisciplinary Perspectives on Urban Metabolism', *Journal of Industrial Ecology* 16, no. 6 (2012), pp. 851–861
39 O. de Schutter, *The Transformative Potential of the Right to Food* (New York: UN Human Rights Council, 2014).
40 K. Pothukuchi and J.L. Kaufman, 'Placing the Food System on the Urban Agenda: The Role of Municipal Institutions in Food Systems Planning', *Agriculture and Human Values* 16 (1999), pp. 213–224.
41 M. De Onis, M. Blössner, and E. Borghi, 'Prevalence and Trends of Stunting Among Pre-School Children, 1990–2020', *Public Health Nutrition* 15, no. 1 (2012), pp. 142–148.
42 De Schutter, *The Transformative Potential of the Right to Food*, p. 4.
43 D.E. Pataki et al., 'Coupling Biogeochemical Cycles in Urban Environments: Ecosystem Services, Green Solutions, and Misconceptions', *Frontiers in Ecology and the Environment* 9, no. 1 (2011), pp. 27–36.

urban expansion tends to go at the expense of (productive) green space in and around cities. The lack of urban green also contributes to urban heat islands, an urban environmental health challenge that is aggravated by climate change.[44] Heat islands 'intensify the energy problem of cities, deteriorate comfort conditions, put in danger the vulnerable population and amplify the pollution problems'.[45]

As the foregoing already shows, these six main food system challenges cannot be understood or addressed in isolation. Their interconnectedness and interdependency is central to emerging nexus-thinking, such as the water-energy-food nexus. It implies that these three domains—water security, energy security and food security—are inextricably linked and that actions in one area more often than not have an impact on one or both of the others. Applying nexus-thinking to the aforementioned food system challenges means that we need to understand sustainable food provisioning as a water-energy-environment-waste-climate change-social inequality-health nexus, within the context of population growth, urbanization and dietary change. These themes, and the interrelations between (some of) them, have been key to the socio-spatial interventions that feature or are proposed in virtually all of the following chapters.

The Spatiality of Food-related Challenges

Although this seven-fold nexus makes sustainable food provisioning a complex issue, we still need to add yet another layer to this complexity, which is the spatial component entailed in this nexus. Food provisioning practices, the conditions that shape these practices and the impacts of these practices are not only of a social, economic, and environmental nature but also manifest themselves spatially. This spatial manifestation of practices, conditions, and impacts is twofold.

On the one hand there are inextricable spatial interdependencies between food provisioning practices. We will illustrate this briefly using pork as an example.[46] Pre-packed pork for sale in supermarkets (at discount prices), is very often linked to a large-scale industrial slaughterhouse, to large-scale

44 T. Susca, S.R. Gaffin, and G.R. Dell'Osso, 'Positive Effects of Vegetation: Urban Heat Island and Green Roofs', *Environmental Pollution* 159, nos. 8–9 (2011), pp. 2119–2126.

45 M. Santamouris, 'Cooling the Cities: A Review of Reflective and Green Roof Mitigation Technologies to Fight Heat Island and Improve Comfort in Urban Environments', *Solar Energy* 103 (2014), pp. 682–703.

46 Inspired by H. Oostindie et al., 'Sense and Non-Sense of Local-Global Food Chain Comparison, Empirical Evidence from Dutch and Italian Pork Case Studies', *Sustainability* 8 no. 4 (2016), p. 319.

intensive livestock farms within and outside the country where the slaughterhouse is located, and to large-scale monocultures of soy for the production of animal feed. This then implies links between practices in places that are geographically far apart. Unpacked meat for sale in specialty shops (at premium prices) is very likely related to a smaller-scale artisan slaughterhouse, to small-scale livestock production with more attention to distinctive quality in texture, taste, and smell, animal welfare and environmental sustainability, and to own feed production or sourcing from nearby farmers. This then implies links between practices that are geographically proximate to one another. But it most likely also implies a different kind and quality of rural landscape compared to the first example of pork provisioning, because of different agricultural practices and scales of operation.

On the other hand, it is important to understand the spatial aspects of the nexus. With this we refer to the existence of spatial differences in climate change effects, in food access and availability, in diet-related ill health, in food waste, and so on. The chapter on food security and food production systems[47] of the report by the International Panel on Climate Change (IPCC) shows, for example, that agricultural productivity is likely to increase in Central and Northern Europe and decrease in the Mediterranean countries as a result of climate change. It also indicates that in particular the currently most food insecure parts of the world, Africa and South Asia, which are also the regions with highest rates of population growth and urbanization, are expected to suffer the highest negative impact of climate change on agricultural productivity. In these most food insecure regions we also witness the highest levels of children under 5 affected by either stunted growth or overweight,[48] both examples of diet-related ill health. Furthermore, there is a strong correlation between the projected climate change impact on agricultural productivity and the availability of water for food production, hence a clear sign of the spatiality of the food-climate change-public health-water nexus. And we can add social inequality to this, as urban slums are mainly located in high risk areas prone to flooding. With

47 J.R. Porter et al., 'Chapter 7: Food Security and Food Production Systems', *IPCC 2014: Climate Change 2014: Impacts, Adaptation, and Vulnerability.* Contribution of working group II to the fifth assessment report of the intergovernmental panel on climate change. Final draft. IPCC AR5 WGII, 2014.
48 Development Initiatives, *Global Nutrition Report 2017: Nourishing the SDGs* (Bristol, Development Initiatives, 2017).

the climate change induced aggravation of extreme weather events the urban poor are more likely to be affected by flooding, and as a result, be more exposed to vector-borne and water-borne diseases and lower availability of and access to food.[49]

Foodscapes

To deal with the spatial aspects of food provisioning practices and the conditions shaping these practices we propose to use the concept of foodscapes. It is a concept that has been introduced relatively recently, primarily in the field of public health and nutrition studies, 'as a tool to describe our food environments and to assess the potential impact on food choice and food behaviour'.[50] An easy way of explaining the term foodscape would be to understand it as an assembly of its two components—food and scape— and thus define it as 'the relationship between food, its spatial context and the viewer—the person to which this image appears'.[51] Following this line of reasoning, a foodscape can be understood as the actual site where we find food.[52] Building on that, the concept of foodscape can be used as a synonym for food environment, which 'encompasses any opportunity to obtain food and includes physical, socio-cultural, economic and policy influences at both micro and macro-levels'.[53] This adds the notion of scale to the definition of foodscape. We can distinguish between macro-, meso-, and micro-scale food environments, or foodscapes. The macro level is shaped by 'global or regional marketscapes that shape food choices through widely dispersed international food systems that include transportation networks, agricultural and food industries, and food distribution outlets'.[54] The meso scale refers to build environments at the community level providing 'food landscapes ... that represent eating outlets available for choosing foods that determine food provisioning'.[55] The micro level then concerns the domestic foodscape, which refers to the physical appearance of the food, how food is served, the amount of food that is served, how, where and with whom (if anyone) meals are eaten, and how and where meals are prepared and food is stored. All this can be described with notions as kitchenscape, tablescape and platescape.[56]

49 S. Altizer et al., 'Climate Change and Infectious Diseases: From Evidence to a Predictive Framework', *Science* 341, no. 6145 (2013), pp. 514–519.

50 B.E. Mikkelsen, 'Images of Foodscapes: Introduction to Foodscape Studies and Their Application in the Study of Healthy Eating Out-Of-Home Environments', *Perspectives in Public Health* 131, no. 5 (2011), pp. 209–216.

51 Ibid., p. 210.

52 S. Freidberg, 'Perspective and Power in the Ethical Foodscape', *Environment and Planning A* 42 (2010), pp. 1868–1874.

53 A.A. Lake et al., 'The Foodscape: Classification and Field Validation of Secondary Data Sources', *Health Place* 16, no. 4 (2010), pp. 666–673.

54 J. Sobal and B. Wansink, 'Kitchenscapes, Tablescapes, Platescapes, and Foodscapes: Influences of Microscale Built Environments on Food Intake', *Environment and Behavior* 39, no. 1 (2007), pp. 124–142.

55 Ibid., p. 126.

56 Ibid.

The inclusion of scale and place (i.e. the physical location of a specific food provisioning activity) in the definition of foodscape points to two important constituting elements of the concept:

1 Foodscapes are *nested*, meaning that the domestic foodscape is embedded in a community or neighbourhood foodscape, which in turn is embedded in a regional or global foodscape. In other words, what is eaten at home is linked to and may be influenced by the kind of food outlets that are present or easily accessible in the neighbourhood or city and by the extent to which these food outlets are supplied with food by local processors and producers or by transnational food industries and farmers in different parts of the world. Simultaneously, food consumption and procurement practices will also reproduce or transform neighbourhood, city region, and global foodscapes.

2 Foodscapes are *interconnected*, meaning that the places shaped by different food provisioning activities—i.e. producing, processing, distributing, trading, preparing and eating—are inextricably linked to one another. Hence, mono-functional suburbs, supermarkets at the outskirts of towns, long-distance food transport systems (harbours, airports, and central distribution centres) and large-scale monofunctional agricultural production systems are interconnected. The same holds true for urban and peri-urban farms, low-cost short-distance modes of food transport, farmer's markets, and street shops.

This nested-ness and interconnectedness also means that the definition of foodscape as developed within the public health and nutrition studies domain, where the emphasis is on the food purchasing and out-of-home eating environment, has to be broadened to encompass all places where food provisioning activities take place, hence from production, to processing, distribution, sales, cooking, and eating.

Given the diversity in agricultural production systems, modes of food transport, the kind of food outlets, and spatial distribution of these outlets, as well as in food culture, the diversity of foodscapes is virtually endless. To simplify and reduce this diversity we have constructed two ideal types of foodscapes (see p. 34), which are one-sided accentuations of more or less interrelated aspects of a specific phenomenon. An ideal type foodscape does not mean ideal in the sense that it is excellent, nor does it refer to the average or common denominator. It is, rather, a constructed ideal of a foodscape used to stress certain elements common to a particular kind of foodscape. As such these two ideal type foodscapes represent the extremes of the contemporary spectrum of foodscapes. Everyday socio-spatial realities are, however, not confined to these two extremes but consist of a variety of hybrid forms of these ideal types. We do, however, consider it important to portray these two extremes as they, on the one hand, often feature (also in this book) as a point of reference for socio-spatial development or change, and, on the other hand, denote different vested and materialized ways of food provisioning that are difficult to change.

The first ideal type is the agro-industrial foodscape. This foodscape is rooted in the agricultural modernization or productionist paradigm and is the outcome of a globalized corporate food regime.[57] Food and the resources needed to produce it are seen as commodities and both entrepreneurs and consumers are best served by free global trade. Food security is perceived as a production challenge and sustainable food production is narrowly defined as optimizing input-output relations. The agro-industrial foodscape is furthermore characterized by an important role for nutrition scientists and food technologists, developing the knowledge and methods that enable the food processing industry to produce safe and healthy food products.

The second ideal type, the agro-ecological foodscape, is rooted in a place-based integrated paradigm with food sovereignty as a leading motto.[58] Food security is primarily seen as a challenge in terms of availability, accessibility, affordability, and adequacy.[59] Sustainability is defined in broad terms, encompassing environmental, social, and economic aspects. Diversified production systems are an im-

57 T. Lang and M. Heasman, *Food Wars: the Global Battle for Mouths, Minds and Markets* (Oxford: Routledge, 2015).

58 E. Holt Giménez and A. Shattuck, 'Food Crises, Food Regimes and Food Movements: Rumblings of Reform or Tides of Transformation?', *The Journal of Peasant Studies* 38, no. 1 (2011), pp. 109–144.

59 De Schutter, *The Transformative Potential of the Right to Food.*

portant prerequisite for nutrition security: 'Diverse farming systems contribute to more diverse diets for the communities that produce their own food, thus improving nutrition.'[60]

↷
Next page: Ideal Types of Foodscapes

A final aspect worth mentioning in relation to the steadily growing body of foodscape literature is the value-laden element of the concept. In that respect, the notion of ethical foodscape is emerging in the debate as a way of 'conceptualizing and engaging critically with the processes, politics, spaces, and places of the praxis of ethical relationalities embedded and produced in and through the provisioning of food'.[61] Foodscape then becomes an agenda for change that focuses on 'the opportunities to challenge the existing ways of food production and consumption and create different future trajectories'.[62] This book primarily builds upon this by exploring how food provisioning could be done differently and by presenting guidelines for the socio-spatial design of future foodscapes.

60 Ibid., p. 9.
61 M. Goodman, D. Maye and L. Holloway, 'Ethical Foodscapes?: Premises, Promises, and Possibilities', *Environment and Planning* A 42 (2010), pp. 1782–1796.
62 Mikkelsen, 'Images of Foodscapes', p. 211.

Dimension	Agro-industrial foodscape	Agro-ecological foodscape
Vision on food and food system	Commodity: seeds/ planting materials and food are owned by en- trepreneurs and trans- national companies; food system benefits from free global trade	Human right (right to food); emphasis on food sovereignty; rights of peoples and nation states to protect and preserve their agriculture and food culture
Food security	Matter of production and logistics (efficient distribution systems)	Primarily a challenge of improving availability, access, affordability and adequacy; Also a matter of production (in some parts of the world) and distribution
Vision on primary production	Cost-efficient pro- duction through scale enlargement, reduction of manual labour, spe- cialization and spatial concentration of food production	Product diversifica- tion, broadening of economic basis, retain more value added, la- bour intensive, embed agriculture in terroir
Sustainability	Improving technical efficiency by minimiz- ing inputs (fertilizer, pesticides, energy, land, labour) per unit of output	Integral & place-based approach: economic (employment, income), social (accessible, affordable & adequate food), environmental (closed loops, local varieties, seasonal products, minimize food transport)
Producer-consumer relations and quality assurance	Quality and safety assurance schemes; industry and retail labels and hallmarks; tracking and tracing	Personal trust-based relations; denomina- tion of origin labels; transparent food networks
Organoleptic quality	End-of-chain diver- sification; created by the food processing industry based on standardized primary product	Created by farmers and/or artisanal food processors; quality linked to region / tradi- tion / nature (terroir)
Health	Nutritionism: nutri- tionally engineered functional foods	Lifestyle, dietary pat- tern and eating habits; diversified production
Spatial implications	Monofunctional urban and rural landscapes; urban-rural divide	Multifunctional urban and rural landscapes; diversity of urban-rural relations and interac- tions

63 B. Born and M. Purcell, 'Avoiding the Local Trap: Scale and Food Systems in Planning Research', *Journal of Planning Education and Research* 26, no. 2 (2006), pp. 195–207.

64 Cohen, 'Urbanization in Developing Countries'.

65 www.milanurbanfoodpolicypact.org/text/ (accessed 22-02-2018).

The title of this book is 'flourishing foodscapes'. So far, this introduction has not sketched a hopeful, flourishing image of our present food system. Rather the contrary, one could argue when looking at present and future food system challenges. However, these challenges do not and should not preclude a more hopeful vision on the future of food.

In this book we present a range of promising and hopefully inspiring examples of flourishing foodscapes and the building blocks for them. From these and other examples that we have studied— some of which we have been actively involved in in various ways—we have derived five socio-spatial design principles for flourishing foodscapes:

1. *Adopt a city region perspective.* This comes down to exploring to what extent and how social and spatial connections between cities and their rural hinterland can be re-established—a kind of Von Thünen revisited—without falling into the local trap,[63] i.e. the implicit assumption that local food systems are by definition sustainable. Hence, what is needed is a better understanding of the pros and cons of increased social and spatial proximity of food provisioning practices. A second reason for adopting a city region perspective is that the city region is increasingly becoming the appropriate level of action as a result of the decentralization of policy responsibilities.[64] Many of the aforementioned food system challenges refer to policy domains for which local governments bear responsibility (e.g. waste management, transport, spatial planning, environmental health) or are expected to develop programmes and strategies (e.g. biodiversity, climate change, public health). The growing number of municipalities that will 'work to develop sustainable food systems that are inclusive, resilient, safe and diverse, that provide healthy and affordable food to all people in a human rights-based framework, that minimize waste and conserve biodiversity while adapting to and mitigating impacts of climate change'[65] is a clear illustration of this.

2. *Link different levels of scale.* This follows from our observation that foodscapes are nested, that reciprocal dependencies exist between different levels of scale: the domestic foodscape, the neighbourhood foodscape and the city region foodscape. For a spatial intervention at a particular level of scale to be effective, it has to be aligned with other levels of scale, and this may thus require spatial interventions at these other levels as well.

3. *Connect flows and close cycles.* Food and food-related waste as well as depletion of resources have been identified as two major food system challenges. Allowing resources in waste to be recovered for flows creating value can be a means to address both these challenges. Using the waste generated by one flow as the input for another flow implies a different approach to and design of waste management: from removing something harmful to developing it into something useful. This is key to notions such as circular metabolism and circular economy, which are increasingly featuring in academic and policy debates about the future of cities: 'the long-term viability and sustainability of cities is reliant on them shifting from a linear model to a circular model of metabolism in which outputs are recycled back into the system to become inputs'.[66]

4. *Enhance spatial diversity and synergies.* There is growing recognition that ecological as well as social diversity is paramount to long-term resilience of food provisioning systems. This implies the need to develop spatial intervention strategies that support and enhance different forms of diversity, instead of reducing it.[67] Some of the aforementioned food system challenges can be addressed by enhancing spatial diversity, thereby achieving multiple benefits from the same place. Rooftop farming is a good example of this, as it can contribute to greening of cities, reducing energy consumption for heating and cooling buildings, combatting urban heat islands, temporarily retaining storm water, generating biodiversity in cities, creating employment in the urban food economy and developing knowledge and skills about urban food production.[68]

66 Broto, Allen, and Rapoport, Interdisciplinary Perspectives on Urban Metabolism', p. 853.
67 J. Norberg et al., 'Diversity and Resilience of Social-ecological Systems', in *Complexity Theory for a Sustainable Future*, eds. J. Norberg and G. Cumming (New York: Columbia University Press, 2008), pp. 46–80.
68 L. Mandel, *Eat Up: The Inside Scoop on Rooftop Agriculture* (Gabriola Island: New Society Publishers, 2013).

5. *Conceive multiple utopias.* Utopian thinking is on the rise in food sociology and food geography. This focuses primarily on making visible the kind of food provisioning practices that tend to remain hidden, unrecognized, and/or misunderstood within the prevailing food provisioning paradigm.[69] In some cases food sociologists and food geographers go a step further by imagining desirable future foodscapes. One of the core businesses of spatial designers is to imagine, and visualize, what the future of a particular place (ranging from a building to a regional landscape) could look like. However, quite often only one future vision is being elaborated. To evoke creativity, stimulate debate, and understand the pros and cons of different future foodscapes, we argue that it is important to conceive multiple food utopias.

As mentioned in the previous chapter this book consists of five parts, each dedicated to one of the five socio-spatial design principles. Each part comprises five chapters, with the first being an introduction to and elaboration of the socio-spatial design principle and the others four cases that illustrate that specific principle. In addition to introducing these socio-spatial design principles and making a case why these are important for designing flourishing foodscapes, we also aim to make clear why it is relevant for spatial designers to look at urban and rural space through a food lens. Food is an integrative theme that connects a range of topics and questions that are highly relevant to spatial designers and planners.[70] The challenge for the designer is to show how these topics are connected spatially and which alternative spatial qualities may emerge if things are connected differently. We argue that the five design principles, around which this book is built, will support spatial designers in meeting this challenge. This will, however, require a different role of the designer; from the creative draughtsman designing a visionary blueprint to the facilitator of a multi-stakeholder process in which spatial designs can be made to envision the present, to visualize different interests and/or to imagine alternative futures.

69 P.V. Stock, M. Carolan and C. Rosin, *Food Utopias: Reimagining Citizenship, Ethics and Community* (Oxford: Routledge, 2015).

70 J.S.C. Wiskerke and A. Viljoen, 'Sustainable Urban Food Provisioning: Challenges for Scientists, Policymakers, Planners and Designers', in *Sustainable Food Planning: Evolving Theory and Practice*, eds. A. Viljoen and J.S.C. Wiskerke (Wageningen: Wageningen Academic Publishers, 2012), pp. 19–35.

Johannes S.C. Wiskerke & Saline Verhoeven

CITY-REGION PERSPECTIVE

As argued in the previous chapter, cities have since long grown beyond the productive capacity of their rural hinterlands and this poses enormous challenges to urban food security and the sustainability of urban food provisioning systems:

> Feeding cities ... arguably has a greater social and physical impact on our lives and planet than anything else we do. Yet few of us in the West are conscious of the process. ... Food arrives on our plates as if by magic, and we rarely stop to wonder how it got there. ... When you consider that every day for a city the size of London, enough food for thirty million meals must be produced, imported, sold, cooked, eaten and disposed of again, and that something similar must happen every day for every city on earth, it is remarkable that those of us living in cities get to eat at all.[1]

Living and eating in cities is inextricably linked to globalized chains of food production, processing and distribution.[2] This globalized food system has brought many benefits to the urban population (in particular to urban citizens in the West): food is usually constantly available at relatively low prices and many food products have a year-round supply. However, as we saw in 'The Spatiality of Food Provisioning' (pp. 17ff.), these benefits have also come at social, environmental, and public health costs: contribution to climate change due to high dependency on fossil fuel of all food provision activities (production, processing, packaging, transport, and storage); environmental pollution by excessive use of pesticides and chemical fertilizer; decline of agro- and biodiversity; increased amounts of waste (food and food packaging); social inequalities in access to and affordability of food; and diet-related ill health (obesity, hunger and malnutrition). These are the fundamental issues[3] that need to be addressed in an integral manner to create a food provisioning system capable of sustainably feeding a growing and predominantly urban world population.

In the past decades, different strategies have been developed and implemented to alleviate some of these challenges. Initially, these strategies primarily had a rural focus as problems and challenges related to food provisioning were seen as belonging to agricultural production and thus to the rural domain. In more recent years, an urban approach to these problems and challenges has emerged in addition to the rural approach. As food provisioning is increasingly being understood as a rural as well as an urban practice, more and more researchers, designers, and policymakers are approaching food provisioning and its related impacts as an interrelated urban-rural issue. To this end, the notion of a city region food system is gaining ground in scientific, design and policy circles. Before elaborating on the city region perspective on food provisioning, we will first briefly introduce and discuss rural and urban approaches to food system challenges.

1   C. Steel, *Hungry City: How Food Shapes our Lives* (London: Random House, 2008).

2   K. Morgan, T.K. Marsden, and Murdoch, *Worlds of Food: Place, Power, and Provenance in the Food Chain* (Oxford: University Press, 2006).

3   T. Lang, 'Crisis? What Crisis? The Normality of the Current Food Crisis', *Journal of Agrarian Change* 10, no. 1 (2010), pp. 87–97.

Rural Approaches to
Food System Challenges

To address some of these aforementioned food system challenges three sets of alternatives to mainstream agriculture have been developed over the past twenty or thirty years:

1. Organic and integrated farming systems to address the environmental impact of primary production. These systems have improved sustainability at farm level in environmental terms (less or no pesticides and chemical fertilizer) and sometimes also in economic (more value added for niche market products) and social terms (better working conditions, more job satisfaction). However, many organic and integrated farming systems followed the dominant development pattern of conventional agriculture, i.e. a specialization on food production alone, a spatial separation from other environmental and social functions, long anonymous supply chains, and a focus on cost reduction through an increase in scale.[4]

2. Alternative food networks and/or short food supply chains to shorten the spatial and/or social distance between producer and consumer. In many cases farmers, individually or collectively, have been the initiators of these networks. Increasing control over the food chain and retaining more value added at farm level have been the driving forces behind the creation and development of short food supply chains.[5] More recently, we witness an increase in new food networks initiated by 'concerned' citizens interested in obtaining healthy food directly from the source in order to gain more control over food quality and production practices.[6] These alternative food networks, whether initiated by farmers or citizens, have helped in reconnecting producers and consumers, preserving (or even increasing) agro-biodiversity by re-introducing and valorizing traditional plant varieties and animal breeds, and improving the environmental performance of the food supply chain by reducing food transport and, in many cases, by producing according to organic or low external input methods.[7] Although alternative food networks have a high potential in delivering multiple sustainability outcomes, their further development is hampered by the lack of an infrastructural stepping stone (medium-sized processing and storage facilities and distribution networks have largely disappeared in the past decades) and by the fact that the vast majority of consumers buy food at supermarkets, which are unable (or unwilling) to incorporate small to medium-sized initiatives into their food delivery chains.[8]

3. Multifunctional agriculture[9] as a means to address the economic vulnerability of conventional, specialized agriculture by broadening the economic basis of the farm enterprise[10] but also to reconnect agriculture and society and enhance societal support for agriculture. Moreover, through the development of multifunctional agriculture new socio-economic networks are developed that contribute to the socio-economic viability of the region.[11]

These three interlinked development paths have, politically as well as scientifically, been addressed, analyzed and promoted from a rural development perspective.[12]

Food on the Urban Agenda

This dominant rural focus has strongly contributed to food being 'a stranger to the field of urban planning'.[13] Many urban residents, especially in most Western countries, are taking food for granted. A second reason for the rural bias to food is that food and agriculture are not viewed as part of the urban public domain. This is rooted in the historical process of urbanization, which led to define certain issues as essentially urban and others as essentially rural. Food and agriculture are generally con-

4   Morgan, Marsden, and Murdoch, *Worlds of Food*.

5   D. Roep and J.S.C. Wiskerke, *Nourishing Networks: Fourteen Lessons about Creating Sustainable Food Supply Chains* (Doetinchem: Reed Business Information, 2006).

6   G. Brunori, A. Rossi, and V. Malandrin, 'Co-producing Transition: Innovation Processes in Farms Adhering to Solidarity-based Purchase Groups (GAS) in Tuscany, Italy', *International Journal of Sociology of Agriculture & Food* 18, no. 1 (2011).

7   J.S.C. Wiskerke, 'On Places Lost and Places Regained: Reflections on the Alternative Food Geography and Sustainable Regional Development', *International Planning Studies* 14 (2009), pp. 369–387.

8   Roep and Wiskerke, *Nourishing Networks*.

9   G. van Huylenbroeck and G. Durand, *Multifunctional Agriculture: A New Paradigm for European Agriculture and Rural Development* (Aldershot: Ashgate, 2003).

10 J.D. van der Ploeg et al., 'Rural Development: From Practices and Policies towards Theory', *Sociologia Ruralis* 40, no. 4 (2000), pp. 391–408.

11 H. Renting et al., 'Multifunctionality of Agricultural Activities, Changing Rural Identities and New Institutional Arrangements', *International Journal of Agricultural Resources, Governance and Ecology* 7 (2008), pp. 361–385.

12 R. Sonnino, 'Feeding the City: Towards a New Research and Planning Agenda', *International Planning Studies* 14 (2009), pp. 425–435.

13 K. Pothukuchi and J.L. Kaufman, 'The Food System: A Stranger to The Planning Field', *Journal of the American Planning Association* 66 (2000), pp. 113–124.

14 Sonnino, 'Feeding the City'.

15 A. Moragues-Faus and K. Morgan, 'Reframing the Foodscape: The Emergent World of Urban Food Policy', *Environment and Planning A* 47, no. 7 (2015), pp. 1558–1573.

16 www.milanurban foodpolicypact.org/ signatory-cities/ (accessed 17 April 2018).

sidered to be typical rural issues. This persistent dichotomy in public policy between urban and rural policy has resulted in three shortcomings[14] in food studies, planning, and policy:

1. The study of chains and networks of food provisioning is confined to rural development studies, thereby missing the fact that the city is the space, place, and scale where demand for food products is greatest, including 'alternative' products (e.g. organics, local, origin labelled).

2. Urban food security failure is seen as a production failure instead of a failure of availability, accessibility, and affordability and this has restrained much-needed interventions in urban food security.

3. It has promoted the view of food policy as a non-urban strategy, delaying research on the role of food and agriculture in sustainable urban development as well as on the role of cities as food system innovators and food policymakers.

However, in recent years a growing number of cities have become very active in the field of food and agriculture. Municipal authorities and city councils appear as new actors in the food policy arena,[15] together with new urban social movements. A recent milestone in this respect has been the signing in October 2015 of the Milan Urban Food Policy Pact by over 100 cities—165 by mid-2018[16]—in which they commit themselves to 'develop sustainable food systems that are inclusive, resilient, safe and diverse, that provide healthy and affordable food to all people in a human rights-based framework, that minimize waste and conserve biodiversity while adapting to and mitigating impacts of climate change'. Key reasons why food policy is increasingly seen as an urban issue is the fact that many social, ethical, and environmental problems of cities are food-related and understood as such by urban policymakers; hunger, nutrition value and food insecurity, access to culturally appropriate food, diet-related ill health, carbon footprint, energy consumption, water contamination, loss of farmland, and rural decline.[17] Nowadays there is a growing awareness that food is more central to many urban problems than urban planners, designers, and policymakers have realized in the past.

The growing recognition that food is as much (or even more) an urban issue than a rural issue has also spurred interest in the development of urban and peri-urban agriculture.[18] In the past, much of the political and scientific attention focused on the often quite tenuous relations between urban development and farming close to and inside cities, as these two activities were thought to compete for the same space (pressure on farm land availability and price due to urban sprawl, city dwellers migrating to the countryside thereby restricting development possibilities of farmers). More recently, there is growing interest however in analyzing urban agriculture and city development in terms of mutually beneficial relationships.[19] The short distance between urban farms and urban residents allows for positive interactions between farmers' needs and urban citizens' demands: locally grown freshly available food, authentic experiences, closeness to farms and farmers, protection of farm land in and around cities (also for leisure purposes), public procurement of regional produce, facilitating farmers markets, and so on. From an urban development perspective, urban and peri-urban farming can contribute to a city's capacity to satisfy the basic needs of its citizens. Furthermore, there is growing awareness among local authorities that multifunctional urban and peri-urban green open spaces have a critical role to play in the environmental management of the city, such as disaster prevention, storm water storage/infiltration and run-off reduction, lowering the 'urban heat island' effect and reduction of cooling costs, natural cleaning of wastewater, climate change mitigation/adaptation, and recycling of nutrients from urban wastes.[20]

The City Region

The growing interest in and importance of 'rural' issues (such as agriculture, food, biodiversity, environment) in urban policies, planning, and development, sometimes phrased as 'the countryside in the city',[21] points to a new focus in policies, planning, and development. A focus that aims to go beyond the urban-rural dichotomy by highlighting the increasing importance of relations and interactions along the urban-rural continuum:

> The dichotomy between urban and rural has been used to support a model of development that is no longer as relevant. It serves present purposes better to think of an urban rural continuum in all regions, with mutually reinforcing and reciprocal relationships, and flows of resources, people, and information.[22]

This is the essence of the concept of the city region.[23]

Despite the widespread and growing use of the notion of city region, there is no commonly accepted definition.[24] The minimum common denominator in all definitions is the presence of a core city connected to its hinterland by economic, social, and/or environmental relations and interactions.[25] The notion of the core city can also be replaced by multiple cores making the city region a polycentric space. This implies that the boundaries of the city region can fluctuate in time and differ according to the relations and interactions that one focuses on.

Starting from the notion that city regions are not just simply geographically or physically bounded locations but places shaped by relations and interactions, implies that important issues of governance need to be addressed as the city region transgresses administrative boundaries and is confronted with the challenge of interlinking and aligning policies that were once considered to be confined to either the urban or the rural domain. Hence, a city-region perspective has several implications for design, planning, and policymaking.[26] First, it requires a shift from a sectoral

17 J.S.C. Wiskerke, 'Urban Food Systems', in *Cities and Agriculture: Developing Resilient Urban Food Systems*, eds. H. de Zeeuw and P. Drechsel (Abingdon: Routledge, 2015), pp. 1–25.

18 R. van Veenhuizen, *Cities Farming for Future, Urban Agriculture for Green and Productive Cities* (Leusden: RUAF Foundation, IDRC and IIRP, ETC-Urban agriculture, 2006).

19 A.M. Viljoen en J.S.C. Wiskerke, *Sustainable Food Planning: Evolving Theories and Practices* (Wageningen Academic Publishers, 2012).

20 De Zeeuw and Drechsel, *Cities and Agriculture*.

21 L. Jarosz, 'The City in The Country: Growing Alternative Food Networks in Metropolitan Areas', *Journal of Rural Studies* 24 (2008), pp. 231–244.

22 T. Forster and A. Getz Escudero, *City Regions as Landscapes for People, Food and Nature* (Washington DC: EcoAgriculture Partners on behalf of the Landscapes for People, Food and Nature Initiative, 2014).

23 A. Rodriguez-Pose, 'The Rise of the "City-region" Concept and its Development Policy Implications', *European Planning Studies* 16, no. 8 (2008), pp. 1025–1046.

24 J.B. Parr, 'Perspectives on the City-Region', *Regional Studies* 39, no. 5 (2005), pp. 555–566.

25 Rodriguez-Pose, 'The Rise of the "City-region" Concept and its Development Policy Implications'.

26 Ibid., pp. 1033–1035.

27 A. Vázquez-Barquero, *Endogenous Development: Networking, Innovation, Institutions, and Cities* (London: Routledge, 2002).

28 N. Brenner, 'Metropolitan Institutional Reform and The Rescaling of State Space in Contemporary Western Europe', *European Urban and Regional Studies* 10, no. 4 (2003), pp. 297–324.

29 Renting, 'Multifunctionality of Agricultural Activities, Changing Rural Identities and New Institutional Arrangements'.

30 H. Renting, T.K. Marsden, and J. Banks, 'Understanding Alternative Food Networks: Exploring the Role of Short Food Supply Chains in Rural Development', *Environment and Planning A* 35 (2003), pp. 393–411.

to an integrated approach.[27] This is particularly relevant in the case of food, which is multi-functional and multi-sectoral by default as it not only relates to production and consumption, but also to policy domains such as transport, waste management, education, employment, social welfare, education, and environment. Second, it calls for a place-based approach to design, planning, and policy-making, building on the economic, social, and institutional specificities of a city region. A consequence of this is that the conventional approach to development, i.e. the reproduction of development models, has to be replaced with custom-made approaches in which a thorough diagnosis of the conditions and needs of each city region is the starting point. Best practices will have to be thoroughly re-tailored to local conditions before they are implemented. Third, it requires more attention to bottom-up and participatory approaches. Many city-regional development strategies count on and in some cases are even initiated by civic groups, such as local economic, social, and/or cultural associations. By virtue of their smaller geographical area of operation these civic groups can play a key role in the design and implementation of a city-region development strategy.[28]

City Region Food Systems

In the growing body of literature on city regions the domains of food and agriculture are generally not considered to be of relevance in shaping city regions, in particular in industrialized economies. However, as a significant share of agricultural activities takes place in highly urbanized settings and as these agricultural activities are becoming increasingly multifunctional,[29] new or renewed ties between urban dwellers and farmers are constructed. In addition, there is a trend among parts of the urban population to consume more fresh and local products, to demand short chain food delivery and to request more transparency about the origin of food products.[30] Hence, citizens are becoming more and more interested in regional urban-focused food networks and are increasingly calling for support to urban and peri-urban farmers to safeguard or even increase the availability of and accessibility to local food. The already mentioned growth in urban and regional food strategies, which often explicitly call for more coherence between the city and nearby rural food production, is a clear indication of the emergence of city region food system thinking.[31] The term was defined in a 2013 Food and Agriculture Organization consultation as:

> The complex relation of actors, relations and processes related to food production, processing, marketing, and consumption in a given geographical region that includes one main or smaller urban centres and surrounding peri-urban and rural areas that exchange people, goods and services across the urban rural continuum.[32]

This definition largely fits our approach to a city region food system, but with one addition and one modification. The addition is that we also need to look at actors, relations, and processes involved in food distribution and food waste. The modification is that we prefer a relational approach to city region food systems to a geographically bound approach. A relational approach allows us to include food provisioning practices taking place outside a given geographical area in our analyses of current food systems and designs of future city region foodscapes.

Introducing the Four Cases

With this first socio-spatial design principle—to adopt a city region perspective on food systems—we imply that the level of the city region is the most appropriate level of scale to develop and implement an integrated and comprehensive socio-spatial design approach for future foodscapes. Due to the diversity in the characteristics, problems, and challenges of food provisioning systems it is impossible to develop an integrated and comprehensive set of solutions that work in all city regions. Each city region has its specific characteristics, challenges, and solutions and hence it is vital that city regions design, develop, and implement their own strategy.

To illustrate this we will present and outline four different examples of city region food system approaches. There are similarities between the different cases as all four have implemented or are implementing integrated approaches to food provisioning by focusing on multiple food system challenges. Yet they also differ in terms of priorities, the role of the local government and other key stakeholders such as civil society organizations and the private sector, and the socio-spatial relations between city and countryside. The four city regions are:

1. Bristol (United Kingdom) as a case of building a food strategy on the activities of civic groups and on an explorative study of how the city is fed from its rural hinterland and beyond.
2. New York City (United States) as an example of improving the resilience of a mega city's food system by promoting regional food planning.
3. Ede (The Netherlands) as an illustration of a small city with a relatively large countryside that aims to strengthen its food system by establishing new connections: between economic and social objectives, between food businesses, research and education, and between city and countryside.
4. Belo Horizonte (Brazil) as an example of a metropolitan food security programme in which the municipality assumes public responsibility for the right to food in adequate quantities and quality for its citizens throughout their lives.

31 M. Dubbeling et al., *City Region Food Systems and Food Waste Management: Linking Urban and Rural Areas for Sustainable and Resilient Development* (Bonn and Eschborn: Deutsche Gesellschaft für Internationale Zusammenarbeit [GIZ] GmbH, 2015).
32 Ibid., p. 8.

Joy Carey, Daniel Keech & Matthew Reed

BUILDING THE BRISTOL CITY-REGION FOOD SYSTEM

CITY-REGION PERSPECTIVE

South Gloucestershire

Bristol

North Somerset

Bath & North
East Somerset

Bristol city region, photo: Joy Carey, from *Who Feeds Bristol: Towards a Resilient Food Plan*, 2011

Bristol is located in England's geographical south-west. It has a population of about 455,000, with an economy historically founded on global colonial trade. Today its commercial importance lies in aerospace technology, finance, and creative industries and it is well known for its vibrant, bohemian culture, thriving arts scene, and diverse population. The West of England Combined Authority—which comprises the following local authorities: Bristol, Bath & North East Somerset, and South Gloucestershire—is generally seen as Bristol's city region. It has a population of about 910,000. Since May 2017, the Bristol city region (formally the West of England Combined Authority) is among the first of seven city regions in England with an elected 'metro-mayor', responsible for economic development, housing, and transport.

The city of Bristol sits at the gateway to the rural southwest, the part of England most economically reliant on agriculture. Food and agriculture are, however, largely outside of the control of local politics. The regulation of food is principally influenced by the multiple retailers that supply about 80% of UK groceries. Spatially, the food system has a profound impact on the urban landscape, defining not only the built edges of the city but also the streetscape. Local authorities have limited powers to control the development or location of individual multiple retailer stores.

Much of the criticism against the dominant food system emerged from an increased awareness in Bristol about its reliance on fossil fuels. This became especially evident during fuel distribution boycotts in 2001, resulting in tangible food shortage threats. Concerns about the food system are also associated with the CO_2 emissions of agriculture, food transport, refrigeration and post-retail consumer practices, all of which exacerbate global warming. Recent flooding in or near the Bristol city region demonstrates how vulnerable the area can be to increasingly extreme weather patterns. The sharp oil price rise during the recession, followed in 2014/15 by a dramatic drop, reinforced the link between volatile oil prices and the price of food in a very direct way. Despite food price falls, many vulnerable households have inadequate family budgets to meet nutritional standards and, consequently, are in need of food support. This widespread food security challenge, affecting people in work as much as those who are jobless, is new in the UK and underlines another type of food system vulnerability.

The City of Bristol and surrounding hills, from: *Who Feeds Bristol: Towards a Resilient Food Plan, report,* Joy Carey, 20

The intersection of the environmental, social, and community factors has provided the driving force for a diverse network of civic food initiatives in the city region. To describe, or even map, food initiatives in the city region is challenging in terms of number, scale, and scope, but we estimate that there are more than 200 groups. In scale, they range from those involving hundreds of people to those focused on several persons sharing a garden in a neighbourhood. In scope, they range from initiatives to fight obesity through operations such as food waste cafes and food banks to those attempting to resurrect artisan food skills. There are areas of overlap and even redundancy; some initiatives are well organized and networked, others fizzle out quickly. Most organizations are no- or low-budget and rely on finding points of leverage to create change.

An important civil-society intervention was the formation of the Bristol Food Network (BFN) in 2009, registered as a community interest company in 2014, to promote a set of key goals, such as: encouraging people to cook from scratch, grow their own produce and eat more fresh, seasonal, local, organically grown food; encouraging the use of good-quality land in and near the city for food production; promoting and encouraging the redistribution, recycling, and composting of food waste; and advancing nutritional education and social cohesion. This wide platform has become one around which a wide range of groups can gather and includes those concerned with radical social transformation of the food system, those advocating diet changes, and locals who wish to cultivate a patch of ground in their neighbourhood. In 2009, BFN wrote a 'Sustainable Food Strategy' for Bristol, which stimulated the City Council to develop its own 10-point food charter. This internal charter effectively became an unofficial food strategy to support public-sector food procurement. The charter was a significant step forward and improved communication among staff from different sections of the Council in a Food Initiative Group.

Another key resource in further developing the food network was the publication of the report 'Who Feeds Bristol? Towards a Resilient Food Plan', commissioned by National Health Service (NHS) Bristol. The study resulting in this report was shaped around the following questions:

— Who feeds Bristol and where does the food come from?
— How does Bristol city's food supply system fit into the wider region's food supply system?
— What are the strengths and vulnerabilities?
— To what extent is the current food supply system that serves Bristol city region resilient to shocks and unexpected circumstances in the longer term?
— Which areas of the city and which groups of Bristol residents would be most adversely affected by vulnerabilities in the food supply system?
— What role and powers do the city's decision makers and key stakeholders have in shaping the food system that serves the city and the city region?
— What are the priority areas that need to be addressed in order to develop a more resilient food supply system for the future?

To this end the study looked at the six key components of the food system: production, processing, distribution, retail, catering, and waste. It investigated the provision of basic staple food items; land use for current and potential food production; and the current food supply capacity from the surrounding region in relation to the food needs of Bristol. It also investigated which businesses were involved in preparing, distributing, selling, and recycling or disposing of food across the city region and within the city itself. Information was gathered from existing reports, databases, websites, surveys, and business interviews. The report was 'primarily a descriptive analysis of the food system serving Bristol' but, for the first time, provided a wide range of information about the op-

Blue Finger Alliance, for protection of Grade 1 agricultural lands, UK, photo: Saline Verhoeven

FareShare South West, Bristol, redistribution of surplus food to charities, photo: Saline Verhoeven

Vegetables for decoration at College Green, Bristol Cathedral, photo: Saline Verhoeven

eration of the food system in the south-west region. Despite its constraints, the report provided a key resource for discussing Bristol's food system and how a closer integration might be created between the productive rural areas and the consumer markets of the city region. The report advocates a 'Food Systems Planning' approach for Bristol in order to build a food culture for the city that has the health of people and planet at its heart.

A further development, in March 2011, was the formation of the Bristol Food Policy Council (BFPC), modelled on precedents in North America, notably Toronto, Canada. With members drawn from a wide range of stakeholders including local food industry, Bristol City Council, Bristol Food Network, universities, and grass-roots bodies, it set itself the goal of promoting 'Good Food', defined as being 'vital to the quality of people's lives in Bristol. As well as being tasty, healthy and affordable the food we eat should be good for nature, good for workers, good for local businesses, and good for animal welfare'. The recommendations from the 'Who Feeds Bristol?' report have now become the basis for the Bristol Good Food Plan framework, launched in November 2013. The Food Plan aims to help different actors to participate in an integrated, sustainable food vision for the city, and represents a mechanism for people to coordinate discussion and work. Although not formally part of Bristol City Council, the BFPC and its Good Food Plan gained the official support of Bristol's first elected Mayor (George Ferguson, 2012–2016).

The networks of Bristol food activists have been able to lever specific strategic changes with well-timed and well-executed discursive interventions (for example, the decision by North Bristol Health Trust to address the sustainability of their food procurement policy and catering operations, or the inclusion of a paragraph about the food system in Bristol City Council Planning Policy). The Bristol Food Policy Council holds a seat open for a representative of the multiple retailers, and that symbolic space captures the food network's struggle to influence mass consumers and producers.

Conclusions

The Bristol example shows that citizens' activism has been highly influential in several ways. Firstly, the ability of people to organize themselves into formal and inclusive networks, particularly BFN and BFPC, has helped to improve strategic coordination and inspired policy engagement with sustainable food within the City Council. Secondly, the effective communications of these networks and their expertise have generated a wealth of food-related knowledge and goodwill with positive implications across public, private, and voluntary sectors. This, in turn, encourages further localized actions that underscore the multiple values and social/environmental functions of urban food production and also present compelling arguments for a more diversified food economy. Thirdly, the nature of Bristol's food initiatives, which include new financial, organizational and retailing methods, have led the city to become a place for food innovation in the southwest. And finally, Bristol has been very influential in the UK, encouraging other initiatives to emerge and grow.

The city region concept has undoubtedly helped cast Bristol within, and not separate from, its productive hinterland. However, a consideration of the food system is not included in the responsibility of the city region's metro-mayor. In the future this could be called for, given the links between the food systems and domains the metro-mayor is responsible for: transport, jobs, and economic development. If Bristol's grass-roots networks can successfully recreate helpful political and financial supports, things could be looking up. The network of food activists has demonstrated that they can deliver new ideas, strategic/policy contributions and practical examples of change. Many key resources to creating wider and more systemic food system change lie within the control of the local state. The challenge for those in local government is to match the constructive and civically-minded contribution of the food activist network.

TRANSFORM BRISTOL'S FOOD CULTURE

SAFEGUARD THE DIVERSITY OF FOOD RETAIL

SAFEGUARD LAND FOR FOOD PRODUCTION

INCREASE URBAN FOOD PRODUCTION

A GOOD FOOD PLAN FOR BRISTOL

REDISTRIBUTE, RECYCLE & COMPOST FOOD WASTE

PROTECT KEY INFRASTRUCTURE FOR LOCAL FOOD SUPPLIES

INCREASE THE MARKET OPPORTUNITIES FOR LOCAL & REGIONAL SUPPLIERS

SUPPORT COMMUNITY FOOD ENTERPRISES

From: *A Good Food Plan for Bristol*, 2013, image: Joy Carey

NEW YORK CITY: THE NEED FOR REGIONAL FOOD PLANNING

CITY-REGION PERSPECTIVE

Routes of food distribution trucks into New York City

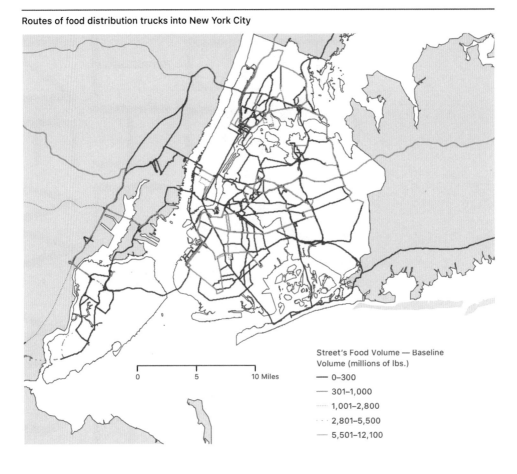

Street's Food Volume — Baseline
Volume (millions of lbs.)

— 0–300
— 301–1,000
...... 1,001–2,800
. . . 2,801–5,500
— 5,501–12,100

0   5   10 Miles

Major clusters of food distribution, New York City

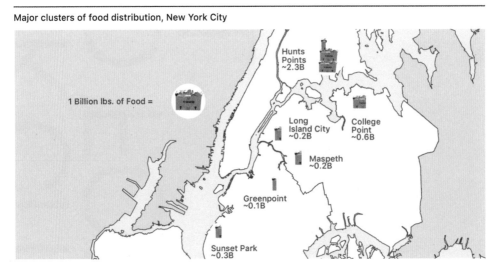

1 Billion lbs. of Food =

Hunts Points ~2.3B

Long Island City ~0.2B

College Point ~0.6B

Maspeth ~0.2B

Greenpoint ~0.1B

Sunset Park ~0.3B

Source: Five Borough Food Flow: 2016 New York City Food Distribution & Resiliency Study Results

In 1921, a planned railroad strike made real the possibility that a city of the size of New York, dependent on distant food supply and losing nearby farmland, would be at risk if food supplies were cut off. This potential strike prompted W.P. Hedden to write a book entitled *How Great Cities Are Fed*,[1] in which he introduced the concept of foodshed: the geographic area from which food flows into a city, town, or village. It includes all the places and spaces of the food provisioning practices that make up a city region's food system. Despite Hedden's concerns about the vulnerability of the food supply of cities, food was, even until recent years, largely absent from the agenda of city planners and urban policy makers.

In the last two decades this has begun to change with a growing number of city governments becoming engaged in food policy and planning. Until recently, municipal food policy and planning tended to focus mainly on the city itself, paying little or no attention to a city's surrounding foodshed.

1   W.P. Hedden, *How Great Cities Are Fed* (New York: D.C. Heath & Co, 1929).
2   www.nycedc.com/system/files/files/resource/2016_food_supply-resiliency_study_results.pdf (accessed 31-12-2017).
3   www1.nyc.gov/site/foodpolicy/about/food-metrics-report.page (accessed 31-12-2017).

Reasons for City
Region Food Planning

However, since 2010, New York City (NYC) has started to address issues associated with its food system that occur both within and outside its five boroughs. This has not been easy as NYC agencies are primarily only responsible for the food system within its five boroughs. While city officials see a clear justification for policies that help New Yorkers, a regional food policy is a much harder sell. The city region includes New York's two neighbouring states, some 31 counties, and roughly 700 separate municipalities. Distinct jurisdictions, competing needs and interests, fractious politics, and the lack of regional governance structures makes coordination complex. And elected officials are often reluctant to invest city tax dollars, and their political capital, on policies that benefit other communities. But two recently released reports, a study of food distribution within NYC's boundaries, called 'Five Borough Food Flow',[2] and NYC's annual 'Food Metrics Report'[3] show that food planning at the city region scale is essential for a more efficient, resilient, and equitable food system. This chapter discusses several reasons why.

Improving Transportation Efficiency
According to the 'Five Borough Food Flow' report, approximately 19 billion pounds of food move throughout NYC each year, transported by thousands of distributors to roughly 42,000 point-of-sale outlets, from bodegas to big box stores. More than half of this food travels over just four bridges and through two tunnels. The last mile of food delivery occurs almost entirely (99%) by truck. Ensuring the efficiency and security of the network of warehouses, food hubs, distribution facilities, transportation routes, and retailers depends on a well-coordinated regional transportation system. The city alone cannot reduce traffic congestion, improve roadway safety, and protect multi-state bridges and tunnels from disruptions. This requires regional planning and infrastructure management by multi-jurisdictional authorities. The benefits of such an effort include reduced air pollution and greenhouse gas emissions, as well as more efficient movement of food.

Moderating Food Costs
through Food Infrastructure

Reducing transportation and wholesale distribution costs would help to moderate food costs. Transportation accounts for about 3.2 cents of every food dollar, while wholesale trade accounts for another 9.1 cents. Reducing both through investments in regional transportation and distribution infrastructure, and government incentives to make distribution infrastructure more efficient, can keep retail food prices down while producing co-benefits such as reduced air pollution and greenhouse gas emissions. One opportunity to reduce such costs involves developing a regional system of food hubs. These would promote regional food, facilitate on-farm processing and aggregation near points of production, increase value-added products, and reduce distribution costs.

Addressing Environmental Injustice
Regional food planning can also address the environmental injustices that arise from concentrations of food businesses in neighbourhoods like Hunts Point in the South Bronx, which is home to the Hunts Point Food Distribution Centre (FDC), the largest geographic cluster of food distribution in NYC. Hunts Point moves 4.5 billion pounds of food annually, half to NYC retailers and half to other retailers in the region. Hunts Point is a predominantly Hispanic (76%) and Black (22%) neighbourhood, with a poverty rate (43%) twice as high as the city average (21%). The diesel trucks travelling to and from the food market emit airborne fine particulate matter at levels higher than the city average, contributing to twice the rate of asthma hospitalization. NYC has already taken numerous steps to improve the environmental conditions of Hunts Point and to reduce the environmental impacts of truck traffic. Regional transportation planning would further reduce the environmental health impact borne by Hunts Point residents by expanding cleaner transportation options for the FDC. This alone will not eliminate the substantial disparities facing the people of Hunts Point, but they can improve environmental conditions in the community.

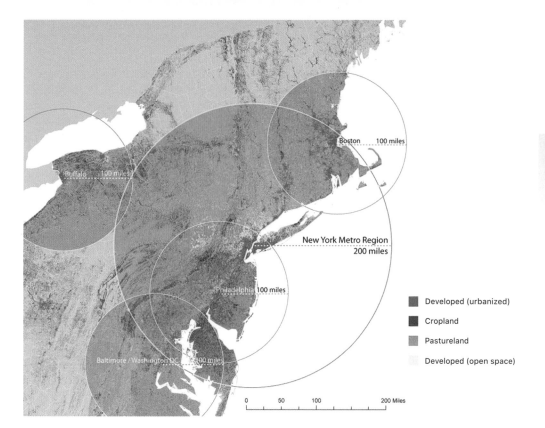

Boston 100 miles

Buffalo 100 miles

New York Metro Region
200 miles

Philadelphia 100 miles

Baltimore / Washington DC 100 miles

■ Developed (urbanized)

■ Cropland

■ Pastureland

□ Developed (open space)

0   50   100   200 Miles

Foodshed of the New York Metro Region, image: Urban Design Lab, The Earth Institute at Columbia University

Share of Total Food Volume

Share of Locations

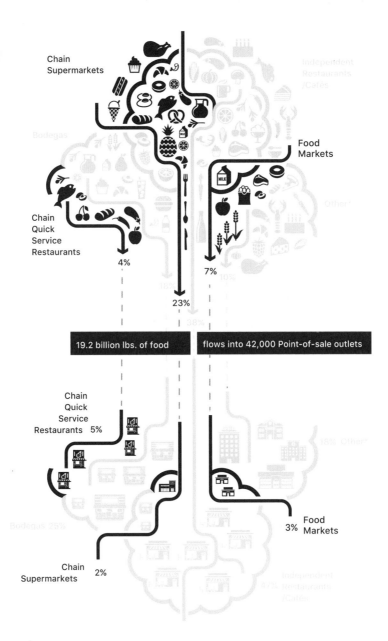

Chain
Supermarkets

Independent
Restaurants
/Cafes

Food
Markets

Other*

Chain
Quick
Service
Restaurants

4%

7%

23%

19.2 billion lbs. of food   **flows into 42,000 Point-of-sale outlets**

Chain
Quick
Service
Restaurants   5%

Food
3%   Markets

Chain
Supermarkets   2%

Food flow of New York City: share of volume and locations.
Source: Five Borough Food Flow: 2016 New York City Food Distribution & Resiliency Study Results

Increasing Resilience

No single NYC food distributor or food hub has more than 15% of the market. This fragmentation makes the food system somewhat resilient. However, the clustering of food distribution businesses in and around the Hunts Point FDC remains a big vulnerability. Protecting the Hunts Point peninsula from flooding and upgrading the market's infrastructure is key to enabling the city's food distribution system to rebound from climate change-induced weather events, as well as disruptions due to power grid failures or acts of terrorism. Planning to support a mix of national, regional, and local food suppliers and distribution firms is crucial to avert the kinds of system-wide disruptions that occur when infrastructure is geographically concentrated or composed of a small number of firms. Protecting regional infrastructure from the effects of extreme weather events is critical. Equally critical is planning to ensure that the region's most vulnerable communities have access to food and water in the event of a disaster. This all requires coordination at the level of the city region.

Protecting Drinking Water

Approximately 90% of NYC's drinking water comes from surface reservoirs in a mostly rural 1,600 square mile watershed in the Catskills. The city's water is treated and purified but is not filtered as NYC has a waiver from the federal filtration rule by committing to land acquisition in the watershed and various programmes to help the farmers and communities in the watershed adopt practices to minimize pollution to the streams that feed the city's reservoirs. The Watershed Agricultural Program, which is funded by city water customers, financially supports farmers to operate sustainably within the city's watershed. By helping them and their surrounding communities to thrive, it forestalls local pressure to permit forms of economic activity that would threaten the water supply and necessitate filtration. This is key to both local food and safe drinking water.

Maintaining Working Landscapes

Maintaining vibrant farms and rural communities is also key to conserve working landscapes in an increasingly densely populated region, preventing automobile-dependent sprawl and reducing carbon emissions that contribute to climate change. This requires regional farmland planning, succession planning for farm owners, agroforestry opportunities for owners of forested land, and zoning and financial assistance to keep farms in food production, efforts best organized at a foodshed scale. Another important mechanism is regionalization of the public plate, i.e. the purchase by local governments of food grown, raised, and processed within the region for school lunches and other public feeding programmes. A better-coordinated regional market for locally grown institutional food could achieve economies of scale, improvements in nutrition, and reductions in food insecurity.

Reducing Pollution of Our Waterways

One of the last remaining major sources of water pollution is combined sewer overflow (CSO), the mix of storm water and untreated sewage that overflows into waterways when it rains. Conventional infrastructure to capture storm water, such as larger sewers and treatment plants, or holding tanks, is costly and unpopular. 'Green infrastructure', by contrast, is a cost-effective alternative. It involves making the city's concrete and asphalt surfaces permeable, allowing rain to percolate into the ground instead of running into the nearest river. Vegetated surfaces not only prevent CSO run-off but also provide environmental and health co-benefits, such as reducing the urban heat island effect and air pollution. Urban agriculture projects have been funded by the city as a form of green infrastructure, a policy that can be greatly expanded, helping to reduce water pollution while producing fresh vegetables.

Regional Food Waste Composting
Organic waste accounts for one-third of the NYC household waste stream, 80% of which is now landfilled in surrounding states. Like San Francisco (see pp. 159ff.) NYC has implemented a 'Zero Waste' initiative that includes commercial composting regulations and pilot household composting programmes. The commercial programme requires businesses generating large quantities of organic waste to separate their food waste for composting. To be successful, however, regional composting facilities will have to be developed, and also a market for the end product. Regional planning for organic waste management is furthermore needed to ensure that facilities are spread fairly throughout the region and do not impose environmental harms on communities already burdened by industrial infrastructure.

Conclusions

Regional food planning holds the promise of a more sustainable, equitable, and rational food system for NYC. It can bring health, economic, environmental, and social benefits that result from an integrated approach to food, agriculture, transportation, and economic development. However, regional planning faces a number of obstacles. Strong ideological commitment to local land use controls makes regional land use planning difficult. The lack of democratic institutions with a mandate and capacity to plan for food makes collaboration among jurisdictions challenging. However, cities as diverse as Philadelphia, Chicago, and Portland have crafted regional food plans that address some of the issues discussed above. These have typically been developed by metropolitan planning organizations, appointed bodies responsible for regional transportation planning, with the involvement of a wide range of stakeholders.

CREATING CONNECTIONS THROUGH EDE'S MUNICIPAL FOOD STRATEGY

CITY-REGION

Nijkerk

Barneveld

Scherpenzeel

Ede

Renswoude

Veenendaal

Rhenen

Wageningen

1 www.regiofoodvalley.
nl/extra/english/
(accessed 19-02-2018).

Ede is a municipality in the Netherlands in the province of Gelderland. It is one of the largest in the Netherlands in terms of surface area and consists of the city of Ede itself and seven villages spread across the surrounding countryside. This means that the municipality includes a large rural area as well as an urban centre and smaller urbanized areas, with an overall population of over 113,000 inhabitants, approximately 72,000 of whom live in Ede city. Ede municipality is characterized by a large variety in landscapes. The region was formed on a moraine ridge, as the elevated area provided opportunities for survival. High (dry) heathland landscapes for sheep, lowland meadows for cattle, interspersed with areas where farming has taken place for centuries. This historical spatial organization can still be found in Ede municipality today. A large part of the municipal area is a national park, De Hoge Veluwe.

Ede is member of the FoodValley region,[1] a partnership of eight municipalities (totalling 345,000 residents) with a focus on research, education, and innovation in the agro-food sector. FoodValley is home to many international food companies, research institutes, and Wageningen University. Within the FoodValley about 15,000 professionals are active in food-related sciences and technological development. Far more are involved in the manufacturing of food products. Through the Food-Valley partnership the eight municipalities intend to create conditions for interactions and collaborations between food manufacturers and knowledge institutes to develop new and innovate food concepts. Special focus lies on health and sustainability. FoodValley has the ambition of becoming the world's dynamic centre of knowledge and innovation for the international food industry, similar to what Silicon Valley is for the ICT industry.

Ede's Food Vision

Ede is considered to be one of the frontrunners in the Netherlands when it comes to municipal food policy and in 2017 was awarded a Milan Pact Award for urban food governance.[2] In 2012, the municipal councillors created a new vision for the municipality to guide the future direction of policy. Ede chose 'food' as the central policy theme for the future and in 2015 a specific food vision document was adopted by the city council. The municipality appointed a special food alderman with his own budget, making Ede the first municipality in the Netherlands to do so. In 2017, Ede was one of the 12 Dutch municipalities to sign the City Deal 'Food on the Urban Agenda', in which the participating municipalities aim to improve their food provisioning system and develop an integrated food policy.

A healthy and sustainable food system for everyone in Ede: that is the ambition Ede pursues through its food vision. This vision is designed to be integrated, meaning it connects several policy areas such as health, economy, and social work. The vision focuses more specifically on improving the economic opportunities of the municipality, while producing food sustainably and becoming a socially stronger, more inclusive and healthier city. Consequently, in the context of Ede's food policy, food is understood as an instrument that can be applied as a solution to other policy domains.

Ede's food vision connects economy and society through knowledge and innovation.[3] In this vision, Ede reveals two main ambitions to be and to stay in a leading food policy position:

1. To strengthen Ede's economic power and competitive position by increasing its attractiveness for business and knowledge institutes, students, visitors, and future inhabitants; supporting innovation in agrifood businesses; supporting food events; and intensifying international cooperation.
2. To strengthen Ede's societal power by creating opportunities for people to meet and connect; strengthening the relation between the city and its rural hinterland; enhancing knowledge and awareness about healthy and sustainable food; increasing cultural attractiveness for recreation and tourism; and facilitating urban agriculture initiatives.

In their vision of 'strengthening by connecting', Ede uses knowledge and innovation to connect the economic and societal side of food. In addition, the food vision of Ede stresses the importance of their 'food partners' that are necessary for implementing the vision. The local government, knowledge institutes, and businesses are mentioned, but above all: the inhabitants of Ede. Their motivations and initiatives are considered to be of vital importance for the success of the food vision of Ede.[4]

Food as a Connector

Central to Ede's food vision is to strengthen economic and societal development and progress by creating connections. Food serves as a connector in different ways: between food businesses and food research and education institutes, between schools, sports and health care organizations, and between city and countryside.

2   www.milanurban-foodpolicypact.org/2017/10/20/the-cities-of-toronto-and-antananarivo-win-this-years-milan-pact-awards/ (accessed 19-02-2018).
3   www.ede.nl/fileadmin/files/ede/gemeente/documenten/20150923_Visie_Food.pdf (accessed 19-02-2018).
4   www.ede.nl/edekiestvoorfood/ (accessed 19-02-2018).

Food Unplugged, annual food festival in Ede, photo: Floris Heuer

City Pigs, Ede, www.stadsvarkens.nl, photo: Emile Nijs

FoodValley: Connecting Businesses and Knowledge Institutes

The economy of Ede and of the FoodValley region is to a large extent based on food. The economic and spatial clustering of food businesses, food research, and food education has supported the growth and competitiveness of food companies as well as new start-ups in the food sector. Thanks to the connections between businesses, research, and education FoodValley has become an attractive location for national and international food companies. For example, the largest Dutch dairy cooperative, FrieslandCampina, has moved its R&D division to the campus of Wageningen University and Research. The economic growth of the food cluster also has a positive economic spin-off for other businesses and employment opportunities in Ede municipality.

Healthy Eating: Connecting Food Education, Sports and Health Care

Enhancing food literacy is, according to Ede municipality, a means to stimulate healthy eating. Towards this end Ede invests in educational food projects for schools, such as in lessons about healthy and sustainable eating and in school gardens for all primary school children. Ede also creates space for urban agriculture and encourages farmers and other food businesses to organize open days. This enables children, young people, and adults to see, hear, smell, and taste what is happening on farms and in food businesses in Ede. A unique collaboration between the municipality and citizen groups Eetbaar Ede and Smaakstad Ede is the FoodFloor: a platform where citizens with a food initiative can find fellow enthusiasts and receive a small subsidy to bring their project a step further.

The municipality also wants to curb the rising prevalence of non-communicable diseases, caused by current eating habits. Social and ethical considerations play a role here—i.e. access to and affordability of healthy food as a basic human right—but also economic ones as diet-related ill health impacts heavily on the health care budgets. Ede municipality collaborates with companies, societal organizations, research institutes, schools, the municipal public health service, and the Gelderse Vallei hospital to stimulate healthy eating patterns. Elderly people and children are important target groups. Healthy food and education about this at schools, in sports canteens, and health care establishments is a focal point for Ede.

Regional Food Networks:
Connecting the Rural and the Urban
Another priority in Ede's food vision is to strengthen the link between city and countryside through urban agriculture, regional food markets, and more local and regional food in food outlets and eateries in Ede city and the villages. Regionally produced and sourced food can meet the needs of consumers who want to know the origin of their food. Moreover, local food creates a new market for agricultural companies, both conventional and organic, and contributes to the liveliness in the centre of Ede. The municipality also expects that shorter food chains and smart logistics offer opportunities to prevent and reduce waste.

Ede municipality has a relatively large rural area with many farms, primarily dairy and livestock. Within a business-as-usual scenario, i.e. specialization and scale enlargement, it is expected that the number of farms in Ede will decline from 700 to about 200 over the next ten years. Creating a market for regional, place-based products may provide an interesting opportunity for some farmers. Additionally, it is one of the ways to make Ede's city region food system more sustainable and healthy by reducing food transport, packaging, and storage and by creating the logistic opportunities for delivering fresh food.

Conclusions

Ede municipality sees it as its responsibility as a local government to address contemporary food challenges. Ede sees integrated food policy as key to address these challenges and to align and create synergies between societal, economic, and environmental objectives. The municipality is not only keen on implementing and practising this integrated food vision in its own region, but also has the ambition to show the importance and value of food connections for sustainable development to a national and international audience of food professionals and interested citizens. Towards this end Ede is planning to develop the World Food Centre, which is to become the iconic (inter)national food experience centre: a place where the societal, economic, and environmental themes of Ede's food policy come together; a place that fosters the dialogue as well as the sharing and co-creation of knowledge between agro-food businesses and society; and a place where consumers can (re)connect to food by experiencing how food is made from farm to fork.

Ground-to-ground track World Food Centre Ede

BELO HORIZONTE: WORLD PIONEER IN REDUCING HUNGER AND MALNUTRITION

Belo Horizonte Metropolitan Region, Minas Gerias, Brasil

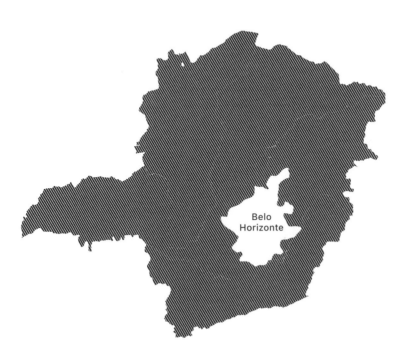

Belo Horizonte

Belo Horizonte Metropolitan Region

Introduction

Belo Horizonte is the capital of the Brazilian state of Minas Gerais. It is Brazil's sixth largest city, with a population of 2.5 million. The city forms the core of the Belo Horizonte Metropolitan Region, which comprises 33 urban and rural municipalities. With a total population of more than 5.7 million it is Brazil's third most populous metropolitan region. Like many cities in Brazil it was, and still is, characterized by high levels of socioeconomic inequality.[1] In the early 1990s it was estimated that 38% of families in the region lived below the poverty line, and 44% of all children lived in poverty.[2] Close to 20% of children aged 0 to 3 years old showed some degree of malnutrition.[3]

Reducing food insecurity became one of the prime objectives of the new municipal government that took office in 1993. The food security programme that was developed under the leadership of mayor Patrus Ananias has become renowned worldwide, receiving national as well as international prizes. It has served as a model for other municipalities in and outside Brazil as well as for Brazil's national 'Fome Zero' (Zero Hunger) policy that was implemented by President Lula da Silva's administration from 2003 onwards.

1   M. Mendonça and C. Rocha, 'Implementing National Food Policies to Promote Local Family Agriculture: Belo Horizonte's Story', *Development in Practice* 25, no. 2 (2015), pp. 160–173.

2   C. Rocha, 'Urban Food Security Policy: The Case of Belo Horizonte, Brazil', *Journal for the Study of Food and Society* 5, no. 1 (2001), pp. 36–47.

3   E.M. Pratley and B. Dodson, 'The Spaces for Farmers in the City: A Case Study Comparison of Direct Selling Alternative Food Networks in Toronto, Canada and Belo Horizonte, Brazil', *Canadian Food Studies/ La Revue canadienne des études sur l'alimentation* 1, no. 1 (2014), pp. 72–87.

Key to the food security programme in Belo Horizonte was the acknowledgement by the municipal government that all citizens have the right to adequate quantity and quality of food throughout their lives, and that it is the duty of governments to guarantee this. This public responsibility for the right to food has been a key factor in putting a coordinated, system-wide municipal policy for food security into practice.

Among the first acts of the municipal government after taking office in 1993 was to create a municipal Secretariat for Food Policy and Supply (Secretaria Municipal Adjunta de Abastecimento—SMAAB) charged with preventing and reducing malnutrition and hunger among vulnerable groups, bringing food to parts of the city that were neglected by commercial outlets, and increasing food production. The unique aspect of SMAAB is that it worked cross-departmentally with all city authorities and important civil society organizations and initiatives to implement food security for the people of Belo Horizonte. Today, SMAAB has grown into the Municipal Secretariat for Food and Nutrition Security (SMASAN), with a staff of 180, including 30 nutritionists, and programmes that benefit more than 300,000 citizens daily. Although its approach has evolved over the years, its basic mandate remains that of ensuring food and nutrition security in Belo Horizonte, especially among low-income residents. It does that through a comprehensive set of programmes aimed at providing access to food and increasing agricultural production both in surrounding rural areas and within the city itself. The creation of SMASAN allowed for an integrated thinking about the food system. It no longer was 'food for hungry students' in a department of education, or 'food for needy people' in a department of social assistance, or 'food from family farmers' in a department of agriculture. Rather than compartmentalizing food security in the municipal policy agenda, SMASAN was able to integrate all the aspects of the food system. Its strategy was to partner with other city departments in implementing its programmes.

SMASAN has organized its programmes along six lines of work:[4] 1) subsidized food sales; 2) food and nutrition assistance; 3) supply and regulation of food markets; 4) support to urban agriculture; 5) education for food consumption; and 6) job and income generation. For the purpose of this book the first four will be briefly described, as they all have socio-spatial implications.

Subsidized Food Sales

Probably the most iconic programme in SMASAN's repertoire is the 'Popular Restaurant' (*Restaurante Popular*). Since 1994, when the first of its four Popular Restaurants opened to the public, Belo Horizonte has been the reference for other cities in Brazil in operating a successful public eatery providing healthy, balanced meals at very low cost to a large number of residents. These restaurants serve a typical lunch of rice, beans, meat, vegetables, salad, and fruit (or juice) for the low price of R$3.00 (about € 0.85). Breakfast can be bought for R$0.75 (€ 0.22) and dinner for R$1.50 (€ 0.45). The city also sells subsidized non-perishable food items through its 'Popular Big Basket' (*Cestão Popular*) programme. Unlike the Popular Restaurant, this is not a universal programme, but restricted to low-income families who must be included in a registry by the Secretariat of Social Services. Registered people receive a magnetic card which gives them access to the subsidized purchases in 26 specific points of sale (vans or trucks operated by the city) in low-income areas.

4   M.A. Girioli, 'Secretaria Municipal Adjunta de Abastecimento: Promovendo a Segurança Alimentar e Nutricional' (2008). Summary text prepared for a visit by the delegation from the Ontario Secondary School Teachers Federation; C. Rocha and I. Lessa, 'Urban Governance for Food Security: The Alternative Food System in Belo Horizonte, Brazil', *International Planning Studies* 14, no. 4 (2009), pp. 389–400.

Lunch at a Restaurante Popular, Belo Horizonte

Food and Nutrition Assistance to At-risk Groups

This line of action focuses on providing direct food and nutrition assistance to children and youth, the elderly, and homeless people. This is all carried out in venues where at-risk people already receive some attention (public schools and day-care centres, health clinics, nursing homes, shelters, and other charitable institutions). The largest programme under this line of work is the 'School Meals Programme', which in 2012 served over 40 million meals to 155 thousand students in 218 public schools. Another programme is the monthly distribution of two kilograms of powdered milk and a litre of cooking oil to families with children presenting some degree of under-nutrition. Since 2004, the 'Food Bank' has been added to SMASAN's projects. Its objectives are to reduce unnecessary food waste and provide additional access to food to marginalized populations not covered by other city programmes. Most of the food received by the food bank is fresh produce. The food bank daily collects remains of fresh fruits and vegetables from farmers' markets and grocery stores around the city. It then selects, cleans, and vacuum freezes perishable foods for distribution to charitable organizations and social service agencies, which will then prepare and serve communal meals.

Supply and Regulation of Food Markets

This aims at improving access to healthy food by increasing the number of commercial outlets supplying good quality foodstuff at lower prices. To this end SMASAN licenses private operators to be located in key regions of the city. In exchange for being allowed to operate in more profitable, city-owned locations, sellers are required to serve low-income, peripheral areas on weekends. Under the license agreement with SMASAN, private operators sell 25 products at a price set by the Secretariat (20–50% below market prices). Prices of other items sold in these outlets are not regulated, allowing operators to make a small profit. Besides prices, SMASAN also monitors the quality of the products sold under the programmes and provides technical assistance and general information on product display, safe storage, and handling. The 'Straight from the Country' and 'The Country Store' programmes aim at facilitating direct interaction between small rural producers and urban consumers. By eliminating the intermediaries that normally operate in bringing the products of small rural producers to urban markets, SMASAN intends to increase the income of small family farmers and artisan processors and still offer high-quality products to consumers at lower prices. The main goal of these programmes is to help rural families to establish themselves in the countryside, halting the rural-urban migration which has inflated Belo Horizonte's populations in the favelas (shantytowns).

Support to Urban and Peri-urban Agriculture

In Belo Horizonte, food production is seen as a legitimate form of land use and as an activity contributing to the social functioning of the city region. Urban and peri-urban agriculture is promoted through participatory community involvement and the use of agro-ecological production methods. At last count, SMASAN's programme for urban and peri-urban agriculture had created 185 vegetable gardens and 48 orchards across Belo Horizonte. This includes gardens in schools and day-care centres, three fully commercial gardens, and non-commercial gardens in health and social welfare centres, nursing homes, shelters, and other public facilities. School gardens are among the most effective tools for promoting urban agriculture. Children can attend workshops on micro-gardening, and SMASAN provides assistance in setting up gardens to schools that join the programme. Close to 100,000 children are involved in school gardening, spending on average one hour a day caring for the plants. SMASAN's orchard programme distributes fruit tree seedlings (typically cherry, carambola, orange, lemon, and tangerine) free of charge to schools, institutions, and community groups, primarily in low-income favelas on sloping land, where trees are also needed to prevent soil erosion.

Family farmers in the rural areas of the city-region also receive support, in particular through public procurement of food from smallholder family farmers for the school meals programme and the Popular Restaurants. This has become mandatory under federal law. In the longer term, SMASAN plans to lower the costs of food production by introducing rainwater harvesting systems and by improving wastewater treatment and the quality of compost. Towards this end collaboration with the city's waste management service is foreseen. Another ambition on the SMASAN agenda is to guarantee urban farmers the use of public land for at least five years. It is also lobbying for the zoning of parcels of urban land specifically for agriculture in order to reduce intense competition for land for real estate development.[5]

Conclusions

Belo Horizonte's food policy is generally considered to be an outstanding example of an integrated and place-based approach to food security and has served as an example for the federal Zero Hunger policy introduced in 2003. Setting up a specific municipal organization (SMASAN) that works across and links various traditional municipal departments (education, health, social services, spatial planning) to develop and implement the city region's food security programme has been a key factor for success. Its lines of action and institutional philosophy—public responsibility for the right to food—have had a major impact on improving the social equity and inclusiveness of Belo Horizonte's city region food system.

5   www.fao.org/ag/agp/greenercities/en/gg-clac/belo_horizonte.html (accessed 19-02-2018).

Johannes S.C. Wiskerke, Saline Verhoeven & Marc C.A. Wegerif

LINKING SCALES

Dar es Salaam

This second part of the book covers the second socio-spatial design principle, that of 'linking scales'. Unlike in the previous part this second principle is illustrated with the example of just one city region, Dar es Salaam. We will first introduce Dar es Salaam and discuss its growth challenges and its food system, and then briefly outline the principle of linking scales and how that applies to Dar es Salaam.

Introducing Dar es Salaam

Dar es Salaam is the largest city of Tanzania and of Eastern Africa in terms of population. Although it is not Tanzania's capital (which is Dodoma), it is the country's most important economic centre and the focus of the permanent central government administration. Dar es Salaam is the third fastest growing city in Africa, after Bamako (Mali) and Lagos (Nigeria), and is in the top 10 of fastest growing cities in the world. Dar es Salaam has a population of around 4.6 million (2017), up from less than 2.5 million in 2002.[1] The average annual population has grown by approximately 4.4% since 2006 and is expected to reach 5.7 million by 2025.

Dar es Salaam is a prime example of the urban or metropolitan centres that take in almost all new population growth and where two thirds of the world's 9 billion people will be living in 2050. Sustainably feeding such cities, where many residents live precarious lives in poverty, is a growing challenge for any food system to meet.[2] Agriculture still provides the primary income for around 80% of the population of Tanzania. Food production is dominated by small-scale agricultural and pastoral production systems, which produce enough to make the country marginally food secure.[3] However, food security at national level does not mean that it covers all the people living in Dar es Salaam.

1 National Bureau of Statistics, *2012 Population and Housing Census* (Dar es Salaam: National Bureau of Statistics, Ministry of Finance, 2013).

2 T. Lang, 'Crisis? What Crisis? The Normality of the Current Food Crisis', *Journal of Agrarian Change* 10, no. 1 (2010), pp. 87–97.

3 FAOSTAT, 2016.

Urban agriculture in Dar es Salaam, photo: Tim Kort

Charcoal and wood fires in the city of Dar es Salaam add to air pollution, photo: David Habets

Small vans and motocycles used to transport live chickens to the market, Dar es Salaam, photo: Anna Maria Fink

Dar es Salaam's Growth Challenges

Economic liberalization in Tanzania has contributed to economic growth, also in agricultural outputs, and international investors including supermarket chains have begun to establish themselves in Tanzania.[4] Along with these economic improvements Dar es Salaam faces multiple challenges, which are not unique to Dar es Salaam as they hold true for many of the fast-growing cities around the world, in particular in Africa:

1. Traffic congestion and air pollution. The speed of urbanization has major infrastructural consequences for Dar es Salaam, just like it has for many other large and rapidly growing urban centres: 'Building infrastructure takes time as well as money, and rapid growth often means that there is not enough of either to keep up with needs'.[5] Dar es Salaam's transport infrastructure is outdated and unable to cope with the growing number of cars, leading to a rapid increase in traffic congestion problems. This is a major source of air pollution.

2. Climate change. Food insecurity induced by climate change in Dar es Salaam will not only be the result of lower or at least highly fluctuating levels of food production, but also of the unavailability and inaccessibility of food in parts of the city. Dar es Salaam is a delta metropole and parts of the metropolitan area will be flooded as a result of heavy rainfall, which may have severe negative impacts on food distribution and the accessibility of food markets.

3. Social inequality and poverty. While in most major regions of the world urbanization has gone hand in hand with economic development, this does not hold true for Africa, where current urbanization seems to occur regardless of economic development.[6] Rather, these cities seem to function as magnets to those seeking a higher quality of life. This results in significant and growing wealth differences between the relatively small upper- and middle-class and the very large low-income class. Manifestations of this are socioeconomic related differences in access to food, housing, clean drinking water, and electricity and adequate sewage and solid waste disposal facilities.[7] The following statistics[8] about Dar es Salaam illustrate this:

- 27% of the households sometimes or frequently have a problem satisfying food needs;
- 26% of 5-year-olds are stunted in their growth due to poor nutrition;
- 16% of the population lives below the basic needs poverty line;
- 10% of the urban households have motorized transport (motorbikes, cars or trucks);
- 41% of the households have only one room in a house they share with other households;
- 74% of the households have three or more members;
- 21% of the population has water piped to their yard or house;
- 45% of the population has electricity;
- 65% of the population cook on charcoal and 24% on wood;
- 23% of the population has a refrigerator.

It is clear that many residents of Dar es Salaam live in crowded conditions with little or no secure storage space for food. Very few have access to refrigerators or private motorized transport and this has a major impact on what food they can buy and from where they can procure it. More than half the people in the city do not have electricity and many of those in houses with electricity still cook on charcoal or firewood.

4. Creating and maintaining space for urban and peri-urban agriculture, which is increasingly recognized for its role in climate change adaptation and mitigation, in environmental and waste management, and in alleviating food poverty and insecurity.[9] It is a means to create and maintain green open spaces and increase vegetation cover in the city. This can

J.S. Crush and G.B. Frayne, 'Urban Food Insecurity and the New International Food Security Agenda', *Development Southern Africa* 28, no. 4 (2011), pp. 527–544.

A. Sorensen and J. Okata, 'Introduction: Megacities, Urban Form, and Sustainability', in *Megacities: Urban Form, Governance and Sustainability*, eds. A. Sorensen and J. Okata (Tokyo and New York: Springer, 2010), pp. 1–11.

B. Cohen, 'Urbanization in Developing Countries: Current Trends, Future Projections, and Key Challenges for Sustainability', *Techology in Society* 28 (2006), pp. 63–80.

V. Broto, A. Allen, and E. Rapoport, 'Interdisciplinary Perspectives on Urban Metabolism', *Journal of Industrial Ecology* 16, no. 6 (2012), pp. 851–861.

M.C.A. Wegerif, *Feeding Dar es Salaam: A Symbiotic Food System Perspective*, PhD thesis (Wageningen: Wageningen University, 2017).

H. de Zeeuw and P. Drechsel, *Cities and Agriculture: Developing Resilient Urban Food Systems* (Oxford: Routledge, 2015).

R.V. Piacentini, 'A Whole-Building, Integrated Approach for Designing a High-Performance, Net-Zero-Energy and Net-Zero-Water Building', in *Mediterranean Green Buildings & Renewable Energy* (Cham: Springer, 2017), pp. 931–940.

Wegerif, *Feeding Dar es Salaam*.

M. Dubbeling, 'Urban Agriculture as a Climate Change and Disaster Risk Reduction Strategy', *Urban Agriculture Magazine* 27 (2014), pp. 3–7.

help to reduce urban heat islands by providing shade and increasing evapotranspiration.[10] Furthermore, green productive urban spaces can help to store excess rainfall and thus reduce flood risks. Urban agriculture can also help to reduce food transport, and thus alleviate the aforementioned problem of traffic congestion. Urban agriculture can also help to reduce the need for cool storage of perishable products and can thereby contribute to lowering GHG emissions. In Dar es Salaam, up to 90% of the green leafy vegetables eaten are produced in the metropolitan area and its fringe. Urban and peri-urban agriculture is also a major source of other food items, such as milk, poultry, and eggs.[11] Finally, urban agriculture can play a role in the productive reuse of urban organic waste and wastewater, which may help to reduce energy use in fertilizer production and in organic waste collection and disposal[12] as well as in lowering emissions from wastewater treatment. These multiple beneficial impacts imply that it is important to maintain space for urban and peri-urban agriculture, spatially as well as regulatory. This is a challenge for the three municipal governments that make up Dar es Salaam and that on the one hand have difficulties governing population growth and the utilization of space and on the other hand have an ambiguous position about urban and peri-urban agriculture. The local authorities do recognize the 'greening and food security' benefits of urban agriculture, but they also point to the health risks (zoonosis) of keeping livestock in urban settings.

These growth challenges need to be addressed when (re)designing Dar es Salaam's foodscapes. Spatial interventions should not lead to more (and should preferably alleviate) traffic congestion, should be adapted to and preferably mitigate climate change, should take into account the specific living conditions of the urban poor, and should help to create and maintain space for urban agriculture.

Access to Food in Dar es Salaam

The main sources of food for the majority of people in Dar es Salaam are:[13]

- the *duka,* a general shop that sells a variety of fresh and processed foods and that can be found in every street;
- the *genge*, a fresh fruit and vegetables stand, which can also be found in almost every street;
- the people's markets;
- direct access from producers in urban, peri-urban and rural areas;
- street food vendors.

The supermarkets are only used by some elite consumers who have access to transport. Getting to the supermarket requires motorized transport, which makes it more expensive and less accessible for the majority of the urban dwellers. The foods that most people rely on are generally more expensive in supermarkets. Other drawbacks of the supermarkets are the fixed quantities and the fact that supermarkets do not sell on credit.

Widely agreed definitions of the 'right to food' include people having 'physical and economic access at all times to sufficient, adequate and culturally acceptable food'.[14] At the micro level of the individual eater or household this access to food entails several aspects:

1. *Low prices* are clearly important and are maintained by having low overhead and getting supplies through an efficient food system. The efficiency of Dar es Salaam's food system is fundamentally different from that of western food systems, which are to a large extent managed by a small number of transnational retailers and food processing industries. Dar es Salaam's food system is based on a large number of self-employed producers, transporters, processors, traders, and cooks who are assisting each other and work together in ways that value collaboration over competition: 'Multitudes of actors are collectively delivering at great scale but with no centralized management from cooperatives, corporations, or the state. The system is instead held together around the ordering principle of symbiosis underpinned by common cultural repertoires and familiarity'.[15]

2. Beyond low prices, accessibility of food for more people also requires the sale of food in *flexible quantities* that match the exact needs and purchasing ability of the eaters at the time they need the food. Whereas the supermarket model tends to only offer their better prices when buying in bulk, such as getting a 25-kg sack of maize rather than a kilo or even half a kilo, the *duka* and the people's markets sell at the same low price regardless of quantity. The system of measuring out the quantities that a customer wants (or can afford), rather than selling pre-packaged foods, is practiced for the main food items in all the *dukas* and markets. Flexibility of quantities is also a necessity for many because of their crowded and insecure living conditions where food cannot be stored safely.

3. *Proximity to place of residence* reduces or, in most cases in Dar es Salaam, eliminates transport costs and saves time. This becomes more important when buying in small quantities and depending on an unreliable income; for most people in Dar it is easy to go to the *duka* when they have the money and need the food. This, combined with the long opening hours of *dukas*, makes it possible to use the fridge and other storage facilities at the *duka* when you have little space at home.

4. *Credit* is used by many in Dar es Salaam, even the relatively wealthy, to secure food when cash is in short supply, and sometimes just for convenience. Not only the *dukas* are prepared to sell on credit to clients they know, street food vendors often supply on credit as well. People who frequently receive a monthly salary run a tab with a particular street food vendor eating their breakfast or lunch there and pay at the end of the

Wegerif, *Feeding Dar es Salaam.*

O. de Schutter, *The Transformative Potential of the Right to Food* (New York: UN Human Rights Council, 2014).

Wegerif, *Feeding Dar es Salaam.*

month. Traders do the same thing, paying the street food vendor once they have sold their stock.

5. *Charity* is another way for a large number of eaters to have access to food. Borrowing money in hard times is also common and overlaps with charity in that the loans are often not paid back. Charity and networks through which sharing and support are obtained play a more important role in Dar es Salaam than they might in a situation where the state providedes some form of a social safety net.

6. *Sharing food and the shared use of cooking and storage facilities* play a very important role in people accessing food, especially when economic circumstances are tough. Children in particular are beneficiaries of a common practice of eating together and sharing food with friends and relatives who are around. Among people with very low levels of capital, the sharing of cooking equipment helps those who cannot afford it and/or have no space to store and keep such equipment. As well as sharing food, even with those who cannot always pay. Cooking equipment is also shared among people who are tenants in different rooms of the same house and sometimes with neighbours as well. The *duka* and street food trader can also be seen as providing shared use of equipment in that the fridge at the *duka*, given the accessibility mentioned above, serves as cool storage for the houses around it. Having a fridge of one's own becomes less important when there is a shop a few minutes away where you can buy fresh milk or cold sodas from morning until late at night. In addition, it is common for a *duka* owner, or indeed a neighbour with a fridge, to let other people put their things in the fridge.

7. An overarching need is for *an income* in order to be able to buy food. The food system cannot provide incomes for all urban residents, but the current system does provide quite a few opportunities. There

are many business and jobs in the sector. Different food systems could create more or less income earning opportunities and therefore contribute more or less to addressing people's right to food. What is clear is that a food system that would reduce the income earning opportunities within it, even if it was capable of producing and distributing more food, would lead to more hunger.

These aspects have to be taken into account when (re)designing Dar es Salaam's foodscapes. It means that proposed spatial interventions should not worsen but rather maintain or preferably improve the access to and affordability of food.

Multi-scalar Foodscapes

The description of the components that determine food access in Dar es Salaam combined with the statistics on social inequalities show that the dynamics and functioning of Dar es Salaam's foodscapes can only be understood by applying a multi-scalar perspective. Having access to food when living in one room with no storage capacity, having a low and irregular income, and not having any means of transport, presupposes living in a neighbourhood with nearby *dukas* and people's markets to have access to food. But these *dukas* and markets have to be supplied through a spatial infrastructure and modes of transport at the city or metropolitan level that are capable of delivering fresh and perishable products in time and that do not worsen traffic congestion problems. And, finally, it requires good connections, in terms of infrastructure and social networks, between the city and Tanzania's rural areas where the majority of the staple products are produced.

As mentioned on p. 30, the scale dimension is well elaborated by Sobal & Wansink[16] by distinguishing between macro, meso, and micro scale foodscapes. These different levels of scale are interlinked. To phrase it differently, foodscape scale levels are *nested*, which means that the domestic foodscape (storage, cooking, and eating, but in some cases also food growing and/or processing) is embedded in a community or neighbourhood foodscape (supermarkets, grocery shops, speciality shops, street vendors, bars and restaurants, but sometimes also urban gardens), which in turn is embedded in a regional, national or global foodscape (food transport, distribution centres, artisan or industrial food processors and urban, peri-urban, and rural farms). In other words, an abundance of processed foods and ready-made meals consumed at home is most likely to be linked to a micro-wave as main cooking device, a neighbourhood with lots of fast food establishments and convenience stores, and a globally sourcing food industry. Or, to return to Dar es Salaam, eating and cooking at home means that meals are prepared from fresh and semi-processed food products, bought at a market or *duka* in the neighbourhood, which get their food partially from urban and perl-urban farms and partially from rural farms further away from the city.

Rethinking and Redesigning the Foodscape of Dar es Salaam: Introducing the Four Cases

This multi-scalar and nested character of Dar es Salaam's foodscape also implies that redesigning it requires an endeavour to redesign at different levels of scale. For example, a redesign of a neighbourhood aimed at introducing supermarkets at the expense of street shops and people's markets will never work if the city's transport infrastructure as well as the eating, cooking, and living conditions of eaters are not changed accordingly. The latter is, of course, not something that can be changed through spatial redesign alone. And above all, given the importance of having an income to buy food and the fact that many people earn an income in Dar es Salaam's food economy, any redesign should avoid proposing a foodscape that reduces the income earning opportunities within it, even if it was capable of producing and distributing more food, as it would worsen food insecurity.

J. Sobal and B. Wansink, 'Kitchenscapes, Tablescapes, Platescapes, and Foodscapes: Influences of Microscale Built Environments on Food Intake', *Environment and Behavior* 39, no. 1 (2007), pp. 124–142. A.M. Fink, 'Looking for a Metamorphosis of the White Elephant', in *Seeing Dar*, eds. J.S.C. Wiskerke, D. Habets, and S. Verhoeven (Amsterdam: Academy of Architecture, 2015), pp. 78–87, https://issuu. com/bouwkunst/docs/ seeingdar/9 (accessed 19-12-2017)

Rethinking Dar es Salaam's foodscape therefore requires us to think in different levels of scale and to connect these. It also requires to take into account the growth challenges of Dar es Salaam, see pp. 88-89 (traffic congestion, climate change, social inequality and space for urban agriculture) as well as the conditions shaping food security (in particular access, affordability, and income), see pp. 90-92. The four cases presented in this second part of the book are an attempt to do so. Towards this end the authors of these four chapters have spent two weeks in Dar es Salaam to explore, experience and understand practices, patterns and socio-spatial relations of eating, preparing, trading, transporting, processing, and growing food, and to use that experience as input for proposing spatial (re-)designs. As Anna Fink, the author of the next chapter, clearly expressed:

> At the beginning of my journey, the markets seemed like an organized chaos of work, rest and trade. After a week of observations and reflection, these actions slowly became habits and finally rituals of people, who together form a place. What started as an experience of oversaturation and a blurry image became a network of relationships formed by traders. And, finally, these relationships appeared in space and revealed an internal logic that organically formed itself.[17]

This is evidently an example of how a sociological understanding of food provisioning can feed into spatial design.

The following four cases will feature in this second part of the book:

1. A building. This case focuses on a recently constructed though largely unused five-storey building for small businesses (food and other commodities). Anna Fink explores why it isn't used and what has to be changed to make it function as a trading place for food and other commodities.

Bicycles used for transporting goods to the market, photo: Saline Verhoeven

Dukas (small shops) at the Shekilango market, Dar es Salaam, photo: Saline Verhoeven

2. A market. This case focuses on the Shekilango market, one of the people's markets in Dar es Salaam that is regularly inaccessible as a result of flooding caused by heavy rainfall. David Habets proposes several small interventions to improve water management in order for the market to be accessible year-round while simultaneously improving working conditions.

3. A neighbourhood. This case focuses on one of the slum areas in Dar es Salaam that are prone to flooding due to the combined problem of heavy rainfall and waterways being used as solid waste dumping sites. Tim Kort proposes to use this waste to create mounts that will better protect the slum areas from flooding and to transform the water ways into areas for urban agriculture.

4. A metropolitan infrastructure. This case looks at the entire metropolitan area with a focus on food transport to and through the city. Jerryt Krombeen suggests redesigning the transport infrastructure by building on what already exists.

THE META-MORPHOSIS OF THE WHITE ELEPHANT

LINKING SCALES

The Machinga complex also known as the White Elephant, Dar es Salaam, photo: Anna Maria Fink

Dar es Salaam is a city that appears to be shaped by a collective of individuals: a society of traders, where everyone seems to be a salesman or saleswoman. In this city, trade is an opportunity that provides a source of livelihood for many and is the heartbeat of this complex organism. Here, self-determination comes before dependence, the collective before the corporate, and the person before the employee.

To 'control' the unbridled growth of informal street food markets, the municipal government of Dar es Salaam decided to build a multiple-floor indoor food market, where vendors could rent market space for selling food and goods. However, the situation at present is that the building is not used and that a new informal street market has been established around the building. This 'White Elephant' is a typical example of failed and culturally inappropriate (or insensitive) architecture.

Public Space

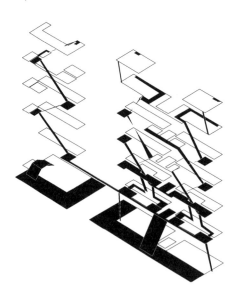

Trade in public space

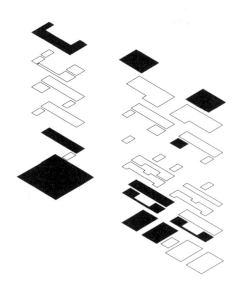

Communal space

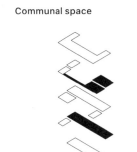

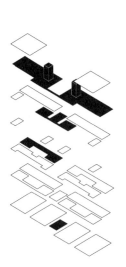

Corporate space

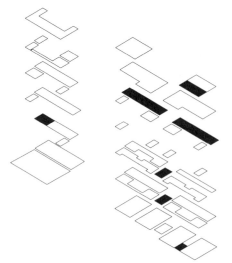

Spatial organization of the Black Elephant, Dar es Salaam, image: Anna Maria Fink

The officially called Machinga complex is a three-part concrete monster, rising five storeys into the air. It was erected in order to host over 5,000 so-called petty traders (small traders selling various goods) doing their business in Dar es Salaam. Equipped with countless empty metal cages the complex is still waiting to fulfil its purpose as a new type of people's market. So far without success, as evidenced by the 'illegal' market that has sprung up around the building, leaving the complex itself empty for most of its time and space. For 200 Tanzanian Shilling everyone can rent a metal cage roughly two square meters in size to store and display their goods.[1] These cages are assembled to form corridors along the open half-floors, reached via a central staircase or a rampway connected to the main street and the bus station.

This White Elephant is a perfect example illustrating the attempts of the government to formalize and structure informal routines. However, without taking into account the fragile balance between the informal and the formal: they provided a building that doesn't fit the daily practices and cultural habits of the people that are supposed to use it. Many traders say that the fee to rent a space is too high for what they get and that the terms of rental are very inflexible. Market traders, for example, are supposed to rent space in the building for three consecutive months, which doesn't match the habit of only renting a market stall for the few hours a day the market vendor actually has goods to sell. Furthermore, the traders complain about the lack of customers and cite various reasons for this, such as the malfunctioning bus station, and blame the council for it.[2]

Observing, understanding, and describing the main qualities of working places in and around successful marketplaces in Dar es Salaam convinced me that the formal structure of the Machinga complex could be transformed into a structure that can stimulate, control, and inspire the informal. Towards this end I propose a spatial design, the Black Elephant, integrating informal daily life into the formal structure in order to empower people to inhabit the building and transform the Machinga complex into a lively market place. The design aims to transform the empty building towards an open and fluid public space. Proposing interventions in the buildings' architectural constitution, its place in the city, and how it is internally governed. Offering traders functionality in space, flexibility in use, and diversity in social interactions.

Routing as a Spine
The first step is to adapt and reshape the structure to create a more functional space with more possibilities of movement that allows development and increased use of the building over time. The emptiness has to be conquered by weakening its power: a new route through the building can create density within it while keeping space for growth and development around it. Changing the main spatial structure from a stack of floors to ranks of routes is the first formal intervention to take in order to reach the goal of functionality in space. This routing space can fill itself informally, without fixed demarcation or a static plan. Step by step, the White Elephant is going to be invaded by this new route of slopes and stairs that introduce a new trading mentality into its empty spaces. Instead of the existing uniform routing directed to floors, the new route is penetrating the whole building.

1   www.streetnet.org.
    za/show.php?id=384_
    (accessed 13-12-2013).
2   www.ippmedia.com/
    frontend/index.
    php/&tfww.ripAti./
    KIKX0Dnx/www/func-
    tion.fopen?l=54634
    (accessed 13-12-2013),

Total space Black Elephant

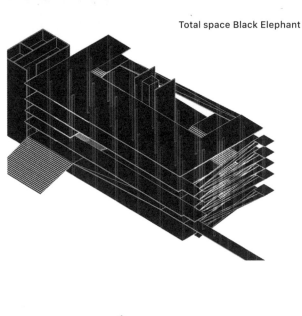

aces

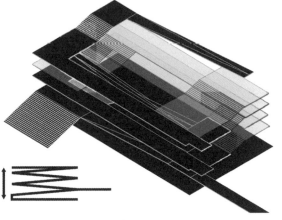

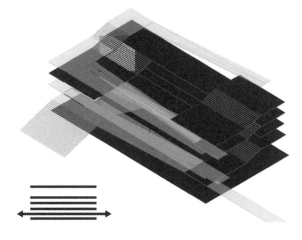

Spatial organization of the Black Elephant, Dar es Salaam, image: Anna Maria Fink

Connection to the Context

A crucial, supporting intervention is to reconnect the building complex with its urban context by extending the ground floor into the trees of the Karume Park, the wall of Karume stadion, and onto the edge of the streets passing it. The Karume bus station interweaves the Dalla Dalla network—small privately operated busses—and is a key element to literally create traffic into the Machinga complex. While the frontside is deconstructed by ramps offering fluid trading space, the backside is opened for market and city functions by stairs. These two design elements offer the base for a shift in perception from empty building to lively space providing routing space as a spine. They also give traders the opportunity to display their products along the flowing route and to form communal space in every transition space between the staircase and the floors.

New Market Stalls

To find flexibility in use and to make the marketplace interesting to a wide range of entrepreneurs, a new system of rent has to replace the metal cages. Just like at a normal market, traders should be able to pay per day, week, month, or year for a clearly defined sum and space. They should not be limited by an object outlining their space (like the cages), but by a wholly self-determined set of assembled materials. The formality of the renting organization should not be translated literally into the space. Therefore, these spatial forms should follow the four main typologies: the defined, closed space or *duka*, the collective roof (chicken traders), the half-open walled space (butchers) and the flexible individual space (vegetable salespeople). These four typologies form the basis of the spaces needed to accommodate traders. Public functions or corporate organizations need their own typologies but should follow the rule of simplicity and openness. Every architectural intervention needs to encourage the purpose that it was made for and widen the opportunities according to individual ideas.

Socio-cultural Space

Looking at successful marketplaces in Dar es Salaam you will see that a marketplace is more than a platform for trade. It is a social space flexible enough to host the diversity of uses and the plurality of relationships, as well as a workplace and a place to live in. As the day progresses, a butcher boy starts by putting on his white boots and white clothes and transforming himself into a professional. In a quiet minute, while waiting for the fire to get going, he drinks a quick coffee at the corner, watching the first chicken middlemen arrive in their white trucks and having a chat with the other guy buying coffee. In his next break, he will change his bloody shirt and have some *chapatti* and soup at his favourite place. With ten minutes to spare until his next shift begins, he plays a quick game of pool over at the vegetable section. At the end of his day he walks to the washhouse to clean his splattered boots and before he finally leaves the market he attends a theoretical driving lesson at the driving school close to the washhouse. A market, therefore, has to provide more than just trading functions and offer facilities for the people working there to fulfil other parts of their lives. It has to be interwoven with facilities extending the traders' opportunities for self-determination. In these routines of working people, the edges of the market and the in-between spaces are of extreme importance for contemplation during the day.

A Future for the White Elephant

As in Tameka market, a formalized market in Dar es Salaam where facilities can be found around the main market programme, in the White Elephant facilities such as food places, washrooms or public services could form a basic structure. Creating a chain of places along a route with a lively diversity of markets and petty trading spaces with public functions as the supporting structure. In addition to this, small businesses, workshops, collectives, and service have to find a safe place. To add a financially strong partner and a business of an international scale, one big capitalist corporation could get a neatly outlined space in it.

Taking these four interventions into account, a careful transformation of the Machinga complex can make it into a functioning, innovative people's market and, more importantly, a new public space within the evolving city. The example of metamorphosis of the White Elephant illustrates the importance of the cultural component in designing a sustainable food system; you can build a structure but it needs to suit the habits of the people that are supposed to use it.

Going from public to private, scheme: Anna Maria Fink

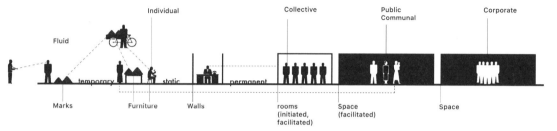

Fluid

Individual

Collective

Public
Communal

Corporate

Marks

temporary

Furniture

static

Walls

permanent

rooms
(initiated,
facilitated)

Space
(facilitated)

Space

Life in the Black Elephant, image: Anna Maria Fink

A ROOF AND A FLOOR

Dar es Salaam

LINKING SCALES

Looking down from the Rombo Hotel one can see the roof of the Shekilango Market, a green view of Michichi along the floodplains, and the long line of the Morrogorro road stretching inland from the centre at the Indian Ocean. The rusty metal sheets piled across and on top of each other make the market, shading it from the blazing sun and keeping it dry during the long rains of the monsoon. Individuals, collectively making the market, built these roofs.

Dar es Salaam's challenges of a rapid urbanization can be seen on its streets. The Shekilango market lies within a dynamic urban context. The Shekilango road, in the district Sinza, will become an important transfer hub for the new, fast public bus line along the Morrogorro road. Hotels rise between the low Swahili houses, bars blast African hip hop beats through the streets, and *dukas* transform themselves to accommodate the upcoming African middle class.

The Shekilango market is a beautiful example of how the city-wide food network provides food to Dar es Salaam nowadays. If and how food trading and provisioning will remain an important activity in the everyday life of the urban dwellers will depend on the metamorphosis of the people's markets within the rapidly changing city, which is increasingly prone to flooding because of increased incidences of heavy rainfall. In this chapter I propose a redesign of the market with a focus on improving water management so that the market is accessible year-round and working conditions improve at the same time.

Markets: Important Nodes for Food Security and Urban Life

Trading flows through Tanzania's veins. Daniel Mbisso, lecturer at the Department of Architecture at Ardhi University in Dar es Salaam, describes it as 'the social glue' of society: 'Selling and buying food at the markets are the small everyday interactions that work as the social glue for the communities of Dar'. The market place is a fluid space, offering opportunities for everyone. In the early morning when the sun paints the Indian Ocean deep red, you'll see a coffee vendor arriving and groups of men huddle together. The coffee vendor creates a social space around himself every time he sets up his vending place. Later, streets become an unloading area for thousands of chickens. Several hours after that they turn into the terrace for *Mama Lishe*—female (informal) restaurateurs—preparing and serving food. The marketplace in Dar es Salaam is used collectively in multiple ways from the eleventh hour of the night to 12-hour night Swahili time, 5 am to 6 pm.

Dar es Salaam has a few dozen officially recognized food markets (also known as people's markets) that fulfil multiple functions (of which selling, preparing, buying, and eating food are among the most important activities). These markets full of traders and vendors provide the city with the food items it needs every day. They form the everyday places where food is purchased, sold, cooked, and eaten. Individuals are working within a couple of square metres from each other and collectively shape the market. The people's markets, petty trading spaces where small traders are selling various goods, are probably the most widely accessible points of distribution for food in the urbanizing areas and therefore can be seen as important nodes in urban food provisioning.

The markets in Dar es Salaam are a collection of individual entrepreneurial activities. Killing chickens and cooking the heads, feet, and intestines are two separate undertakings. The pool table used for recreation during slow hours is the property of a third party. Clean and fresh water is the business of a fourth. The people's markets show a great variety of small interdependent economic activities coming together in a single space. They provide an income for several people in a multitude of ways. Every single one of them is self-employed, responsible for their place in the space and in the group. There is friendly competition amongst them. Social values, such as the faithful return of regular customers, the spontaneous encounters between seller and customer, and the game of negotiating prices create a sense of unity among suppliers. In organizational terms, this translates into sales clusters with the same merchandise.

Growing Challenges

This social structure of the people's markets that transcend self-interest is one of the ways in which food builds up a realm that enables all people to act in public. Understanding this meaning of space in formal and informal trade in Dar is crucial for understanding the city's transformation.

The city of Dar es Salaam is facing the enormous task of accommodating a rapidly growing population while improving the quality of life within the city. Providing the basic needs for all urban dwellers, now and in the future, is a huge challenge. The infrastructure for food and water has to be secured and further developed. Affordable fresh food, clean drinking water and protection from the seasonal extremes are baselines on which the city can flourish. Many of the people living in Dar buy their food on a daily basis. Especially for the poorest amongst them, the opportunity to buy small quantities day-by-day at an easily accessible market is of the utmost importance.

These markets, however, are usually difficult or impossible to reach in times of heavy rainfall, due to the lack of a water management infrastructure. Climate change with more extreme rainfall puts the accessibility of the markets under even more pressure.

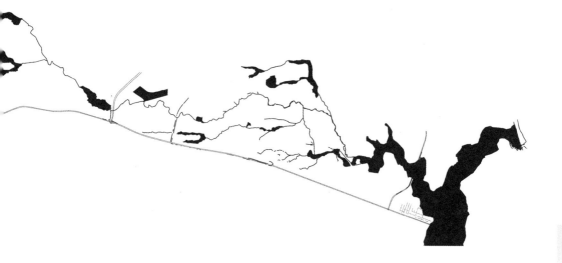

The Shekilango People's Market

The Shekilango Market, situated on the Shekilango Road in the district Sinza, is one of the formal people's markets in Dar es Salaam. It has approximately 550 vendors who sell their products from 6 in the morning to 6 in the evening, 7 days a week.

Selling and slaughtering chickens is a core activity here. In addition, there many sewing shops and a number of *dukas*. These are established in individual permanent cubicles, comparable to a 'garage', where men and women usually work separately from each other. Only women run the small restaurants at the market, called *Mama Lishe*.

The vegetable stands are owned by women and are built as a temporary structure from materials in poor condition. In addition, there are the portable sales, such as petty traders (usually men who present their goods on an extension of their bodies, for example a basket in their hands), male water sellers and women who buy and clean the remains of chickens. These sellers have a specific place at their disposal and are located in the scarcely available traffic space at the market.

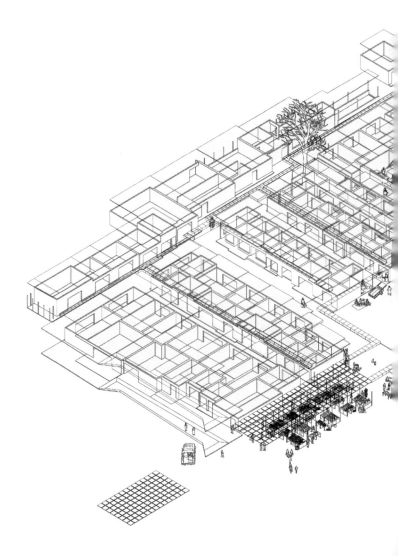

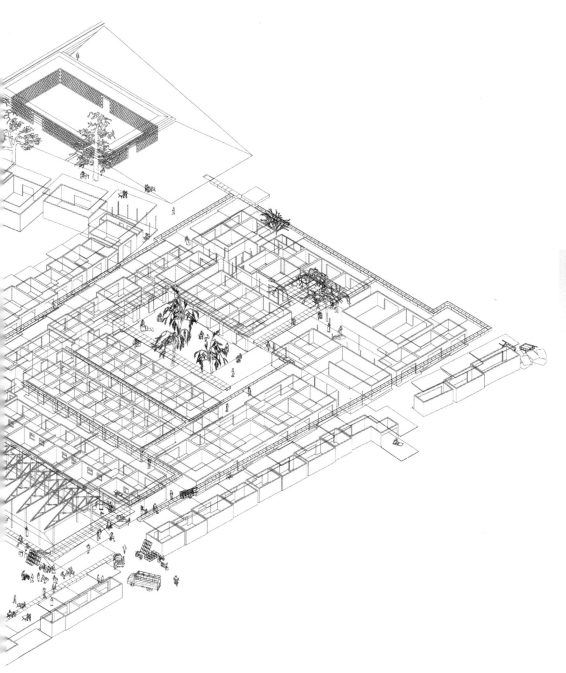

Proposed new roof and floor for the Shekilango market, Dar es Salaam, exploded view: David Habets

Small and Tailor-made Interventions

It is within this market space—which is to be understood as an assemblage of self-employed individuals who collaborate in multiple ways and material aspects—that the water management infrastructure has to be constructed that will keep the market accessible during heavy rainfall. Taking stock of the Machinga complex as an example of failed architecture (see the previous chapter) I propose small interventions that traders can implement at the individual level. A new roof and gutter will collect fresh water during monsoons. The introduction of a concrete ditch between the street and the pavement in front of the shops will drain the streets and keep them accessible. Together, these interventions will create a system for fresh water collection and drainage of the market.

In addition, the square at the back of the Shekilango market, an open area around the public community centre, is redesigned for water storage. The height differences and stairs provide places to sit, linger, and chat during dry periods and retain the surplus of rainwater in the monsoon season. Located on the Sinza river valley it will help to retain the water during heavy rains, and prevent flooding in the urban areas downstream.

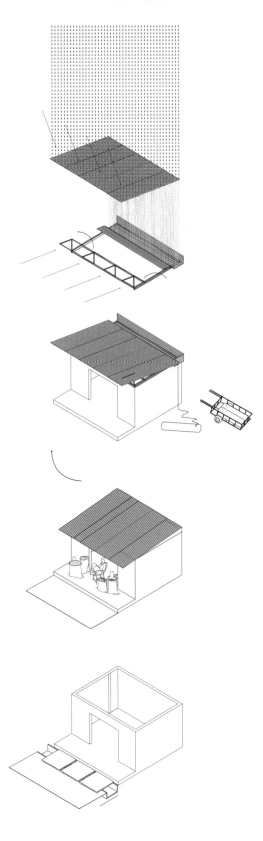

Water collection and drainage per individual shop or duka at the market, Dar es Salaam, diagram: David Habets

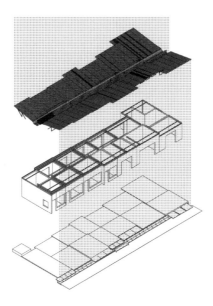

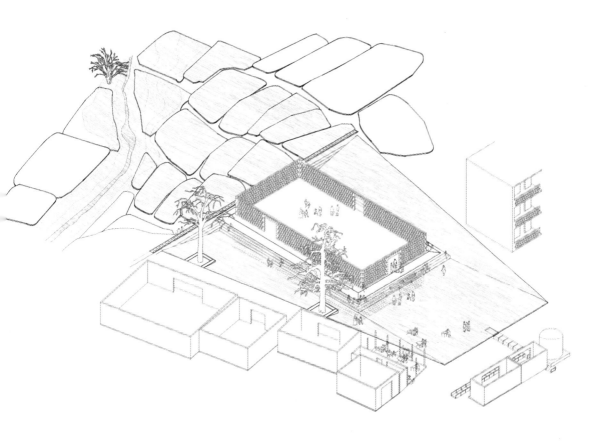

Water collection at the public square at the back of the Shekilango market, Dar es Salaam, scheme: David Habets

Though many food places are firm and real objects, such as the tables and roofs of the food markets, the ground on which the bananas are laid out, and the pushcarts of the sugar reed vendors, many of the words describing these spaces are loose, like fluid, intimate, and welcoming. These are aspects of human activities that inhibit the simple spaces and structures of food trading. They are not carved in stone, nor fixed. They wash away when the people aren't able to develop their activities anymore.

Food makes up part of Dar es Salaam's public space, but it depends on the fluidness of the city's space, where the people themselves can act and trade. So, when responding to climate change and great challenges in the fast-growing city it is not only major structural interventions one should think about. As this example shows, simple solutions for the retention of water can guarantee access to the market. As such these simple solutions help maintain the fluid rhythm of everyday life in Dar es Salaam's lively market places that provide basic public services.

Tim Kort

MOUNDS FOR F(L)OOD VALLEYS

LINKING SCALES

Introduction

The growth rate of Dar es Salaam is so high that the municipal authorities have difficulties meeting the numerous challenges for a healthy and safe living environment for all its citizens. As a result of climate change, excessive weather incidents are likely to occur more frequently. And as approximately 40% of Dar es Salaam is located in areas prone to flooding, many people will be affected by heave rainfalls, in particular the urban poor.

Land in these flood zones is relatively cheap and available for developing settlements. As a result, these flood zones are home to many of the urban slums of Dar es Salaam. The river valleys are also used as landfills for domestic waste, both organic and inorganic solid waste. This results in poor water quality, diseases, and contaminated soil. In addition to being a source of health problems the landfills also become barriers for water. During heavy rains the river valleys fill up with excessive storm water, turning them into extensive flood zones. But when they are filled with garbage, the excessive storm water cannot flow through and infiltrate the soil, thereby aggravating the risk and negative impact of floods.

That this situation can have a major impact on the slum dwellers became clear in 2011. During a long period of intensive rain, a large part of the city was flooded. Approximately 50,000 people were severely affected and 40 people died. People had to flee to rooftops to survive. With an increasing population density in slum areas and more excessive rainfall, flooding problems will likely become worse in the future, in particular when the flood valleys continue to be used as landfills for domestic waste.

Since the municipality of Dar es Salaam lacks the financial resources to realize a large-scale and coordinated flood risk management strategy, it is important to develop a stepwise approach that can be implemented by the urban dwellers themselves. In designing this approach, I was inspired by the existence of mounds in various parts of the world as a means to prevent or reduce flood risks.

1   J. Abrahamse and J. van der Wal, *Waddenzee: Kustlandschap met vijftig eilanden* (Amsterdam: Uniepers, 1989).

2   P. Kelder, *Landschappen rondom de Zuiderzee* (Enkhuizen: Vereniging Vrienden van het Zuiderzeemuseum, 1984).

3   Abrahamse and Van der Wal, *Waddenzee*.

4   www.archeolog-home.com/pages/content/watson-brake-sapelo-island-poverty-point-usa-were-mounds-originally-built-to-protect-native-americans-from-floods-part-1.html (accessed 06-01-2018).

5   log-home.com/pages/content/watson-brake-sapelo-island-poverty-point-usa-were-mounds-originally-built-to-protect-native-americans-from-floods-part-2.html (accessed 06-01-2018).

6   J.L. Gibson, *The Ancient Mounds of Poverty Point: Place of Rings* (Gainesville: University Press of Florida, 2000).

Mounds

Around 500 BC, when the fertility of the higher, sandier soils in the Netherlands deteriorated and sand storms threatened the fields, people moved to the lower lying salt marshes. Initially people only lived there during the summer. This changed with the creation of the first raised settlements, which were named *terpen* or *wierden*,[1] in English known as mounds. They were made of clay sod or by stacking waste such as manure and construction materials.

The first mounds that were built only provided room for one or at most a couple of farms. Later on, entire raised villages were developed by connecting several mounds. The mounds were not only a safe haven for people but also for their livestock. The mounds were also used to store goods, fuel (wood) and building materials. Usually these mounds were just one or two meters high. However, there are also mounds up to ten meters high.[2] Although the need to build mounds was significantly reduced when the Dutch started to build dikes to protect the land from the sea from the 11th century onwards, the construction of mounds continued until the end of the 17th century.

The mounds are not a typical Dutch phenomenon but can be found in the other countries along the Wadden Sea—Germany and Denmark—as well.[3] But also in many other countries across the world there are mounds or remnants of mounds to be found. For example, in the USA a formation of 11 man-made hills, known as Watson Brake, can be found in Northern Louisiana.[4] Based on radiocarbon dating it is estimated that the construction of the Watson Brake mounds began in 3500 B.C. Another example is the village at Poverty Point,[5] which consist of six semicircles intersected by five radials. These mounds were built between 1650–700 B.C. and cover an area of 3.7 km² making it the largest raised settlement in the USA. Made by native Americans, it is assumed that Poverty Point mounds were built as a means of flood protection but also had a spiritual meaning and function.[6]

When reading about the history of mounds that were built in many parts of the world it becomes clear that these remarkable historical landscape elements would not have existed without the collective effort of people.

Designing a Safe and Productive Neighbourhood in the Flood Plains of Dar es Salaam

I found inspiration in the opportunities that can be created through collective work and have incorporated this in my proposal for a redesign of a neighbourhood in one of the vulnerable flood plains of Dar es Salaam. Towards this end I propose a bottom-up strategy as a way to improve the quality of life of the people living in and close to the valleys, as the municipality lacks the organizational and financial capacity to take on the responsibility for creating a safer living environment for the slum dwellers. My proposal can be seen as a toolkit that can help empower communities to work together to build a safe, healthy, and green living environment in the flood valleys of Dar es Salaam. Thereby creating a future in which waste is not a problem, but a resource that generates income and opportunities, and above all a safe haven during future floods.

It all begins with cleaning the river valleys by removing all the garbage and no longer using the valleys as landfills. This has to be combined with deepening the riverbed. Excavating sand and collecting the waste will give room to the river carrying excess water during and after heavy rainfall. With the sand and the garbage dikes can be built along the river. The collected garbage mixed with organic waste can also be used to create mounds close to existing public facilities in the neighbourhood. The hills will serve as safe refuge when the city is flooded. By enlarging the mounds, additional public facilities can be built. Such a system of safe havens will begin to develop at the edges of the valleys, always within 5 to 10 minutes walking distance.

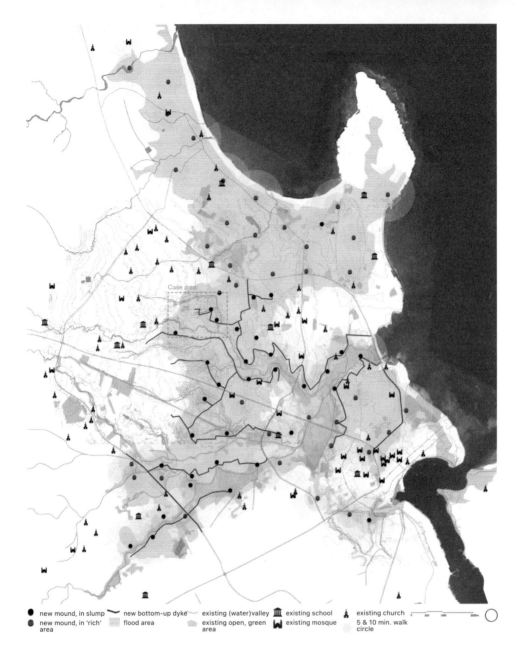

● new mound, in slump
● new mound, in 'rich' area
〰 new bottom-up dyke
▨ flood area
◡ existing (water)valley
▨ existing open, green area
🏛 existing school
🕌 existing mosque
⛪ existing church
5 & 10 min. walk circle

A system of safe havens, public facilities and dikes along the edges of the flood valleys, Dar es Salaam

Example of a more climate change-proof neighbourhood

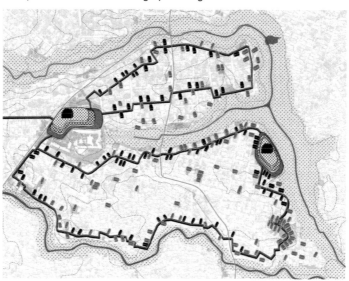

🔲 damaged area because of a flood
🌾 new urban agriculture area
▒ new mound
🖤 new mound house, improvement of existing house
🖤 new mound house, on a green/open spot
🖤 new mound house, on a spot where houses were
▲ organic garbage
⬛ new public facility
〰 new bottom-up dike
🕐 ⟶

Cleaning and deepening riverbeds and creating a mound from waste will make the flood planes safer

Schemes of reprofiling of the flood valleys

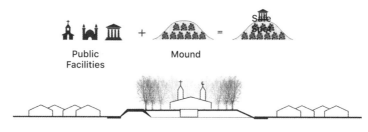

Public Facilities   +   Mound   =

Schemes of the public safety mounds

Schemes of the bottum-up dike

Emptying the flood planes will create green open space in the city. People living on the edge of the valley, who are mostly poor, will have the opportunity to start practicing urban agriculture and grow their own food or sell their produce at the market, providing a (extra) source of income. Thus the function of the valleys changes from landfill into food provisioning, income generation and adaptation to climate change. The new public facilities can, for example, be used to educate people on how to grow their own food. The valleys with urban agriculture turn into green ribbons through the urban fabric.

Conclusions

Building dikes and mounds to create more climate change proof neighbourhoods in Dar es Salaam's flood plains is a process that takes time and requires a collective effort of the people living in those neighbourhoods. Through this work of excavating and cleaning the river beds new job opportunities and income generating activities in the domain of food provisioning may emerge. As the valleys become a source of income this will hopefully prevent the further use of the valleys as landfills.

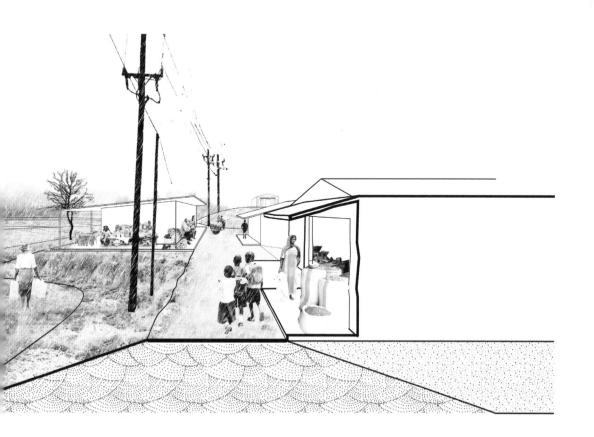

Jerryt Krombeen

LOGISTICS AND THE CITY

LINKING SCALES

The Von Thünen model modified for Dar es Salaam, image: Jerryt Krombeen

HOW TO ACCESS A CITY WITH FOOD

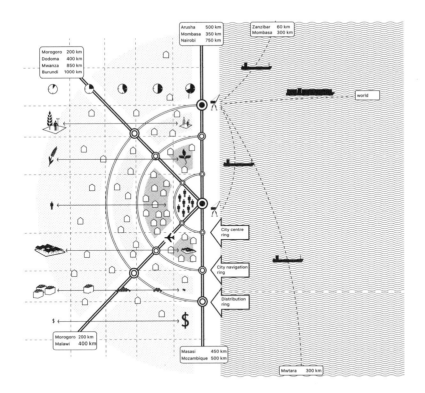

TWO WAYS TO FEED THE CITY

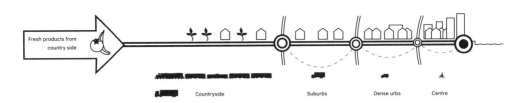

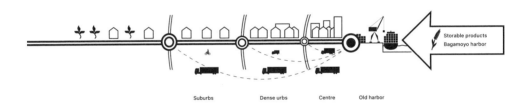

Different modes for transporting fresh produce and storable products into the city, image: Jerryt Krombeen

Dar es Salaam's population increases on average by 4.4% per year. Getting food to and through the city is already an enormous challenge at present. And it will definitely get worse if no spatial interventions are made to tackle the problem of traffic congestion. Almost 90% of the food eaten in Dar es Salaam comes from outside the city, mainly from its rural hinterland, but also by sea. The remaining 10% is produced within the metropolitan region.

Looking at the city's current infrastructure one can only conclude that Dar es Salaam is not ready to feed its projected population size in 2030 and beyond. The more so, since not only the number of inhabitants will grow, but also the size of the city, the number of houses, the number of private cars, and so on. The unplanned organic growth of the city predominantly occurs along the roads that connect the city and its rural hinterland. This leads to an increasing number of intersections along these roads and, as a result, to more traffic congestion.

At present Dar es Salaam does not have a modernized transport system and the country largely runs on second-hand vehicles. With other modalities besides motorized traffic being underrepresented in the traffic system, the limiting factor is that all traffic purposes (goods and people, long and short distance travel) share the same road space. These roads, which are often in bad condition, become increasingly congested due to urban population growth and the associated increase in vehicles. This creates a poor flow, which sometimes means that food is no longer fresh when it arrives in the city. In addition, transport in the city itself takes a lot of time. Urban systems are already overburdened and when in the future large trucks also enter this traffic system, the chaos will only increase.

Missing Links

Dar es Salaam lacks the time and money to develop an infrastructure that is capable of keeping up with its rapidly growing size and population. If a distinction were made between long-distance systems and urban systems, the city's transport system could function more efficiently. The old sea harbour in the city's centre will soon become redundant because of a newly planned one just north of Dar es Salaam, in Bagamoyo. This is to become the biggest sea harbour on the African continent. However, by using this new harbour to transport storable bulk food by boat to the old harbour a new opportunity to supply the city with food arises. This will create a supply route from the opposite direction, from the city's centre harbour to the outskirts of the city.

Additionally, to further assure food provision for the fastgrowing city, a redesign of the city region's transport infrastructure is proposed, by making use of the existing infrastructure. By mending a few missing links in the current network of Dar es Salaam the city's infrastructure could function as a well-planned grid city. By investing in the missing links, the city could create a system that is tailored to the way it already functions. Roughly, the city would be divided into a radial system of three street hierarchies that serve three types of economy: a) the national economy along the BRT-roads, b) the city economy along the city streets, and c) the local economy along the neighbourhood streets.

The National Economy
Along the BRT-roads

The four most important roads, connecting the city with the rest of Tanzania and surrounding countries, meet at rings that connect the city and newly built main ports. The rail network will be extended, creating another modality beside the motorized infrastructure. This will create opportunities to make a parallel system to feed the city.

The nationally important roads clearly show their supra-local importance with the presence of multinationals and, for example, the head offices of AZAM and Tanesco, the energy company. The type of transport for which the road has to be suitable, matches the function and the role it has in the city.

On these four important roads, a fast, modern bus line is introduced, called the Bus Rapid Transit (BRT). Its goal is to transport people within the city limits over long distances. This system could also be implemented for food logistics. It could provide a reliable system of national roads meeting the city network. A connecting system that can transport large quantities quickly and over long distances and that, because of high investments, can combine food logistics, with, for example, passenger transport and transportation of other products and raw materials.

By delivering food to the city relatively fast, the freshness of the products can be guaranteed and the scope of the city region food system can be enlarged. Food can be picked up from further destinations, because it can be kept fresh over longer distances.

The City Economy along the City Streets

On the ring roads, where the BRT and the city ring roads intersect, *dala dalas* (small buses) take over passenger transport from the BRT. This privatized public transport is deployed for further distribution and navigation within the finer fabric of the city. On the urban *dala dala* ring roads, at city level, you find the city economy, i.e. businesses whose markets are within Dar es Salaam. Here the people's markets and *dukas* are located; food trading places that capitalize on the needs of the passer-by and the *dala dala* user. By completing the national embranchments and urban ring roads, which is already largely done, a strong framework for growth at the smallest level of scale also emerges.

The Local Economy along the Neighbourhood Streets

Within this bigger framework the residential streets with the local merchants can be found: the people who offer goods and services from their home. It is at this smallest level of scale that the municipality should not want to plan, because it would harm and disrupt the identity of Dar es Salaam; an identity of winding streets that come to life with food vendors and other merchants. The links in the network will develop naturally in line with the capacity of the infrastructure, the type of economy along the roads and the needs of the urban dwellers.

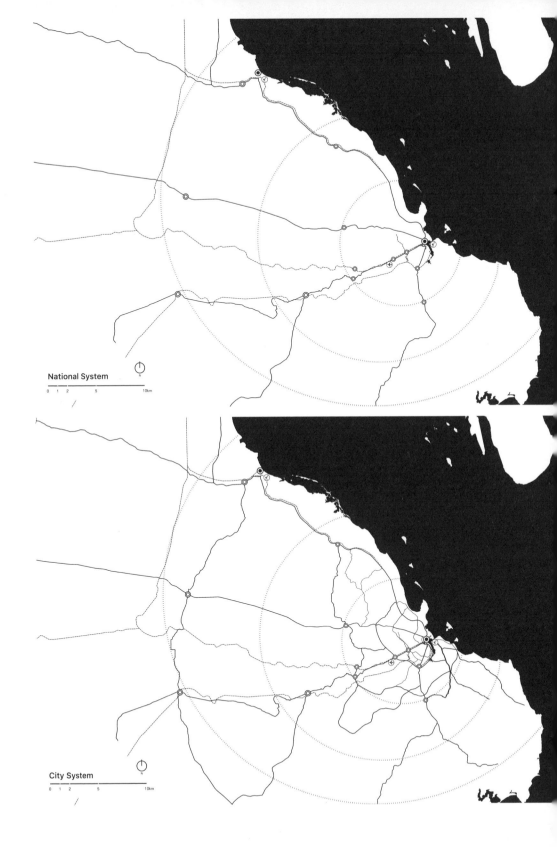

National System

0   1   2   5   10km

N

City System

0   1   2   5   10km

N

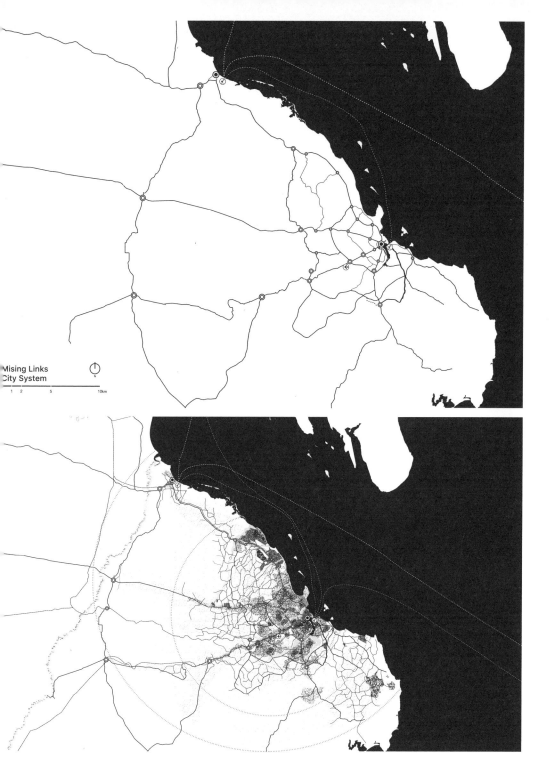

Mising Links
City System

N

1 2   5   10km

Plan for a new transport system, scheme: Jerryt Krombeen

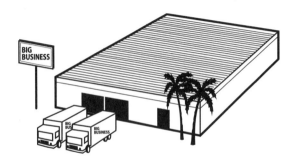

Economy at national, city and local level represented along different roads, scheme: Jerryt Krombeen

Food Hubs

In order to enable the three hierarchies in the city—the (inter)national connections, the urban scale level, and the local entrepreneurs—to work together, hubs have to be realized at the interfaces of these hierarchies. The enhanced infrastructure network with the four major national branches and the three tangential ring roads constitute the basis of this system.

Along the distribution ring large food hubs are already emerging that accommodate the delivery of food from the rural areas. These are transhipment points where the urban traffic systems and the long-distance logistics meet. Various types of transport come together on these multi-modal hubs. People transfer to the BRT network, for example, which starts here.

This also applies to a food provisioning system based on the storability of food. Goods and food are transferred from a system that can transport large quantities quickly and over long distances, to a more urban system and taken to distribution markets.

The different speeds of traffic of the food logistics are linked to the storage life of the product. The protein-rich, dried fish from Lake Nayara and rice from Mwanza, for example, are products that can be stored for longer periods of time. Tomatoes and bananas from Arusha, near the Kilimanjaro, have a medium shelf life. The leafy vegetables cannot be stored and need to be delivered to vendors and eaters within several hours after harvest.

Collecting non-perishables or storable products and their further distribution can take place at the new main seaport, making Bagamoyo also a food hub for the city. Additionally, the old harbour, which has partly fallen into disuse, can be used to bring food from the city centre farther out. A system can be set up with coasters to transport large quantities of bulk from Bagamoyo into the city. This would be a complementary food provisioning system to the train, capable of transporting large quantities from the opposite direction, from the sea instead of the land. By transporting food from the sea via the city centre to the outskirts of the metropolitan region it will be less vulnerable to traffic jams since the trucks will move in the opposite direction and drive on relatively empty roads during rush hour.

As a result of the existing food procurement culture and the daily routine of going to the markets, the system of food hubs already *de facto* exists and is well embedded in the daily life of the urban dweller. With food hubs a supra-local system can emerge that forms a fast and efficient connection with the countryside, both via land and via sea; a system that is capable of feeding the growing city.

Conclusion

The city of Dar es Salaam is increasingly dependent on a good connection with its surrounding countryside and distant rural areas where some of the important staples such as rice and maize are produced. By rethinking the transport modalities along the urban-rural continuum, by intensifying the use of existing roads through a bi-directional food delivery system (i.e. by land from the countryside towards the city centre and by sea from the city centre towards the city's outskirts) and by linking existing roads, a perfect tangential system can be created. Such a system fits in with the modern aspiration of the city, yet it builds on and utilizes the way in which the city functions and works nowadays. This new transport system is based on the morphological and cultural values of the city and its economic diversity; a system that helps everyone move a step forward and keeps food accessible for the entire city, not only by bridging large distances, but also by keeping food affordable and having it available in the places where the urban eaters are used to procure their food items.

Johannes S.C. Wiskerke & Saline Verhoeven

CONNECTING FLOWS

Introduction

The principle of connecting flows and closing cycles in the context of food provisioning aims to address the double relationship between food and waste. That is, on the one hand it refers to food and food packaging going to waste and ending up in landfills or incineration plants. Approximately 40% of the food produced is not consumed due to harvest losses on the farm and post-harvest losses further up the food chain, including post-consumer waste. In industrialized economies food losses primarily occur in the latter stages of the food chain: in supermarkets and restaurants, and at home. Food is removed from supermarket shelves or is not bought or consumed because it is close to or past the expiry date, because people buy too much of it or because the portions served are too large to consume.[1] According to Lang[2] approximately 33% of all food purchased in the United Kingdom is thrown away. In many developing countries food waste primarily occurs in the first stages of the food chain, i.e. during harvest, storage, and transport.[3] Especially for perishable products such as fruits and vegetables harvest and post-harvest losses are high.

On the other hand, the relationship between food and waste refers to solid and liquid waste not being used as a resource for food production. For centuries, waste management used to be viewed from a sanitary-environmental urban perspective following the idea that waste is harmful to city dwellers and to the urban environment. A focus on connecting flows and closing cycles implies a shift from waste being treated as nuisance to waste being seen as a resource. This is particularly relevant for food provisioning as scarcity of resources, such as water and nutrients, is becoming a bigger challenge by the day, while different waste streams are not (yet) or insufficiently recovered and reused for food provisioning.[4]

1   C. Steel, *Hungry City: How Food Shapes Our Lives*, London: Chatto and Windus, 2008.

2   T. Lang, 'Crisis? What Crisis? The Normality of the Current Food Crisis', *Journal of Agrarian Change* 10, no. 1 (2010), pp. 87–97.

3   J. Aulakh and A. Regmi, 'Post-harvest Food Losses Estimation-Development of Consistent Methodology', *Agricultural & Applied Economics Associations*, 2013, pp. 4–6.

4   O. Cofie and L. Jackson, *Thematic Paper 1: Innovative Experiences with the Reuse of Organic Wastes and Wastewater in (Peri-)Urban Agriculture in the Global South*, SUPURBFOOD deliverable 3.2, 2013, www.supurbfood.eu/scripts/document.php?id=71 (accessed 07-01-2018).

5   http://ec.europa.eu/environment/waste/framework/ (accessed 06-01-2018).

6   C.M. Agudelo-Vera et al., 'Harvesting Urban Resources towards More Resilient Cities', *Resources, Conservation and Recycling* 64 (2012), pp. 3–12.

7   V.C. Broto, A. Allen, and E. Rapoport, 'Interdisciplinary Perspectives on Urban Metabolism', *Journal of Industrial Ecology* 16, no. 6 (2012), pp. 851–861.

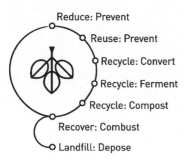

Reduce: Prevent

Reuse: Prevent

Recycle: Convert

Recycle: Ferment

Recycle: Compost

Recover: Combust

Landfill: Depose

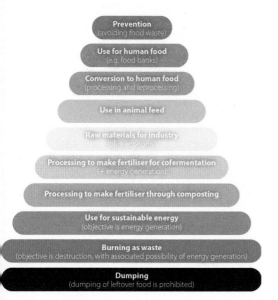

Prevention
(avoiding food waste)

Use for human food
(e.g. food banks)

Conversion to human food
(processing and reprocessing)

Use in animal feed

Raw materials for industry
(blue economy)

Processing to make fertiliser for cofermentation
(+ energy generation)

Processing to make fertiliser through composting

Use for sustainable energy
(objective is energy generation)

Burning as waste
(objective is destruction, with associated possibility of energy generation)

Dumping
(dumping of leftover food is prohibited)

Towards Waste as a Resource: A Summary of Different Perspectives

The idea that waste management is not or not only about removing or preventing something harmful but also about actually adding something useful has gradually gained importance in scientific and societal debates as well as in new waste management policies, such as the European Commission's Waste Framework Directive.[5] In the literature several perspectives are relevant to connecting flows and closing cycles: circular urban metabolism, cradle to cradle, and circular economy. These perspectives embody different but cross-cutting technological and socioeconomic principles with increasing emphasis on creating value from resources that are currently viewed as waste streams. The reason to discuss these perspectives is that they are complementary to the different aspects of sustainability. Some tend to be primarily technological approaches with a strong focus on environmental issues, while others are more socioeconomic approaches with attention for social and economic sustainability.

Circular Urban Metabolism

Analogous to human metabolism, urban metabolism is a model to facilitate the description and analysis of the flows of the materials and energy within cities,[6] by viewing the city as an ecosystem. It provides researchers and designers with a conceptual framework to study exchange processes that produce the urban environment and to develop new ways of thinking about how cities can be made sustainable.[7] A key methodological component of urban metabolism is material flow analysis, which can, for example, be applied to mapping and quantifying the (biogenic) waste flows of a city. The aim of such an analysis is to understand how these material flows impact on the environment and to develop, design, and implement strategies to reduce the impact of these flows on the environment. Transitioning from linear flows to circular flows, whereby the output (waste) of one flow becomes the input (resource) of another flow, is central to the concept of circular metabolism.

Cradle to Cradle

Cradle to cradle is a design perspective developed by the American architect William McDonough and the German chemist Michael Braungart. In 2002 they published their design manifesto entitled *Cradle to Cradle: Remaking the Way We Make Things*,[8] in which they call for the transformation of industrial manufacturing processes through ecologically intelligent design. Cradle to cradle takes nature's biological metabolism, in which the 'waste' of one system becomes food for another system, as a model for developing a technical metabolism for industrial materials and products. This implies that all products have to be designed for continuous recovery and reutilization as biological or technical nutrients within either of these metabolisms.[9]

Circular Economy

Contrary to the linear 'take, make, dispose' extractive industrial model, the circular economy concept envisages an economy in which products are remade, repaired, resold, or recycled. The contemporary understanding of the concept and its practical applications to economic systems and industrial processes has evolved to incorporate different features and contributions from a variety of concepts that share the idea of closed loops.[10] Circular economy thinking is inspired by cradle to cradle, industrial ecology, blue economy,[11] and biomimicry. The Ellen MacArthur Foundation, established in 2010 with the aim of accelerating the transition to the circular economy, defines a circular economy as restorative and regenerative by design with the aim to redefine products and services to 'design out' waste, while minimizing negative impacts.[12] Based upon a review of different definitions of circular economy, Geissdoerfer et al. define the circular economy as 'a regenerative system in which resource input and waste, emission, and energy leakage are minimized by slowing, closing, and narrowing material and energy loops', which can be achieved 'through long-lasting design, maintenance, repair, reuse, remanufacturing, refurbishing, and recycling'.[13] From the perspective of circular economy it is, for the focus of this book, in particular relevant to identify how the nutrients and water in different waste flows (e.g., organic waste and sewage) can be processed in such a way that they can be fed back into the food production process. Or more in general, to identify and develop processes and business models that can strengthen mutually beneficial relations between cities and agriculture.[14]

Waste Management Hierarchies[15]

The change in waste management towards resource management is, as mentioned above, reflected in the EU Waste Framework Directive which proposes a European waste hierarchy. It should be noted that the EU waste hierarchy takes an ecological perspective to waste management. The social perspective is not reflected. A further elaboration on the social aspects is therefore necessary. We present therefore two other waste management hierarchies that consider both ecology and society: a biogenic waste management hierarchy and Moerman's Ladder for food waste.

Biogenic Waste Management Hierarchy

Within the context of the EU-funded project SUPURBFOOD[16] a biogenic waste management target hierarchy has further developed the EU waste hierarchy by considering relevant concepts and approaches. This has primarily been elaborated by Fritschi[17] for the use in SUPURBFOOD. This target hierarchy[18] aims to provide a guideline for the wider public and policy makers towards sustainable biogenic waste management. The following targets are being distinguished:

1. *Reduce or prevent.* This calls for lowering the amount of waste by creating more awareness about the generation of waste in processes of production and consumption. It is about eco-sufficiency: reducing or preventing biogenic waste by a reduction of the level of production and consumption. Don't buy or buy less and buy mindfully. The first

M. Braungart and W. McDonough, *Cradle to Cradle: Remaking the Way We Make Things* (North Point Press, New York, 2012). https://mbdc.com/project-cradle-to-cradle-book/ (accessed 06-01-2018).

M. Geissdoerfer et al., 'The Circular Economy: A New Sustainability Paradigm?', *Journal of Cleaner Production* 143 (2016), pp. 757–768.

G.A. Pauli, *The Blue Economy: 10 Years, 100 Innovations, 100 Million Jobs* (Taos, NM: Paradigm Publications, 2010). www.ellenmacarthurfoundation.org/circular-economy (accessed 06-01-2018).

Geissdoerfer et al., *The Circular Economy*, pp. 757–768, quote p. 759. Towards this end it is very important to deal with the power question in waste management: Who actually owns the waste and is entitled to make a business from waste and who sets the criteria for deciding the type and scale of operations and the operators? This power question is not really addressed in this book.

In the sections 'Waste Management Hierarchies' and 'Challenges for Connecting Flows and Closing Cycles' are primarily based on the results of SUPURBFOOD, an EU-funded project that was coordinated by the first author of this chapter.

16 www.supurbfood.eu.
17 R. Fritschi, *Assessment of Biogenic Waste Flows in the City-Region of Zurich*, Master Thesis (Zurich: Swiss Federal Institute of Technology, ETH-Zürich, 2014).
18 See also Ellen MacArthur Foundation, *Towards the Circular Economy: Economic and Business Rationale for an Accelerated Transition* (Cowes: Ellen MacArthur Foundation, 2012); FOEN, *Swiss Biomass Strategy* (Berne: Swiss Federal Office for the Environment, 2009); and FOEN, *Grundlagen für ein Biomasse- und Nährstoffmanagement in der Schweiz* (Berne: Swiss Federal Office for the Environment, 2010).
19 R. Wagner, *Wohin mit unserem Grüngut?* (Zurich: Zurich Department of Waste, Water, Energy and Air, 2008); B. Wanner, *Betriebe Schweiz: Umweltleistung Anlagenpark* (Glattbrugg: Axpo Kompogas AG, 2013).

target level mainly refers to food, food waste, and food loss, but also to municipal waste in general, cellulosic goods and waste, and consumer goods and waste out of skin, leather, pelt, or wool.

2. *Reuse, repair, or spend.* This refers to reducing the amount of waste by a greater awareness in dealing with consumer goods. The basic message is: don't throw away, but reuse or repair first, or spend. Again, it is about people's mind-sets, their awareness and attitude towards consumer goods. The second target level basically refers to the same goods and types of waste as the first level.

3. *Recycle by converting.* This comes down to decreasing the amount of waste by designing consumer goods out of reusable and recyclable materials (producer's point of view) and by buying and recycling these consumer goods (consumer's point of view). Waste is seen as a natural resource. The conversion of products into raw materials to be re-manufactured into new products is the central element of this target level. This is key to approaches such as zero-waste (see also pp. 159ff.) and cradle-to-cradle design (see also pp. 151ff.). This level is applicable to consumer goods and waste out of cellulosic material, skin, leather, pelt, or wool, but also to food, food loss, and food waste.

4. *Recycle by fermenting.* This concerns the use of waste as raw material or substrate in anaerobic digestion processes. This target level refers directly to the biogenic waste management process of fermentation. Besides the production of an energy carrier (gas), soil conditioner and fertilizer are co-products of this target level and process. Compared to composting processes, fermentation is preferred in some aspects.[19] This target level mainly refers to food loss, green and food waste, but also animal and human excreta.

5. *Recycle by composting.* This refers to using waste as raw material or substrate in composting processes. Through composting, waste is trans-

formed to a material of higher quality and increased functionality. Compost is the resulting product that can be used as fertilizer in food production. This target level is applicable mainly to public green, home garden, and food waste.

6. *Recover by combustion*. This is a process in which waste is directly used to produce energy. The output of combustion is heat and/or electricity as well as combustion residues. Almost every kind of biogenic waste can be processed through combustion. At present this is not a preferred option as the nutrient and raw material recovery from combustion residues (ash, slag, and filter sludge) is still difficult or not fully used. However, if residues become recyclable to a certain degree, the status of combustion within the target hierarchy may have to be re-evaluated.

7. *Depose by landfill*. The combustion of waste to residues can help to reduce the weight and volume of waste that ends up in a landfill. This may be slightly better than disposing waste without any previous treatment. However, without combustion, disposition of combustion residues or untreated waste results in the loss of re-usable materials and nutrients. It means that flows are disconnected and cycles cannot be closed. Therefore, this is the last and least preferred target level and contradicts the basic idea of circular economy.

Moerman's Ladder for Food Waste
When it comes to food waste, a relevant example is the Moerman's ladder, which has many similarities with the aforementioned biogenic waste management hierarchy. The preferred option in closing the waste cycle is upscaling rather than dumping. In this logic a certain priority scale should be followed:

1. Prevention (avoid food waste, for example by not buying or cooking more than you can eat);
2. Use for human food (e.g. donating food to food banks);
3. Conversion to human food (by processing and reprocessing);
4. Use in animal feed;
5. Raw materials for industry (bio-based economy);
6. Processing to make fertilizer for cofermentation (and energy generation);
7. Processing to make fertilizer through composting;
8. Use for sustainable energy (objective is energy generation);
9. Burning as waste (objective is destruction, with associated possibility of energy generation);
10. Dumping in landfill (dumping of leftover food should be prohibited).

The basic idea is that when food waste cannot be avoided through prevention, then direct use for human or animals has the highest priority. Furthermore, instead of disposing of food waste through burning or landfill, it can be used by the industry to produce various products, to make fertilizer, or to generate energy.

Challenges for Connecting
Flows and Closing Cycles

The biogenic and food waste management hierarchies discussed in the previous section show that there are lots of possibilities to prevent (food) waste or to use or re-use it in a better way than incinerating it or disposing of it in a landfill. Yet, there is still a significant discrepancy between opportunities and the current reality. However, in recent years a wide variety of approaches and organizational and business models have been designed, developed, and implemented with the aim of improved recycling of waste, nutrients, and water. As part of the aforementioned SUPURBFOOD project several of these approaches and models have been reviewed.[20] These reviews also indicate that regional and national policies in the domains of waste management, land use, water protection, and energy can have a significant impact on bottlenecks and opportunities for connecting flows and closing cycles.

O. Schmid et al., *Closing of Nutrient, Water and Urban Waste Cycles in UPA*. Final WP4 Report, SUPURBFOOD Deliverable 4.4, 2015, www.supurbfood.eu/scripts/document.php?id=161; Cofie and Jackson, *Thematic Paper 1.* www.rotterzwam.nl/en_US/page/homepage (accessed 07-01-2018)

The growing recognition that (biogenic) waste has an economic value as resource for different usages implies that cost-efficiency considerations, both for public administrations and for private enterprises, are gaining importance. This has led to larger, centralized waste plants, primarily for energy generation, in cities such as Zurich, Vigo, and Rotterdam. At the same time, smaller decentralized waste operations have been established in peri-urban and rural areas. Often these are farmer groups, companies or organizations making compost from green waste from municipalities, horticulturists, or from common land areas. This compost often has different qualities and usages. These usages are not only recycling biogenic waste but also creating benefits like maintaining soil fertility and organic matter, landscape diversity, and recreational quality or even reducing the risks of fire (as in Vigo). But in some cases, biogenic wastes have been used directly to produce food, such as producing mushrooms on coffee waste substrate in Rotterdam.[21]

Further progress regarding efficient and sustainable biogenic waste management is hindered by regulatory constraints and difficulties in accessing finance. Laws and regulations still define some waste streams as waste in the sense of garbage to be disposed of. Ingredients that can be or have been up-scaled are not always officially recognized in their new role as valuable resources. Kitchen waste, for example, is not recognized as animal feed. This means substantial adjustments are needed in the respective regulations to create more opportunities for connecting flows and closing cycles.

As most initiatives concern practices that are alternatives to mainstream practices, they have to overcome many challenges to obtain societal acceptance. An important issue influencing this is the choice of organization and scale of the technical processes. Both large-scale centralized and small-scale decentralized processes face challenges in obtaining societal acceptance, sometimes due to a lack of awareness, other times because of resistance to environmental or behavioural changes. For example, separate garbage collection for large-scale waste processing facilities requires a behavioural change in large group of consumers. In decentralized processes where small-scale local solutions are applied, sorting of domestic waste may be easier to realize as people who produce the waste also process it and benefit from its recycling. However, the technical knowledge and competence required by such processes also pose challenges to the functioning of such processes. Another issue negatively influencing the societal acceptance is the possible nuisance (odour, noise, etc.) related to collecting and processing organic waste. This is more relevant if decentralized waste processing takes place in a residential environment rather than on industrial sites.

The challenge becomes more complicated when food production is involved. Food is a multi-attribute product, which means general principles from industrial ecology may not apply to food when it is grown with inputs previously classified as waste. There are sanitary and legal issues here, but also issues of culture and taste. For example, when coffee waste is used to grow mushrooms, it is readily accepted by consumers. Insects grown on food waste, however, will likely negatively affect the appetite of consumers not used to eating insects. And using fertilizer made from human excreta as nutrient source for food production[22] is probably an even bigger taboo. New ways of re-using and valorizing waste must therefore take cultural norms and values into account.

Introduction to the Cases

This third socio-spatial design principle is thus a plea for developing creative solutions that can help to transform food and other biogenic waste into a resource for food production. Towards this end four cases are presented and discussed. These four cases also build on the second design principle – linking scales – as they represent different levels of scale in connecting flows and closing cycles:

1. In 'A Building that Breathes Life' Louise Vet describes and explains the rationale behind the recently (2011) built office and laboratory of the Netherlands Institute of Ecological Research, which was entirely designed according to the cradle-to-cradle philosophy.
2. 'Revitalizing the Mokattam Ridge' is a design proposal by Mark van Vilsteren, focusing on the Mokattam neighbourhood—also known as Garbage City—in Egypt's capital Cairo. He proposes a spatial intervention to close the food waste flow while also making the neighbourhood a safer place to live.
3. In 'San Francisco: A Zero Waste City by 2020' we discuss the ambitions and approach of San Francisco as the frontrunner city of the zero waste municipalities.
4. In 'Green Tides of Brittany: Mending the Broken Loop' Maxim Cloarec addresses the environmental problems of intensive animal husbandry in the French region of Brittany by proposing a strategic landscape intervention at regional level that embraces the whole ecosystem, including agriculture, cities, and the sea.

22 www.ruaf.org/productive-reuse-wastes-wastewater; Cofie and Jackson, *Thematic Paper.*

Louise E.M. Vet

Wageningen

CONNECTING
FLOWS

A BUILDING THAT BREATHES LIFE

Introduction

Since 2011, researchers of the Netherlands Institute of Ecology (NIOO), one of the research institutes of the Royal Netherlands Academy of Arts and Sciences (KNAW), have been working in their new headquarters in Wageningen. Laboratories and offices are surrounded by greenhouses, trial ponds, and a range of other facilities. The design and construction of the building and its surroundings are inspired by the cradle-to-cradle (C2C) principles, developed by the German chemist Michael Braungart and the US architect William McDonough.[1] C2C is a design framework for going beyond sustainability and designing for abundance in a circular economy.[2]

Building the new headquarters of NIOO-KNAW according to the C2C principles implied the ambition to take it a major step further than most sustainable buildings realized in the Netherlands until then.[3] Constructing sustainable buildings had been mostly limited to a focus on reducing energy use. Taking it further meant that we included circularity and biodiversity in addition to energy as pillars for the design and construction of the premises of the research institute.[4]

The building has fast become an architectural showcase of sustainable construction and is a testing ground for the latest eco-technology, where innovation and experimentation are given room to grow.[5] The unconventional green roof, for instance, not only filters water and air and aids temperature control, but also contributes to biodiversity and helps *Plant-e*[6] to test and further develop generating of electricity from plants.

1 M. Braungart and W. McDonough, *Cradle to Cradle: Remaking the Way We Make Things* (New York: North Point Press, 2012).

2 www.cradletocradle.com/ (accessed 21-12-2017).

3 In 2009, when the building was under construction, I gave a TEDxAmsterdam lecture entitled 'Towards a Circular Economy: Let's Be Positive!' (http://tedx.amsterdam/2009/12/video-louise-vet-on-the-marriage-between-economy-and-ecology/). This was one of the first, if not the first time in the Netherlands that we talked about circular economy within the domain of construction.

4 L. Vet, 'Learning from Nature: Need, Challenge and Implementation of Eco-Technology', *Communications in Applied Biological Sciences*, Ghent University, 76, no. 2 (2011), pp. 85–88.

5 See also www.nioo.knaw.nl/en/building for more information about the building. Several parts of this chapter include sentences that were taken from the website texts about the building.

6 www.plant-e.com/en/ (accessed 18-02-2018).

7 R.J. Cole, 'Transitioning from Green to Regenerative Design', *Building Research & Information* 40, no. 1 (2012), pp. 39–53.

8 Vet, 'Learning from Nature', p. 86.

Design and Construction Process, and Specifications

Sustainable design or sustainability in general tends to focus on what we can do to limit or avoid environmental damage. The C2C approach, however, asks how we can make a valuable contribution to our environment and our everyday life. This is the essence of regenerative design.[7] The C2C guiding principles as applied to this building are using renewable energy, celebrating biodiversity, and closing as many cycles as possible. The latter basically comes down to making everything in such a way that it can, at some point in time, serve again as raw material for use in the natural environment or in new products.

Claus and Kaan Architects—who secured the European tender for designing the new NIOO-KNAW building—were instructed to keep as close to this philosophy as possible. Having clarified the design brief, the next stage was to tackle the construction process. What materials could be used, what kind of flooring, how to generate energy, how to close the wastewater circuit, and use the residual heat? How can we contribute to and increase the variety of plants and animals in the surroundings?

Material

The designers had to comply with rigorous specifications regarding the use of materials. In order to become a people- and environment-friendly building, it had to made from renewable raw materials without any harmful emissions: 'The hull is made of durable concrete without any artificial additives and no sealant, solvents or such like were used in the process. Using materials such as wood, glass, steel, flax, ground limestone and granular debris creates a streamlined building with an open and natural appearance.'[8]

Energy

The NIOO-KNAW building is designed to reduce energy consumption (compared to other office buildings and laboratories) and to produce energy sustainably using solar panels and excess heat. The building has thermal solar panels to store the sun's heat using High Temperature Storage (HTS). In addition, the HTS also stores the excess heat from the building and the greenhouses. The temperature storage is located at a depth of 300 meters. This allows the excess heat produced during the summer to be stored for use the following winter. From there, hot water is brought up to release heat back into the building through hoses in the concrete (concrete core activation). Additionally, in winter, cold outside air is collected using cooling towers and stored in the soil (7 °C), allowing us to cool the building in summer. In this way the temperature in the building can be kept comfortable in winter without using additional energy. For energy provision photovoltaic (PV) foil has been placed on two roofs. At present this does not generate enough power to meet the building's energy needs. The building uses presence detection and daylight regulated switching. It is the first office/laboratory complex with complete LED lighting, wherever possible.

Water

Water is being recycled as much as possible. This means that wastewater is purified so that it can be discharged locally. Hence, a connection to the sewer system was considered to be redundant. Unfortunately, building regulations required the construction of a sewer, which NIOO would rather not use. Three different water circuits can be distinguished: wastewater from the toilets, domestic water (which includes water from the laboratories) and rain water. After purification (mining valuable nutrients from the wastewater) the streams flow into a constructed wetland, also called a helophyte filter. Helophytes are aquatic plants such as reed and cattails, which remove contaminants from the wastewater, thus reducing the ecological impact. The purified water can then flow into a pond and the open ditches in the surrounding area. However, as a lab we are legally not allowed to do this because of the risk of contamination. If it was only an office building it would have been possible.

Waste = Food

One of the main principles of the C2C philosophy is not to generate waste. To accomplish this the NIOO-KNAW building has been designed to retrieve valuable nutrients from faeces and to simultaneously limit the use of water, which is also purified in the same process. The building has a decentralized sanitation system that starts with vacuum toilets that use up to 90% less water compared to conventional toilets. For flushing, the NIOO uses groundwater instead of drinking water. An anaerobic reactor for urine and faeces produces biogas and effluent that is rich in phosphorus, nitrogen, and potassium. The next stage consists of a microalgae reactor and helophyte filter. The microalgae and plants 'eat' the effluent, purifying the wastewater. Being a scientific institute the NIOO also studies the ability of algae in removing micro-pollutants in the waste water such as pharmaceutical rest products, an emerging problem in wastewater treatment. By harvesting and drying the algae, valuable nutrients such as nitrogen and phosphate can be recovered to be used as agricultural fertilizers, thereby closing the nutrient cycle. The purified water may not be clean enough to drink, but it has the same quality as groundwater and can potentially be used to flush the toilets. This means that the water cycle can also be closed!

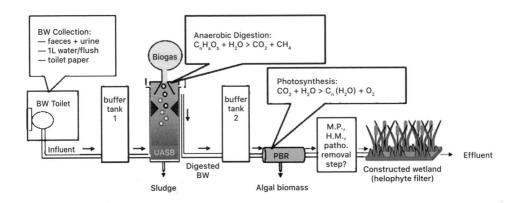

BW Collection:
— faeces + urine
— 1L water/flush
— toilet paper

Biogas

Anaerobic Digestion:
$C_nH_aO_b + H_2O > CO_2 + CH_4$

Photosynthesis:
$CO_2 + H_2O > C_n(H_2O) + O_2$

BW Toilet

buffer tank 1

buffer tank 2

M.P., H.M., patho. removal step?

Influent

UASB

Digested BW

PBR

Effluent

Constructed wetland (helophyte filter)

Sludge

Algal biomass

Black water treatment diagram at NIOO, Wageningen, image: Tania Fernandes

NIOO aims for maximum biodiversity; the green roof is also a research site, Wageningen

Biodiversity

The NIOO-KNAW building has a green roof, which filters water and air and aids temperature control. But the green roof is also a research site to explore and better understand how different green roofs function and contribute to sustaining the variety in species of plants and animals. Furthermore, NIOO aims for maximum biodiversity in its grounds:

Initiatives include the restoration and renewal of old hedges. Old alder pollards were returned to their original location after the end of the construction work, and all around the grounds distinctive ditches and wooded banks have been constructed. These wooded banks are home to a range of indigenous plants including hawthorn, blackthorn, pedunculate oak, rowan, hazel and cardinal's hat. After a number of years of growth, the banks are used to form woven hedges: a kind of ecological barbed wire. Wild plant and insect gardens in the grounds are rich and varied. Other projects include a hotel for swifts and a bat cellar in a repurposed bunker located along a quiet section of the bank.[9]

By now we can conclude that biodiversity has increased since the building was completed. We hope that our building and its surroundings are an example for office and business parks that also want to contribute to biodiversity.

Integrated Approach

At the NIOO-KNAW premises materials, water, energy, waste, and vegetation are not separate but interrelated entities. They come together in an approach of exploring possibilities and finding desirable solutions by closing as many cycles as possible and by creating effective links between various systems and residual flows. By doing so we aim to provide a valuable contribution to the surrounding environment instead of focusing on minimizing the negative impact on the environment. This is why the NIOO-KNAW building and its premises are an example of regenerative design and circular economy. As a building that breathes life the NIOO-KNAW building and its surroundings will never be 'finished': 'There will always be room for improvement and experimentation in the future. The building mirrors the dynamics found in nature and will continue to adapt to new understandings and new technologies'.[10]

9   https://nioo.knaw.nl/en/
    bringing-nature-city
    (accessed 18-02-2018).
10 Vet, 'Learning from
    Nature', pp. 87–88.

CONNECTING FLOWS

REVITALIZING THE MOKATTAM RIDGE

Every year around 932 billion metric tons of wastes are produced worldwide. This is equivalent to the weight of the Cheops pyramid, the biggest pyramid in the world, multiplied by 150 million. To lower the emission of CO_2 recycling is of prime importance. The ... garbage collectors in Cairo's Mokattam settlement manage to recycle op to 80 percent of the daily household waste of Cairo. ... These efficiency rates ... are the aim of the Western governments to reach within the next five to ten years.[1]

Introduction

Mokattam is the name of a range of hills as well as of a neighbourhood belonging to the administrative area of Manshiyat Naser and located in south-eastern Cairo, the capital of Egypt. The Arabic name Mokattam, which means cut off or broken off, refers to how the low range of hills is divided into three sections. The highest segment is a low mountain landform called Mokattam Mountain. In ancient Egypt the low mountain range was an important quarry site for limestone, which was used in the construction of temples and pyramids.

The Mokattam neighbourhood is approximately 0.25 square kilometres and with a population of about 30,000 inhabitants it is one of the densest populated areas of the world. Historically, Mokattam was located at the outskirt of the city. But as Cairo expanded towards the Mokattam mountain the neighbourhood nowadays has a central position in the city of Cairo. The vast majority (over 90%) of Mokattam's population is Coptic Christian. The neighbourhood is well known for its cave church, also known as the Monastery of Saint Simon, which has a seating capacity of 20,000 and is the largest church in the Middle East.[2]

1   V. Joos en F. Conrad, 'Mokattam: World's Largest Recycling Hub' (Basel: ETH Studio Basel Contemporary City Institute, 2010), p. 11.
2   www.amusingplanet. com/2013/09/the-cave-church-of-zabbaleen-in-cairo.html (accessed 24-12-2017).

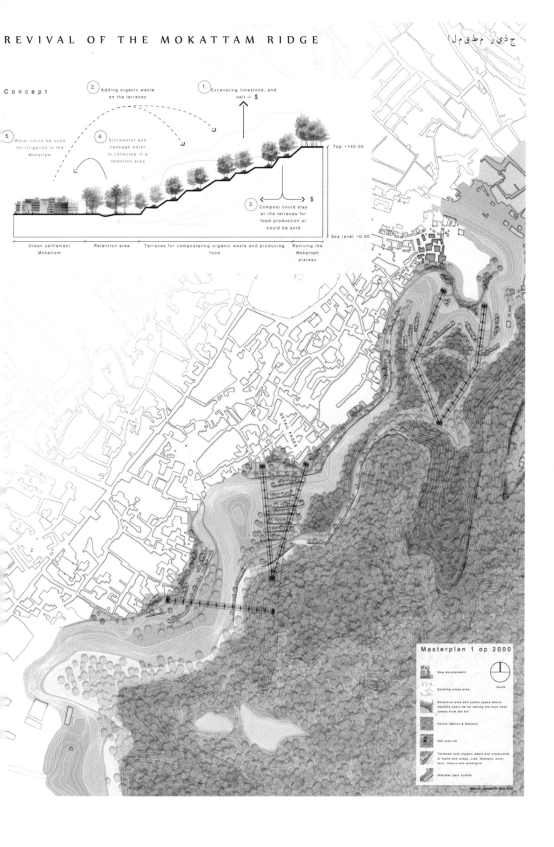

Concept

1. Excavating limestone, and sell it $

2. Adding organic waste on the terraces

3. Compost could stay at the terraces for food production or could be sold

4. Stormwater and seepage water is collected in a retention area

5. Water could be used for irrigation in the Mokattam

Top +140.00

Sea level +0.00

Urban settlement Mokattam | Retention area | Terraces for compostating organic waste and producing food | Reviving the Mokattam plateau

DETAIL FASE

Masterplan 1 op 2000

North

New development

Existing urban area

Retention area and public space where markets could be for selling the food what comes from the hill

Forest (Morus & Robinia)

Hill side lift

Terraces with organic waste and production of fruits and crops. Like, Oranges, potatoes, onions and aubergine

Informal path system

Mark van Vilsteren PS UbA1 2014

Plan for the revival of the Mokattam Ridge, Cairo, image: Mark van Vilsteren

Top down action (Municipality)

Bottom up action (Zabbaleen)

Excavating hill regarding erosion

Creating terraces

Planting trees

Creating the 'green gutter'

Terraces

Hill side lift

Connections

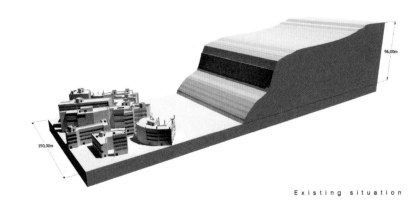

96,00m

150,00m

Existing situation

Adding trees on top of the Mokattam Hill
Excavating limestone at high risk areas

Excavating first terraces

Adding organic waste

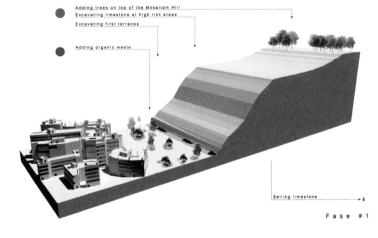

Selling limestone $

Fase #1

Adding trees on top of the Mokattam Hill
Excavating limestone at high risk areas

Excavating terraces
Adding Fruite trees or crops
Adding organic waste

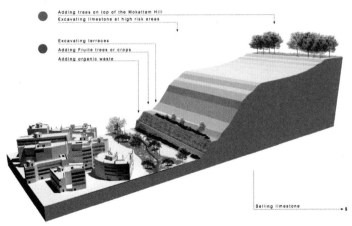

Selling limestone $

Fase #2

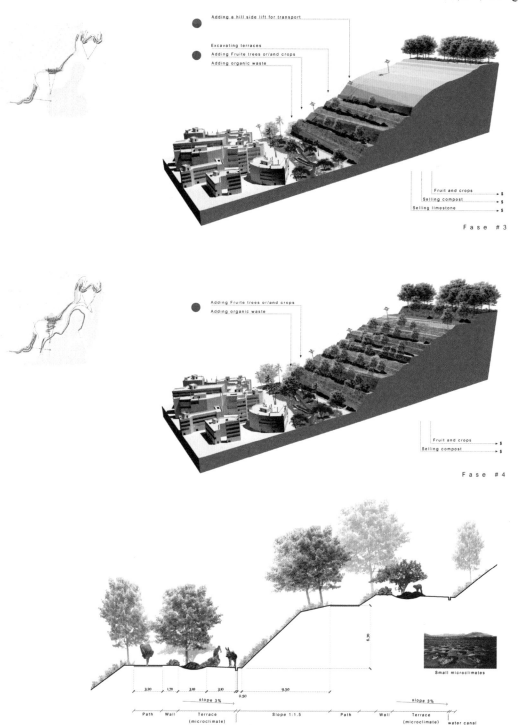

Different stages in the redevelopment of the Mokattam Ridge, Cairo, image: Mark van Vilsteren

Garbage City

However, the Mokattam neighbourhood is best known as Garbage City and its inhabitants as the Zabbaleen, meaning garbage people or garbage collectors. The Zabbaleen men collect a large part of Cairo's trash by picking it up door-to-door. They use donkey-pulled carts and pickup trucks to transport the trash to their neighbourhood. As there is no formal system of separate waste disposal and waste recycling in Egypt, the collected trash is completely un-sorted. Most of the trash is then sorted by women. Many families specialize in sorting certain materials such as paper, plastic, aluminium, glass, and so on. Sorting garbage is a time-consuming task on which women and children may spend up to 10 to 12 hours each day.[3]

First, the trash is sorted into the main 16 categories, such as paper, plas-tic, cardboard, cans, and so on. Then sorting within the category takes place. For xample, the major category of paper is sorted into white paper, yellow paper, thick paper, newspaper, thin paper, etc. Each sub-sorted material is then sold to factories and middlemen for a marginal profit. The Zabbaleen recycle thirty to forty per cent of all the garbage within Cairo and they used to play a key role in recycling urban organic waste.

The initial and very integral step of sorting the trash used to be the respon-sibility of Zabbaleen community mem-bers who owned pigs. The pigs were fed the organic waste. After the organic waste had been eaten by the pigs, the rest of the trash was sorted into differ-ent categories. In addition to their use in sorting out organic waste, pigs were an important source of income. When the pigs had grown, the Zabbaleen sold the pork to large tourist facilities.

Challenges Facing Garbage City and the Zabbaleen

The Zabbaleen's system of garbage collection and recycling, in which pigs played a crucial role, was disrupted in 2009. In that year, many pigs in differ-ent parts of the world were suffering from classical swine fever. Although no incidence of classical swine fever was noted in Egypt, the national government culled more than 300,000 pigs and closed Egypt's two pig slaughterhous-es. According to government officials this was necessary to contain swine fever, however many Zabbaleen re-garded the move as a sectarian slight.[4] As a result the Zabaleen did not only suffer financially by losing half of their income, but their overall waste manage-ment process suddenly missed a vital component.[5] Organic waste started rot-ting in the streets, not just in Mokattam but all over Cairo, causing major health problems.

Another challenge the inhabitants of Mokattam are facing are the rockslides, which occur because of erosion of the limestone. This is caused by water seepage further up the hill in combina-tion with uncontrolled piping of seepage water by the Zabbaleen at the bottom of the ridge. This makes the Mokattam ridge unstable. In 2008, 31 people were killed and 23 injured when a massive rockslide hit Mokattam, sending rocks and boulders crashing down on dozens of houses.[6]

W. Fahmi and K. Sutton, 'Cairo's Zabaleen Garbage Recyclers: Multi-nationals' Takeover and State Relocation Plans', *Habitat International* 30 (2006), pp. 809–837, p. 812.
www.theguardian.com/global-development/poverty-matters/2014/mar/27/waste-egypt-refuse-collectors-zabaleen-cairo (accessed 24-12-2017).
W. Fahmi and K. Sutton, 'Cairo's Contested Garbage: Sustainable Solid Waste Management and the Zabaleen's Right to the City', *Sustainability* 2 (2010), pp. 1765–1783, p. 1772.
www.reuters.com/article/us-egypt-landslide/killer-landslide-hits-east-cairo-shanty-town-idUSL 6294 965 2008 0906 (accessed 24-12-2017).

My design proposal aims to address these two main challenges that the Zabbaleen are facing: 1) restoring the organic waste cycle that was broken with the removal of the pigs and 2) preventing further erosion of the Mokkattam ridge. I want to address both challenges with one spatial intervention by creating new possibilities for organic waste processing and food production on the ridge, thereby generating a new source of income for the Zabbaleen.

The main intervention is terracing the Mokattam Ridge. To prevent further rockslides, this terracing should be kick-started by excavating the most dangerous parts of the Mokattam ridge. At the same time, creating terraces at the bottom of the ridge will give the Zabbaleen the opportunity to start transporting the organic waste within Mokattam to the ridge. Planting trees on the top of the Mokattam ridge will prevent further erosion of the ridge.

Once the ridge is stabilized, the Zabbaleen can start excavating further terraces and sell the limestone. Meanwhile the organic waste that was moved to the first terraces is transforming into compost. This compost can be sold or used to fertilize the soil on the terraces. By fertilizing the soil on the terraces, it is possible to plant and produce crops and fruits. The crops and fruits can be sold at the bottom of the hill in small markets.

An important pre-condition for growing food is the management of fresh water supply. The climate in Cairo is very dry. It only rains a couple of days a year. The Kashmee, a dust storm, blows wind with sand from the Mokattam plateau towards the urban area of east Cairo. A couple of times a year there are rainstorms. Those storms lead to water problems at the bottom of the hill and within the neighbourhood.

To provide the fresh water needed for growing crops and fruits a small canal along the paths and on the terraces is proposed. The terraces are a bit sloped backwards towards the mountain. That is a small catchment area where the water that comes out of the

Mokattam

composting organic waste is retained. It will provide more water for the planted crops, fruits, or trees.

Eventually small microclimates are expected to develop on the terraces. After a while vegetation will grow. On the longer term, the whole ridge will become greener and retain more water, also in combination with the planted trees on top of the Mokattam ridge. This will prevent a Kashmee and the whole area becomes more fertile and less dry.

During a rainstorm, the storage of rainwater can be regulated by the canals. Surplus water is caught in a bigger 'green gutter' at the bottom of the hill. The green gutter eventually will become a green oasis where small markets can be held. Together with the rest of the ridge, this creates a microclimate, which should eventually lower the temperature in Mokattam. The water that is stored could be used to irrigate the small backyards that are now filled up with organic waste. In this way urban agriculture also becomes possible.

Closing Circles, Revitalizing Landscape

When realized, this spatial intervention would imply that the Zabbaleen can use the Mokattam ridge instead of fearing it for its rockslides. Terracing the ridge and transforming it into a site of food production can also help to address the two problems that arose when the pigs were removed: the broken organic waste cycle and the loss of a source of income. It will help get rid of the organic waste that is now piling up in the neighbourhood and city, causing hygiene problems and health issues. At the same time, the new system of organic waste management creates new possibilities for food production on the ridge, provides the Zabbaleen with crops, fruits, and compost to sell and makes the ridge a fertile and safer area, which is also better adapted to the effects of climate change.

Saline Verhoeven & Johannes S.C. Wiskerke

SAN FRANCISCO: A ZERO-WASTE CITY BY 2020

CONNECTING FLOWS

San Francisco

Introduction

Waste is the symbol of inefficiency and a token of misallocated resources. Waste also implies the depletion of non-renewable resources. To prevent this, sustainable consumption and strategic waste management systems are urgently needed. This essentially comes down to reducing and preferably avoiding waste and recovering resources from waste. Disposing of waste in landfills or incinerating waste are to be prevented as this requires lots of energy (which in turn contributes to global warming) and does not lead to resource recovery.

More and more cities worldwide are adopting zero-waste policies and have the ambition to become zero-waste cities in the near future,[1] meaning that nothing ends up in a landfill or is incinerated. Although strategies, goals, and actions of zero waste cities differ, a comprehensive urban zero-waste approach includes the following key components and activities:[2]

1. Awareness, education, and research, by developing zero-waste programmes, providing transformative education, and carrying out zero-waste research.
2. New infrastructure and system thinking. This implies developing infrastructures and technologies that can be supportive of preventing, re-using and recycling waste. It also includes developing a zero-waste governance approach at city level, also specifying the roles and responsibilities of the municipal government, the private sector, and civil society.
3. 100% recycling and recovery, which means that all efforts should be geared towards reducing waste, repairing or re-using products to prevent them going to waste, and recycling and recovering waste.
4. Sustainable consumption and behaviour; focusing on establishing a fundamental and permanent change in lifestyles and in consumption practices and patterns.
5. Transformed industrial design, which calls for cradle-to-cradle design, cleaner production of goods and producer responsibility for reducing waste.
6. Zero depletion legislation and policies, which involves all sorts of legislative and other incentives to prevent waste going to landfills or being incinerated.

1 www.huffingtonpost.com/mariel-vilella/zero-waste-cities-at-the_b_12029704.html (accessed 07-01-2018).
2 A. Zaman and S. Lehmann, 'The Zero Waste Index: A Performance Measurement Tool for Waste Management Systems in a "Zero Waste City"', *Journal of Cleaner Production* 50 (2013), pp. 123–132.
3 www.seeker.com/how-san-francisco-is-becoming-a-zero-waste-city-1893330043.html (accessed 24-12-2017).
4 https://sfenvironment.org/news/press-release/mayor-lee-announces-san-francisco-reaches-80-percent-landfill-waste-diversion-leads-all-cities-in-north-america (accessed 05-01-2018).
5 https://sfenvironment.org/zero-waste-faqs#what-prompted (accessed 05-01-2018).
6 https://sfenvironment.org/carbon-footprint (accessed 03-01-2018).
7 www.bluegreenalliance.org/resources/more-jobs-less-pollution-growing-the-recycling-economy-in-the-u-s/ (accessed 30-12-2017).
8 https://sfenvironment.org/policy/mandatory-recycling-composting-ordinance (accessed 30-12-2017).
9 https://sfenvironment.org/zero-waste-faqs#-fantastic-three (accessed 23-09-2017).
10 E. Lombardi, The secret to San Francisco's Zero Waste Success, 2016, www.waste360.com/waste-reduction/secret-san-franciscos-zero-waste-success (accessed 23-09-2017).
11 www.recology.com/recology-san-francisco/ (accessed 23-09-2017).

San Francisco's Approach

The city of San Francisco (California, USA) plans to be a zero-waste city by the year 2020.[3] In 2002 the city launched its ambitious zero-waste programme and has had considerable success in achieving its goal of 75% diversion of waste from landfill and incineration in 2010. Currently, San Francisco has an 80% diversion rate and has the highest recycling and compost rate records of any city in North America.[4] It is therefore recognized as the national leader in waste management within the USA.

Three Key Sustainability Goals

By increasing diversion of waste from landfill and incineration and pursuing zero waste the municipality of San Francisco aims to achieve three key sustainability goals.[5] First it intends to conserve valuable resources. When materials are send to a landfill instead of being reused or recycled, valuable resources are wasted. Recycling and composting can greatly increase the amount of recyclable materials available to make new products, reducing the need to extract more virgin materials. Food scraps create nutrient-rich compost that can be used as resource for the production of fruits and vegetables in local farms. Compost also helps farms retain water, a precious resource. Second, the objective of the San Francisco municipality is to reduce environmental impacts such as climate change and environmental pollution. For instance, when food scraps and yard trimmings are sent to landfills they produce methane, a potent greenhouse gas which is up to 72 times more potent than carbon dioxide. With its Zero Waste programme San Francisco significantly reduces these emissions, making it an essential component in achieving the City's ambitious greenhouse gas reduction goals.[6] The third sustainability goal to achieve through the Zero Waste programme is to benefit the economy and create green jobs. Composting and recycling save residents and businesses money. Furthermore, higher recycling rates hold the potential to produce new jobs, strengthen the local economy, reduce pollution, and improve public health.[7] According to the San Francisco Mandatory Recycling and Composting Ordinance,[8] which was passed in 2009, recycling and composting waste is mandatory for San Francisco businesses and households.

The Three-stream Waste Collection System

One key element of San Francisco's successful approach towards becoming a zero-waste city is its so-called Fantastic Three programme.[9] This refers to the door-to-door three-stream waste collection system for businesses and households that is easy to use. Blue bins for recycling collect recyclable materials such as paper, glass, plastic, aluminium, and steel. Food scraps, plant trimmings, and compostable paper and fibre are collected in green bins for composting. Other waste is collected in black bins for landfill. All resident and businesses have all three bins. This 3-way collecting system guarantees a maximum recovery of resources. Crucial to its success are the partnerships with local organizations to raise awareness and consumer and producer responsibility, and the pay-as-you-throw philosophy for the collection service. Like with utilities such as electricity, water, or gas you pay for what you use. Residents pay only for trash in the black bin, i.e. the waste that cannot be recycled and goes to landfill. Businesses get a discount on the volume-based waste bill using the business' diversion percentage: i.e. one black, one blue, one green means 66% discount.

Public-private Partnership

Another key to making the Zero Waste programme a success is the partnership of the municipality and Recology.[10] Recology[11] is a private, employee-owned company that has created around 210 jobs, most of them drawn from Bayview-Hunters Point, one of the city's poorest neighbourhoods, where the plant is. Recology is the city's official refuse hauler. There is no competitive bidding for Recology's contract. When the Zero Waste programme started in 2002, the company had to convert its business model based upon landfilling into landfill diversion, composting, and recycling. The city agreed to share the risk for the time needed to make the transition, making it possible for Recology to still make a profit during the change. The plant now deals with recovering recyclable raw material and composting. Recovered resources such as plastic and aluminium are shipped to manufacturers. San Francisco's food waste is processed into fine, coffee-like grounds that is sold as processed compost to organic farms, wineries, and small-scale residential gardeners as fertilizer. Also worth mentioning is that the methane gas generated by the landfill is captured and converted into energy by G2 energy. This provides 1.6 megawatts of electricity, enough for 1,600 households.

Textile Recycling

Textiles are harder to recycle but are one of the most wasted materials. In San Francisco 4,500 pounds of textiles are disposed of in landfills every hour. Most of this can be reused or recycled into insulation material, flooring, packaging, or cushioning in stuffed toys, insoles, and bags.[12] In 2014 San Francisco launched a new programme to reduce and ultimately eliminate textile waste by facilitating the reuse and recycling of clothing, shoes, and textiles.[13] Towards this end the city has partnered with I:CO (I Collect),[14] an international company specialized in reducing textile waste. In San Francisco I:CO and its retail partners have set up more than 100 collection bins at retail stores, apartment complexes, schools, and public buildings around the city. In addition, I:CO had launched awareness campaigns to encourage residents to recycle their shoes and clothes. After the items are picked up by I:CO, the company works with third party sorters and graders to break them into 400 different categories to allocate as second-hand clothing, reuse as cloths, recycle into fibres and paddings, or upcycle into a product of equal or higher quality.[15]

12 https://sfenvironment.org/textiles (accessed 23-09-2017).
13 N. Gonzalez, 'The ROI of San Francisco's Zero-Waste programme', 2015, www.triplepundit.com/special/roi-of-sustainability/the-roi-of-san-franciscos-zero-waste-program/ (accessed 07-01-2018).
14 www.ico-spirit.com/en/ (accessed 07-01-2018).
15 M. Mazzoni, 'San Francisco Program Provides a Roadmap for Eliminating Textile Waste', 2014, www.triplepundit.com/special/sustainable-fashion-2014/san-francisco-program-provides-roadmap-eliminating-textile-waste/ (accessed 07-01-2018).

Easy to understand three-stream waste collection system, San Francisco, image: Recology

The three stream waste collection system, San Francisco

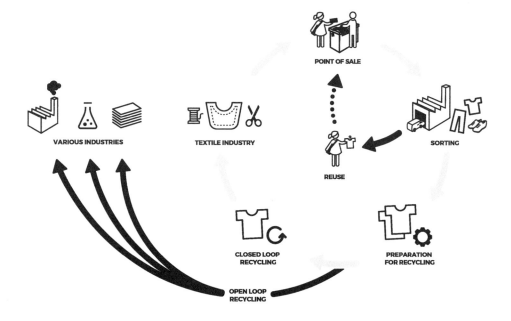

Circular economy in the textile industry, San Francisco, image: I:CO

Conclusions

San Francisco is an inspiring example of reducing, reusing, and recycling waste at city level. Around 80% of the urban waste is recycled and landfill disposal is at the lowest level in decades. There are several reasons for this success. The first one is the implementation of a convenient three-bin system that is to be used by all citizens and companies. Second is that there are economic incentives for residents to reduce the amount of waste going into the black bin (for landfill waste). Third, San Francisco has issued a large range of policies[16] that promote zero-waste goals (such as a ban on the use of Styrofoam or polystyrene foam for food service ware). And fourth it has developed and implemented an extensive outreach and education programme to residents and businesses about recycling and composting. Despite its successful strategy to become a zero-waste city by 2020, San Francisco's Zero Waste Program is sometimes criticized for its emphasis on the recycling of waste rather than on reducing consumption (and thereby waste) and reusing products.[17] That would be an even better strategy to save natural resources and reduce energy use in and costs of waste management.

16 https://sfenvironment.org/zero-waste-legislation (accessed 07-01-2018).

17 Gonzalez, 'The ROI of San Francisco's Zero-Waste programme'.

GREEN TIDES OF BRITTANY: MENDING THE BROKEN LOOP

CONNECTING FLOWS

Introduction

After World War II, the French government focused on increasing agricultural production. Traditional small-scale farming was replaced by large-scale intensive agriculture, which was able to grow rapidly by importing feed and fodder. As a consequence, animal production was no longer constrained by the amount of feed and fodder a farmer could produce and this resulted in an imbalance between the manure that was produced and the soil's ability to absorb it.

Brittany is one of the French regions that is facing an important challenge due to its intensive agriculture. While the region covers only 6.5% of the national territory, it accounts for 57% of the pork production, 33% of the poultry production and 21% of the milk production. The pressure on the natural environment and especially the water is incredibly high: 75,000 tons of nitrogen leach into the water system each year. This oversupply of nutrients in the ecosystem provokes macro algae biomass development, also called the 'green tide phenomenon'. The particular environmental conditions of the coast of Brittany enhance this rapid growth of algae. The bays offer a perfect configuration for rapid water warming and weak currents. Thus, trapping the nutrients and allowing fast photosynthetic activity, the bays are the most affected spots of the region.

1   D. Gravier, A. Wulff, and A. Torstensson, 'Monitoring of Green Tides on the Brittany Coasts (France)', *Primary Producers of the Sea* (Bio458), 2011–2012, pp. 1–9.

Green tides have numerous and varied effects on the environment, human health, and the economy. Biodiversity and floral richness are under threat because of the excessive growth of an invasive kind of algae, 'Ulva', taking light and oxygen from the system. With the tide, algae are washed ashore and accumulate on the coast resulting in biomass decomposition. This causes sediments to transform into organic mud and the decomposition of stranded algae processes significant quantities of hydrogen sulphide gas.[1] This gas is unhealthy and produces an unpleasant odour, inconveniencing both inhabitants and tourists. Some bays have been deserted because of this strong odour, which impact the everyday life of people.

Green tides also have negative economic consequences for the whole region and the local communities, which have to pay the cost of this pollution. Negative media attention has changed the image of Brittany. Formerly famous for its beautiful coastline, the region is now also known for its green tides. Consequently, tourism has decreased since the seventies and part of the most affected bays have been abandoned. The impact on the regional economy, one of the most touristic places of France, is significant. And on top of all, local communities have to pay for the removal and disposal of algae.

The most efficient solution would be to significantly reduce the production and subsequent leaching of nitrogen. Keeping less animals and developing alternative farming systems, which would be beneficial to the environment and to the community, would be the best solution. However, due to a powerful agricultural lobby there is no real ambition for a shift in that sense.

Another, though end-of-pipe solution would be to use the algae for different purposes. These curative attempts have potential but most of the time result in really costly solutions or non-profitable uses. The re-introduction of an ancestral tradition of using the algal material as a fertilizer for instance would worsen the situation causing aquifer pollution and increasing the amount of nitrogen released into the water system. The potential to use algae in foods is also restricted as animals can only eat very few quantities of algae and there is a really limited market for it in terms of human food. Recent experiments for biogas production indicate that this is a feasible and efficient way to produce energy but unfortunately not economically profitable at the moment.

Landscape Strategy and Toolbox

As intensive agriculture only benefits few people whereas the rest of the community has to cope with the green tides phenomenon, there is a real need for a fundamental shift: we need to rethink the way we produce food and the way we plan our territory. This implies a shift from curative means to preventive actions. As the green tides result from nitrogen flows coming from farms located in the entire watershed, the intervention needs to be done at a regional scale. It is fundamental to work on a landscape level in order to understand the complexity of this pollution and the interconnection between agriculture, city, water system, and the specific morphology of the coast. The green tides also impact the everyday life of thousands of people and thus concern everybody, from farmers to local citizens.

I therefore propose to develop a strategic landscape intervention, which not only deals with farmers and small-scale interventions, but embraces the whole ecosystem including agriculture, cities, and the sea. The design intervention focuses on Saint-Brieuc bay, one of the most polluted bays of the region.

The design shows how the relation between animal production and landscape can be re-established, and how the Brittany coast can recover from the green tide pollution. The proposal is a landscape strategy that rethinks the way the region is organized. How can one create a *water machine* that catches the nutrients and cleans the water before it reaches the sea while generating new public spaces and raising awareness about environmental protection? The challenge is to implement a preventive design that combines ecological systems and the public use as one structure.

The strategy consists of a *landscape toolbox,* which includes the implementation of new ditches in-between the fields, new wet areas in the river beds and the creation of salt marshes in the bay. Inspiration for the proposed landscape toolbox came from natural processes of slowing down water flows and the need for recycling nitrogen as a valuable nutrient. Nitrogen is a key component of chlorophyll, amino acids, proteins, and enzymes and is required for plant metabolism. Increasing the time the water spends in the system reduces the downstream transport of nutrients, which then can become available by infiltrating the water upstream.

My proposal is an interconnected ensemble of interventions along the course of the water from the fields and the riverbeds to the bay. The implementation of new ditches and small embankments between the fields—a traditional way to deal with water in the region–prevents water runoff (and thus manure) from being discharged with the water. Ditches and small embankments placed perpendicularly to the general slope of the terrain create a new network that makes the water journey longer and slows down the flow rate. They also bring quality to the existing open landscape and create beautiful scenery.

Dikes are built in order to enlarge the riverbeds and allow the implementation of new wet areas. The existing linear river is therefore transformed into a meandering flow that runs through grasslands and wetlands. The creations of new wet areas are a key element in the improvement of the actual purification of the streams. Interposed between the land and the sea, they intercept a significant fraction of land-derived nitrogen and thus reduce downstream nutrients transport. In addition, these wet areas produce feed and fodder for animals and consequently propose an alternative to the massive feed import. They work together to close the nitrogen cycle transforming the nitrogen surplus into plant growth. Additionally, the dikes create a new system of pathways for both local citizens and tourists and generate a new relation between the fragmented parts of the city.

Finally, the embankments protecting the existing polder are partly opened to permit the re-establishment of a salt marsh. The fields are thus transformed into salty wet areas and become a key element of the filtration system. Salt marshes are an efficient way to lower

Brittany

The proposed landscape strategy at a regional level, Brittany, image: Maxime Cloarec

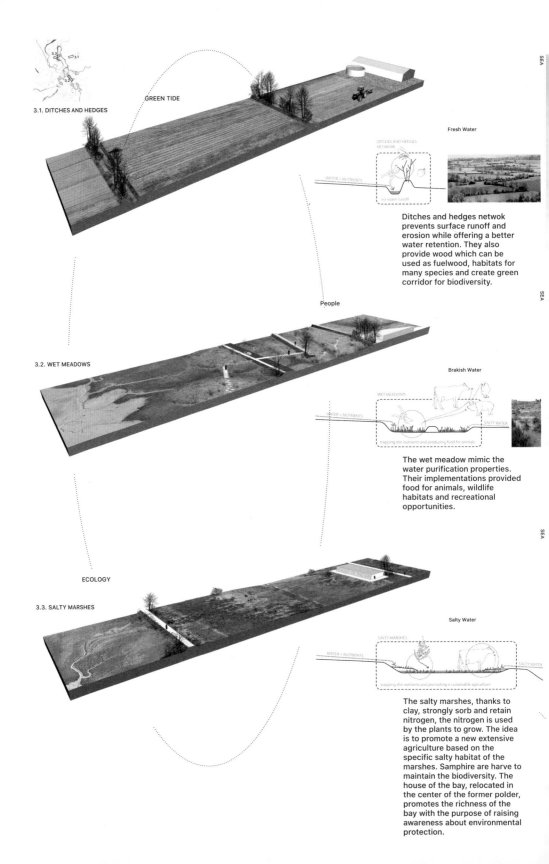

3.1. DITCHES AND HEDGES

GREEN TIDE

SEA

Fresh Water

Ditches and hedges netwok prevents surface runoff and erosion while offering a better water retention. They also provide wood which can be used as fuelwood, habitats for many species and create green corridor for biodiversity.

People

3.2. WET MEADOWS

SEA

Brakish Water

The wet meadow mimic the water purification properties. Their implementations provided food for animals, wildlife habitats and recreational opportunities.

ECOLOGY

3.3. SALTY MARSHES

SEA

Salty Water

The salty marshes, thanks to clay, strongly sorb and retain nitrogen, the nitrogen is used by the plants to grow. The idea is to promote a new extensive agriculture based on the specific salty habitat of the marshes. Samphire are harve to maintain the biodiversity. The house of the bay, relocated in the center of the former polder, promotes the richness of the bay with the purpose of raising awareness about environmental protection.

Recycling nutrients against green tides, Brittany, images: Maxime Cloarec

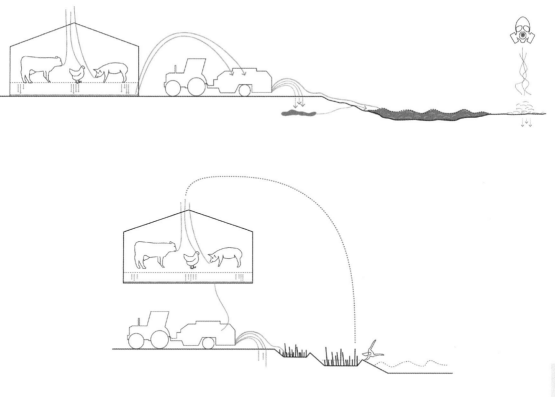

Brittany

Recycling nutrients against green tides, Brittany, images: Maxime Cloarec

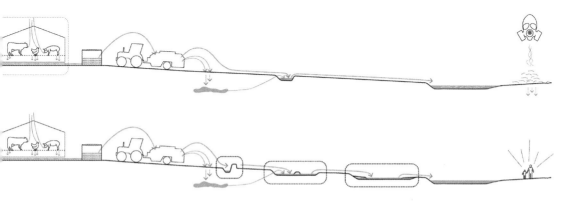

the pollution through percolating and a de-nitrification process. Indeed, they are capable to transform huge quantities of nitrogen into plant production. The salt marshes also allow cattle grazing, which contributes to maintaining high biodiversity while promoting extensive agriculture. In addition to this, they produce products of quality that can be harvested, such as salty herbs (samphire) and thus participate to promote environmentally friendly farming. Furthermore, this part of the project offers recreational public spaces by creating a new system of pathways and by relocating the existing 'House of the Bay', which aims to raise awareness about environmental protections. The purpose is to create a new relation between the existing city and its bay.

Conclusions

To conclude, the green tide phenomenon and eutrophication in general is a worldwide problem that opens up new perspectives and underlines the need for new strategies. This proposal does not intend to resolve the whole pollution problem of the region but wants to show, as a case study, that we need to think about innovative designs and bold interventions if we are to recover from the green tides phenomenon. Many scientific reports have been written on the subject but it has never been thought through in terms of a specific design intervention. To end with: Dealing with the green tides phenomenon through a landscape strategy is an incredibly potential way to create new synergies between technical solutions and landscape quality, ecology and culture, economy and recreation.

Johannes S.C. Wiskerke & Saline Verhoeven

SPATIAL DIVERSITY

Introduction

Our fourth socio-spatial design principle—enhancing spatial diversity and synergies—touches upon two issues related to food provisioning that we will outline in this chapter. The first one is the trend of foodscapes becoming increasingly mono-functional. The second one concerns the rapid decline of (agro)biodiversity. We will conclude this chapter with a short introduction to the four cases that feature in the next four chapters as examples of this fourth socio-spatial design principle. However, before we introduce and discuss these two issues of concern we need to clarify the importance of this fourth principle in general.

The significance of enhancing spatial diversity and synergies lies in the relation between diversity on the one hand and the vulnerability and resilience of ecological and social systems on the other hand. Much research has been done about the importance of biological diversity for maintaining or even improving the resilience of ecosystems, 'which is required to secure the production of essential ecosystem services'.[1] Specific attention is given to the significance of 'response diversity', which is defined as 'the diversity of responses to environmental change among species that contribute to the same ecosystem function'.[2] Erosion of response diversity will reduce ecosystem resilience and lead to 'social and economic vulnerability, changes in nature's capacity to supply human society with essential ecosystem services, and ultimately degraded socioecological systems'.[3]

What holds true for ecological systems—diversity as a prerequisite for resilience—also seems to apply for social communities: 'Diversity ... is critical to a community's ability to move beyond adaptive management to proactively maintain and enhance resiliency.'[4] It does, however, depend on the kind of relations that people have or establish and by which social networks are shaped:

1   T. Elmqvist et al., 'Response Diversity, Ecosystem Change, and Resilience', *Frontiers in Ecology and the Environment* 1, no. 9 (2003), pp. 488–494, quote p. 488.

2   Ibid., p. 488.

3   Ibid., p. 493.

4   L. Newman and A. Dale, 'Network Structure, Diversity, and Proactive Resilience Building: A Response to Tompkins and Adger', *Ecology and Society* 10, no. 1 (2005).

5   Ibid.

6   C. Folke et al., 'Social-ecological Resilience and Biosphere-based Sustainability Science', *Ecology and Society* 21, no. 3 (2016).

7   C. Folke, 'Resilience: The Emergence of a Perspective for Social-Ecological Systems Analyses', *Global environmental change* 16, no. 3 (2006), pp. 253–267.

8   J. Hodbod and H. Eakin, 'Adapting a Social-ecological Resilience Framework for Food Systems', *Journal of Environmental Studies and Sciences* 5, no. 3 (2015), pp. 474–484.

Research suggests that not all social networks are created equal; networks composed of 'bridging' links to a diverse web of resources strengthen a community's ability to adapt to change, but networks composed only of local 'bonding' links, which impose constraining social norms and foster group homophily, can reduce resilience.[5]

Hence, it is the combined diversity of social relations, of values, and of the resources that people and communities can draw from that builds resilience.

In recent years we have seen that research on resilience is no longer confined to either biological or ecological research on ecosystems and anthropological and sociological research on communities and social networks, but also focuses on the interaction between people and nature, between communities and their ecological environment, or between society and the biosphere. The social and the natural depend on one another, mutually shape one another and co-evolve.[6] This is the essence of the social-ecological systems approach. Key to building resilience in social-ecological systems is to maintain, enhance, and celebrate diversity.[7] This is, for instance, also paramount to achieving food security as this 'will require functional redundancy and enhanced response diversity, creating multiple avenues to fulfil all food system objectives'.[8]

From Monofunctional to Multifunctional Urban and Rural Foodscapes

Typical for 20th-century modernization of cities and countryside has been the creation of mono-functional urban and rural landscapes, and, consequently, of mono-functional urban and rural food-scapes. Post-World War II suburban areas are characterized by the spatial separation of functions or activities such as living, working, education, sports, leisure, and shopping. This spatial divide between functions requires and thus goes hand in hand with roads, parking lots, and cars in order to travel between these different places and related functions that are part and parcel of everyday life. The iconic manifestation of this type of urban development in the realm of food provisioning is the supermarket in the shopping mall, generally located at the outskirts of the suburban neighbourhood and surrounded by ample parking space. And for suburban dwellers this may well be one of the few if not the only place relatively close by where food can be bought. This spatial separation of functions in urban space, such as dwelling and food procurement, reduces the vitality of cities:

> Downtown districts bustling with people in day hours become eerily deserted at night, when people swarm to the indoor shopping mall, which, despite the best efforts of designers, is boring and frenetic. Residential neighborhoods find few people on the streets either day or night, because there is nowhere to go and not much to look at without appearing to encroach on the privacy of others.[9]

One of the early and very influential writers criticizing this mono-functional development of cities was Jane Jacobs, with her book *The Death and Life of Great American Cities* in which she states that cities need 'a most intricate and close-grained diversity of uses that give each other constant mutual support, both economically and socially'.[10] In order to foster the cultural, social, and economic development and resilience of cities an encounter of differences and diversity is required.[11]

A similar spatial configuration holds true for the 20th century, and more specifically for post-World War II rural development. Large parts of the countryside have been transformed to create optimal conditions for modern agriculture, with other areas being designated for functions such as leisure, recreation, and nature. In the 20th century, farm size has increased while farms have also become more specialized: in the USA, for example, the average farm size increased from 150 acres to 450 acres (while the number of farms decreased by almost 70% in the same period of time) and the average number of products produced per farm has decreased from 5.1 to 1.2, implying that many farms have specialized in the production of just one commodity.[12] If we try to visualize these figures of farm size growth and specialization, it means that in 1900 a 150-acre farm would consists of five 30-acre plots with a different product being produced on each plot, while in 2000 a 450-acre farm would consist of one 450acre plot on which only one product is produced. As similar agricultural development patterns can be seen in many parts of the world it becomes apparent how monotonous agricultural landscapes have become. Extreme examples are the soybean farms in Brazil's state Mato Grosso with an average size of 1300 ha,[13] the feedlots in the USA ranging in size from 50 to 175 thousand heads of cattle per feedlot,[14] and the largest pig farm in the Pskov region in Russia with a capacity of 1 million pigs and a planned capacity of 2 million in the near future.[15]

These large-scale agricultural production complexes are interlinked to one another—e.g. part of the soy grown in Mato Grosso is feed for cattle and pigs produced elsewhere in the world—but also to the supermarkets in shopping malls at the outskirts of town and global distribution networks connecting rural food production environments and urban food procurement environments.

I.M. Young, *Justice and the Politics of Difference* (Princeton, NJ: Princeton University Press, 2011), p. 246.

J. Jacobs, *The Death and Life of Great American Cities* (New York, NY: Vintage, 2016), p. 14.

S. Cozzolino, 'Insights and Reflections on Jane Jacobs' Legacy: Toward a Jacobsian Theory of the City', *Territorio* 72 (2105), pp. 151–157.

C. Dimitri et al., *The 20th-Century Transformation of US Agriculture and Farm Policy, Vol. 3* (Washington, DC: US Department of Agriculture, Economic Research Service, 2005).

K. Strohm, D. Velazco Bedoya, and M. Osaki, *The Typical Farm BR1300MT in Mato Grosso, Brazil* (s.l.: Agribenchmark, 2012). https://agr.wa.gov/FoF/docs/feedlot.pdf (accessed 16-02-2018). www.pigbusiness.nl/artikel/12247-varkensbedrijf-voor-2-miljoen-dieren/ (accessed 16-02-2018).

E. van Leeuwen, P. Nijkamp, and T. de Noronha Vaz, 'The Multifunctional Use of Urban Greenspace', *International Journal of Agricultural Sustainability* 8, nos. 1-2 (2010), pp. 20–25.

F.A. Uribe et al., 'Walkability Makeover for Suburbia: Retrofitting Calgary's Suburbs, an Economic Evaluation (breakout presentation)', *Journal of Transport & Health* 7 (2017) S55.

M. Horst et al., 'Toward a More Expansive Understanding of Food Hubs', *Journal of Agriculture, Food Systems, and Community Development* 2, no. 1 (2016), pp. 209–225;

Z.C. Zhuang and A.X. Chen, 'The Role of Ethnic Retailing in Retrofitting Suburbia: Case Studies from Toronto, Canada', *Journal of Urbanism: International Research on Placemaking and Urban Sustainability* 10, no. 3 (2017), pp. 275–295.

19 S. Lovell, 'Multifunctional Urban Agriculture for Sustainable Land Use Planning in the United States', *Sustainability* 2, no. 8 (2010), pp. 2499–2522.

20 L.G. Horlings and T.K. Marsden, 'Exploring the "New Rural Paradigm" in Europe: Eco-economic Strategies as a Counterforce to the Global Competitiveness Agenda', *European Urban and Regional Studies* 21, no. 1 (2014), pp. 4–20.

21 J.D. van der Ploeg, A. Long, and J. Banks, *Living Countrysides: Rural Development Processes in Europe: The State of the Art* (Doetinchem: Elsevier Business Information, 2002); G. van Huylenbroeck and G. Durand, *Multifunctional Agriculture: A New Paradigm for European Agriculture and Rural Development* (Farnham: Ashgate Publishing, 2003).

22 J.S.C. Wiskerke, 'On Places Lost and Places Regained: Reflections on the Alternative Food Geography and Sustainable Regional Development', *International Planning Studies* 14, no. 4 (2009), pp. 369–387.

23 H. Renting et al., *Innovative Experiences with Multifunctional (Peri-) urban Agriculture in City Regions in the Global South*, SUPURBFOOD deliverable 3.4 (Leusden: RUAF Foundation, 2013).

In 'The Spatiality of Food Provisioning' (pp. 17ff.) we referred to this as the interconnectedness of foodscapes.

However, beside the still prevailing trend of increasing mono-functionality in the use of urban and rural space, we can see an increase in social practices and spatial planning activities that support and foster multifunctionality of space, both in urban and rural areas. Examples are plans, projects, and practices dedicated to enhancing the multifunctionality of urban green space;[16] retrofitting suburban neighbourhoods by increasing walkability[17] and diversifying food outlets in (sub)urban areas;[18] and creating space for multifunctional urban agriculture.[19] Furthermore, in many European countries there is a significant increase in the number of farmers diversifying their farm business[20] by combining food production with functions such as tourism, education, care, direct selling, energy provision, and nature and landscape management.[21] This diversification of spatial functions in both urban and rural areas is likely to result, if we follow the general line of argumentation introduced in this chapter, in more resilient places and spaces. Additionally, urban-rural relations may be strengthened through new food networks.[22]

Enhancing spatial diversity is also a means to foster spatial synergies, i.e. achieving multiple benefits from the same place by creating synergies between food provisioning and different societal challenges and policy objectives. This especially holds true for what we phrased as the food and water-energy-environment-waste-climate change-social inequality-health nexus on p. 28. Multifunctional urban and peri-urban agriculture and agroforestry spaces in city regions may serve different purposes simultaneously. For instance, the cultivation of rice in the flood plains in Antananarivo (Madagascar) provides a staple crop for a large part of the urban population, mitigates floods during the rainy season, contributes to income generation and job creation for farmers, and reuses urban wastewater that flows onto urban and peri-urban agricultural land.[23] Another example is rooftop farming, which can contribute to greening of cities, reduce energy consumption for heating and cooling buildings, help to combat urban heat islands, be used for storm water containment and generate biodiversity in cities.[24]

By rethinking and redesigning foodscapes several components of the nexus can be addressed simultaneously, for instance reducing the ecological footprint, mitigating climate change, and alleviating poverty and nutrition insecurity. Global food sourcing and concentrating food outlets at the outskirts of suburban neighbourhoods implies motorized food transport (both by food suppliers and by consumers). As a consequence, such a food provisioning system results in greenhouse gas emissions and thus contributes to air pollution and climate change. To significantly reduce this impact, there is an urgent need for measures to reduce food transport and use modes of transport that emit less greenhouse gas, fine particles, and lead. Creating and protecting space for urban and peri-urban farming and establishing food markets and other food outlets within walking distance of as many people as possible would be important measures to reduce air pollution caused by food transport, enhance food and nutrition security for the urban poor, and safeguard jobs and income generation in the urban and peri-urban food economy. Other policy domains that can be addressed by redesigning food provisioning systems are, for instance, public health, community building, and education.[25] Creating synergies between sustainable development goals by rethinking and redesigning how and where food is produced, transported, sold, and eaten is therefore of the utmost importance.

Biodiversity

Biodiversity is key to food production and food security as well as to environmental conservation. The modernization and industrialization of agricultural production and food processing has resulted in a dramatic reduction in agro-biodiversity: 'Predominant patterns of agricultural growth have eroded biodiversity in, for example, plant genetic resources, livestock, insects, and soil organisms.'[26] Due to the focus on increasing productivity in the post-World War II period, agricultural production systems have increasingly been based on a few high productive plant varieties or animal breeds: 'Modern agricultural practices, stemming from the rise of a modern breeding industry and from the Green Revolution, have caused massive genetic erosion, the disappearance of many diverse populations of crops maintained by farmers and adapted to local circumstances.'[27]

In addition to genetic erosion in farm crops and animals, the modernization of farms and the countryside has also resulted in the loss of biodiversity in natural habitats. Land reconsolidation measures that were implemented to make the countryside suitable for modern farming have led to the destruction of natural habitats and historico-cultural landscapes. And natural habitats, such as large parts of the Amazon rainforest, have disappeared due to the expansion of agricultural land:

> Across the tropical regions, the total net increase in agricultural area was more than 100 million ha during the 1980s and 1990s ... and more than 55% of this new agricultural land came from intact forests. This finding confirms that agricultural expansion ... has been a major driver of deforestation and the associated carbon emissions.[28]

The erosion of genetic diversity of agricultural crops as well as the loss of biodiversity due to the destruction of natural habitats to enable the expansion of agricultural land, seems to point to tension or conflict between food production and biodiversity. There are, however, many ways in which synergies can be created between agriculture and biodiversity. For example, the activities of the Slow Food Foundation for Biodiversity[29] are aimed at enhancing biodiversity through agricultural production and other food provisioning activities,

K. Ackerman et al., 'Sustainable Food Systems for Future Cities: The Potential of Urban Agriculture', *The Economic and Social Review* 45, no. 2 (2014), pp. 189–206; L. Mandel, *Eat Up: The Inside Scoop on Rooftop Agriculture* (Gabriola Island: New Society Publishers, 2013).
K.H. Brown and A.L. Jameton, 'Public Health Implications of Urban Agriculture', *Journal of Public Health Policy* 21, no. 1 (2000), pp. 20–39; B.E. Mikkelsen, 'Images of Foodscapes: Introduction to Foodscape Studies and Their Application in the Study of Healthy Eating Out-of-home Environments', *Perspectives in Public Health* 131, no. 5 (2011), pp. 209–216.
L.A. Thrupp, 'Linking Agricultural Biodiversity and Food Security: The Valuable Role of Agrobiodiversity for Sustainable Agriculture', *International Affairs* 75, no. 2 (2000), pp. 265–281.
B. Visser, 'Effects of Biotechnology on Agro-biodiversity', *Biotechnology and Development Monitor* 35 (1998), pp. 2–7.
H.K. Gibbs et al., 'Tropical Forests Were the Primary Sources Of New Agricultural Land in the 1980s and 1990s', *Proceedings of the National Academy of Sciences* 107, no. 38 (2010),16732–16737.
www.fondazioneslowfood.com/en/what-we-do/ (accessed 16-02-2018)
www.terra-genesis.com/wp-content/uploads/2017/03/Regenerative-Agriculture-Definition.pdf (accessed 16-02-2018).
R.J. Cole et al., 'A Regenerative Design Framework: Setting New Aspirations and Initiating New Discussions'. *Building Research & Information* 40, no. 1 (2012), pp. 95–111.

such as:

— Creating 10,000 gardens in Africa and activating a network of young African food professionals who will work to save Africa's extraordinary biodiversity, promote traditional knowledge and gastronomy, and encourage family farming and small-scale agriculture;
— Developing the Ark of Taste, which is a catalogue of quality food products at risk of extinction.
— The Slow Food Chefs' Alliance, an international network of chefs—active in Italy, Morocco, the Netherlands and Mexico—who source their ingredients from local food producers and who promote these agricultural products to their customers;
— The Earth Markets, a network of farmers' markets where small-scale producers directly sell local, seasonal and sustainably grown food products at fair prices.

Another example of creating synergies between agriculture and biodiversity, and which has a lot in common with some of the aforementioned activities of Slow Food, is regenerative agriculture. This is defined as

> a system of farming principles and practices that increases biodiversity, enriches soils, improves watersheds, and enhances ecosystem services. By capturing carbon in soil and aboveground biomass, regenerative agriculture aims to reverse global climate change. At the same time, it offers increased yields, resilience to climate instability, and higher health and vitality for farming communities.[30]

The concept of regenerative agriculture has inspired the development of regenerative design frameworks[31] that can be used for the green as well as the built environment at different levels of scale. To a large extent, the NIOO building described in 'A Building that Breathes Life' (pp. 151ff.) is an example of regenerative design.

Hence, combining biodiversity maintenance with agricultural practices is a strategy that can have multiple ecological and socio-economic benefits, particularly to ensure food security. Practices that conserve, sustainably use and enhance biodiversity are necessary at all levels in farming systems, and are of critical importance for food production, livelihood security, health, and the maintenance of ecosystems.[32]

This is also why protection and enhancement of biodiversity through agricultural practices feature in several of the cases that have been selected as illustration for the socio-spatial design principle of enhancing spatial diversity and synergies.

Introduction to the Cases

In the following chapters four different cases of spatial diversity and synergies will be presented and discussed. These cases also represent different levels of scale and are therefore an illustration of the second socio-spatial design principle:

1. *Food Forest Vlaardingen* is a one-hectare food forest at the border of the city of Vlaardingen and the countryside of Midden-Delfland (The Netherlands). It is primarily a demonstration project to explore and show how food can be grown in a natural way while enhancing biodiversity and creating opportunities for recreation and education. As such, Food Forest Vlaardingen is to become a showcase of spatial synergies between biodiversity and food production as well as between food production and other functions.

2. *Cultivating the city* focuses on designing a network of productive urban green spaces with predominantly native plant and tree species, in Porto Alegre (Brazil). It is based on the assumption that urban agriculture can improve access to food but also enhance urban spatial quality. This requires that all urban agriculture spaces become connected through a city-wide network of food producing spaces. As such this design is also an example of linking scales: urban agriculture sites at neighbourhood level as building blocks for a productive green infrastructure at city level.

3. *The Urban Agriculture Programme of Rosario (Argentina)* is an excellent example of the participatory design and development of multifunctional spaces for urban agriculture. Through the programme, vacant and often unused public spaces have been made accessible for agroecological food production. These intra-urban spaces have been developed into public spaces that not only serve production purposes but are also spaces of social encounter, training, and leisure and contribute to various ecological functions, such as biodiversity and adaptation to climate change. In recent years, peri-urban production areas are also being developed and protected as part of the city-region's greenbelt strategy.

4. *Creating edible landscapes through common land use in the Vigo city region (Galicia, Spain)* discusses development and management of the mountainous forest and scrubland locally known as Monte. Typical for the Vigo city region is that a significant part of the Monte is managed by Associations of Commons, which promote more sustainable uses of their common land, stressing the importance of recovering multifunctional land use and quality (food) products as well as biodiversity and leisure functions.

32 Thrupp, 'Linking Agri-
    cultural Biodiversity and
    Food Security, p. 265.

Paul de Graaf

FOOD FOREST VLAARDINGEN

SPATIAL DIVERSITY

Vlaardingen

Introduction

Location of food forest Vlaarding:
where urban meets rural, map:
Paul de Graaf

Food Forest Vlaardingen (FFV) is a bottom-up initiative in which almost one hectare of food forest has been developed at the border of the city of Vlaardingen and the countryside of Midden-Delfland. It is a productive, biodiverse park that shows how food can be cultivated in a natural way. FFV was initiated by the Rotterdam Forest Garden Network, which sees food forests as a means to connect urban needs and interests to the challenges of the countryside.

FFV is a pilot project to explore the scope for agro-food forestry, now and in the coming 15 to 20 years, and to see how this 'agro-inclusive nature' can be embedded in the landscape. The FFV pilot is a microcosm in which small solutions are sought for rural ecological aspects such as soil, water, and biodiversity as well as for urban aspects such as accessibility and societal support. The knowledge and experience gained through this pilot can be used to develop food forests on a larger scale, although lessons learnt will have to be de- and re-contextualized. Among other things, FFV examines how food forestry can play a complementary role in relation to agricultural sectors such as dairy farming and horticulture, which have been traditionally present in the landscape of Midden-Delfland.

The result is a vision of an agro-ecological landscape in the urban delta, a set of compelling stories about food forestry, and, last but not least, a food forest that is realized through collaborations between different stakeholders and is socially, economically, and spatially well embedded in the delta landscape.

The Principles of the Food Forest

A food forest is a garden or landscape set up as a natural ecosystem but focused on the production of food and other products that people can use. A well-functioning food forest can have a substantial yield per hectare, without the fossil fuels, artificial fertilizer, pesticides, and intensive tillage that characterize the current food production. But a food forest is more than an alternative form of agriculture. Because of its ecological and spatial diversity, it also enriches the increasingly monotonous urban, peri-urban, and rural environment. Its functioning as an ecosystem, with all the stories and principles related to it, makes a food forest an environment where people can learn about and from nature.

A food forest is composed of trees, shrubs and plants, which have been collected for their usefulness for the productive ecosystem as well as for people. This includes natural and cultivated species as well as native and exotic species. In addition, careful consideration is given to how the species fit into the food forest ecosystem. Often, species are applied that are related to native species or that grow in a similar climate. A food forest is a collaborative result made by people and nature.

The characteristics of a food forest are:

- Construction in layers. The food forest is organized as a natural ecosystem. The planting can consist of up to seven layers: crown layer (large trees), small trees, shrubs, herb layer, ground cover plants, root crops and climbers (the 'vertical' layer). Mushrooms and animals also play a role.
- Layers and species support and complement each other. Within the diversity of species and layers, each plant finds its ideal place for growth, where it also contributes optimally to the whole. Each part of the system has several functions: food production, fertilization, crop protection, ground cover, shelter from sun, wind, cold, and so on.
- Soil life plays an essential role in the cooperation between the plants, shrubs, and trees. A fertile, well-rooted, and undisturbed soil has a rich life with all kinds of small creatures, bacteria, and fungi that convert organic matter into nutrients for the crops, retain moisture, and capture CO_2.
- Fungi fulfil a special role in the food forest ecosystem. They form networks in the soil that can extend over kilometres and through which nutrients are distributed. Additionally, networks of fungi enable trees and plants to 'warn' each other about diseases and pests.

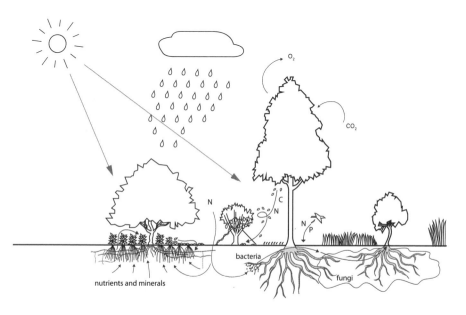

Principal section of a food forest Vlaardingen, section: Paul de Graaf

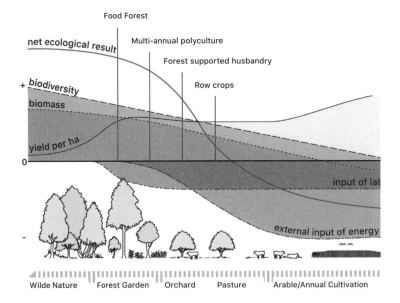

Design and Development Challenges

FFV is a place to test food forest principles in practice. In the design different conditions are created in which various tree-shrub-plant combinations are tried and monitored. This provides important information about how a food forest can function in this landscape. Elevation differences have been created that form ecological gradients from wet to dry and which in a small way simulate the landscape conditions (with creek ridges and peat pasture) in the area. Also, the productive effect of different distances between plants is explored. The most important function of FFV is its role as a source of knowledge about agro-food forestry and permaculture. At the same time, it also serves as a model for hybrid use of space, combining food production, recreation, and nature. The expectation is that within five years the yield from harvest, processing, and activities such as guided tours, courses, and company outings will create a stable economic basis for the continuation of the food forest.

From Citizens' Initiative to Agricultural Company

An important next step is the crossover from a citizens' initiative to an agricultural company. This transition is not self-evident given that a food forest differs radically from agricultural production: polyculture instead of monoculture, no tillage, and harvesting different layers in different seasons. In addition, there is a lack of practical experience with this approach in the Netherlands. To support interested farmers (and new entrants) in this transition a strategy is needed that carefully searches for niches: physical, conceptual, and financial space alongside and, where possible, in collaboration with the current farming practices to experiment with agro-food forestry.

Spatial Framework:
The City Region Foodscape

In pilots like FFV factors such as finances, a benevolent landowner, and the skills and expertise of the (new) farmer are often seen as decisive. Landscape factors, on the other hand, are often only taken into account to a limited extent. As a result, opportunities may be missed out on. Certainly for the longer term it is indispensable to outline a larger spatial framework that looks at location factors from an integral systemic perspective (ecological, economic, social, cultural). Only in this way can food forestry be structurally embedded in the Dutch landscape. This spatial framework must be in line with (future) policy frameworks. These are determined on the one hand by national and regional authorities. On the other hand, the role of cities (and hence municipal authorities) is of increasing importance, as expressed by the notion of city region food systems (see also pp. 45ff.). The further development of the FFV is therefore accompanied by socio-spatial research exploring the future foodscape of the Metropolitan Region Rotterdam.

Complementary and Symbiotic Part of the Metropolitan Foodscape

The future will likely be a hybrid of (continuation and development of) conventional agriculture, greenhouses, food production on and in buildings, and forms of agro-ecology that go 'beyond organic'. From a spatial perspective, conscious and focused choices can be made about which types are needed and wanted, where they are to be located, and how they can complement each other. Due to its biodiversity, food forestry can deliver a range of food, feed, and non-food products. For example, willows are now being produced in Midden-Delfland as feed for the elephants and giraffes in Rotterdam's Blijdorp Zoo. And in the Fodder Trees project, we studied how edible hedges can serve as cattle feed. But food forestry can also produce building materials (bamboo), raw materials for medicines, or dyes. All this in addition to both better and lesser-known edible plants in the food forest: nuts, fruits, leaves, shoots, and tubers.

Conclusions

The relevance of the design discipline lies in bringing together different perspectives and interests and its ability to translate these into spatial scenarios in which promising forms of agroforestry are explored according to food forest principles. This is done on the basis of an opportunity map that provides both an image of the potential for the region and identifies promising locations for pilots. For a number of these locations, example designs are made that show how opportunities can be seized. A special challenge here is the time aspect: the time that trees need to grow, both as a productive unit and in spatial terms, and all aspects that are linked to this, such as the payback time of investments. In addition to a systemic, analytical view, the design of change (transition) requires a strategic approach to the development of the landscape. That is why we are working towards a strategy for implementation in which potential food forest farmers are involved.

The development of the food forest landscape gives rise to new stories to develop and new ways to tell them. Food forest products such as nuts and fruits, but also many unknown shoots and leaves, offer new culinary challenges and questions for recipes. The gradual development of a food forest (over 20–50 years) and the changing, more mixed use that this entails (with more space for nature and recreation) requires a less rigid picture of what an (agricultural) landscape is and how it ought to look. How a food forest produces can give us more insight into how nature works and how we can apply this in our society. By telling these stories the accessibility of the landscape is increased. Interpretive architecture can be used for this, from analogue objects in the landscape to digital apps. This aspect is also taken into account in the implementation strategy as the farmers who start working with the food forest (in various forms) become important ambassadors and food forest storytellers.

Jacques Abelman

CULTIVATING THE CITY: INFRA- STRUCTURES OF ABUNDANCE IN URBAN BRAZIL

Porto Alegre

Introduction

1   W. Baudoin and A. Drescher, *Urban Agriculture for Sustainable Poverty Alleviation and Food Security* (Rome: FAO, 2008).

As urban populations continue to expand, cities in Brazil must adapt to the spatial as well as the social needs of all their inhabitants in order to move towards just and sustainable urban models. New spatial practices must therefore be articulated in order to offer successful strategies for attaining these goals. Urban agriculture is a practice that can potentially address urban spatial quality and access to food at the same time. Urban agriculture can create a secondary food network in the city, creating both opportunities for livelihoods and new economic activities[1]. At the same time, networks of food producing spaces can potentially increase the spatial quality of the city.

Urban agriculture, if it is to become integrated into the city, needs landscape architectural thinking in order to be woven into the larger urban fabric. Thinking on the scale of ecosystems running through a city creates a framework for spatial change; thinking in assemblages of stakeholders and actors creates a framework for social investment and development. These overlapping frameworks are informed and perhaps even defined by the emergent field of landscape democracy. Landscape is understood as the relationship between people and place, both shaping each other. Landscape democracy allows one to see urban space as a field of negotiation between people, places, and power.

This chapter is the outcome of working with the principles of landscape democracy. Within this field, finding the everyday practices that link people and place makes it possible to augment and connect these practices into a larger strategy. Landscape architecture acts as a mediator in these processes of spatial evolution in order to envision just and sustainable urban landscapes. This chapter focuses on designing a network of productive urban green spaces in Porto Alegre, the capital of Brazil's southern state Rio Grande do Sul. Through a series of hypothetical designs for new productive spaces in the city, the potential of landscape architecture to create new green infrastructure is illustrated.

Creating a Productive and Multifunctional Green Infrastructure

In order to design a productive and multifunctional green infrastructure built on people and place it is essential to study the city first-hand. I explored the city on foot, by public transport, by bike, and by car, and engaged in dialogue wherever and whenever possible. I immersed myself in the processes of the city and discovered relationships and tensions present in a variety of sites. Based on this I was able to develop a grounded typology of urban agriculture sites. In this chapter I will present three of them.

Praça Bernardo Dreher: Suburban Food Forest Park

The Ipanema suburb of Porto Alegre is a middle-class neighbourhood far away from the bustle of downtown. The areas tree-lined streets frame well-maintained homes with fences and gardens. Security is an issue here. In this suburb there is a small park, Praça Bernardo Dreher. The park has lawns, some swing sets, large trees, and a football field. A dozen new fruit trees planted here over the years enhance this neighbourhood landscape. Small acts of guerrilla gardening have become a shared neighbourhood practice, bringing residents out to meet each other. The trees yield abundant fruit and in this neighbourhood the harvest is free for all who care to pick it. The municipal workers who come to mow the park lawns steer clear of the protected seedlings, and once these are established they seem to be absorbed into the design of the park. Eyes and ears in the vicinity are on the trees, also creating a safe area for children to play. An atmosphere of unease sometimes prevails in the suburbs, as if danger or violence could erupt if the wrong conditions arose. However, small children playing in the park with no parents to watch over them attests to the network of awareness around the Praça.

Praça Bernardo Dreher, Porto Alegre as a suburban food forest park, collage: Jacques Abelman

The Praça Bernardo Dreher is a good example of bottom-up and top-down meeting halfway. As the act of neighbourhood guerrilla fruit tree planting is integrated into the life of the park, social cohesion is increased. The results are accepted and even maintained by municipal workers. Augmenting this practice could mean providing seedlings for free to those who want to plant them; almost all native fruit trees and medicinal plants are available at the botanical garden or the municipal plant nursery. A landscape architect or planner's role could be to coordinate these plantings into better designs than haphazard planting. It would take a small number of interventions to achieve this; information could even be posted on site. The resulting food production could be distributed among neighbours, or simply left to those who need or want it.

Harvest moments create occasions for people to meet each other around meals or celebrations. Fruit can also be gathered for sale in other areas, from a cart or a small stand, or even brought to the farmer's market. Processed fruits become fresh juices, preserves, and a variety of other products with potential small-scale market value.

Vila São José:
New Partnerships for
Intensive Production

'Spontaneous occupation' is the term used to qualify urban slums in Brazil. Cities are their own ecosystem; an individual or family whose concern is food, shelter, and the business of survival soon fills whatever niche can support life. The pressure on empty urban land is great; those arriving to the city who cannot afford conventional housing quickly claim spaces. However, over time favela areas can evolve into thriving neighbourhoods of ingenious architectures as residents climb the economic ladder out of poverty. Temporary shelters solidify into lower-middle or middle-class housing made of brick and masonry.

The favela Vila São José niches in an empty band of land behind a row of wealthy villas with impenetrable razor wire and walls topped with glass shards. Tiny manicured gardens are attached to many houses, often with similar plantings of medicinal, culinary, and religious plants. For example, Espada de São Jorge, or Sanseveria, is thought to protect houses from evil spirits. Mature fruit trees planted intentionally or as remnants of natural areas pepper the housing area and are carefully maintained as sources of extra food.

Many residents of favelas have come to the city from rural areas to look for employment. Many are from families who left agricultural production to benefit from the economic and social possibilities offered by the city. Favelas are reservoirs of human labour and knowledge.

The location of peri-urban favelas next to agricultural or public land makes agricultural projects potentially possible. Public projects could be created on land belonging to the University in collaboration with experts from agronomy and horticulture. The city could encourage entrepreneurs to start peri-urban agricultural projects by donating land, offering tax breaks, offering social support for worker training, and so on. Here high intensity fruit production could create jobs as well as large quantities of fresh food to be brought to market via the normal distribution chains. Many of the native fruit varieties are not commercialized because they are either too labour-intensive to pick, or too fragile to travel long distances. In a short food supply chain this problem is avoided. Fruits and berries could also be processed into a variety of products, from juices to cosmetics, to be sold locally. Because the maintenance of the trees and the harvesting of the fruit is labour-intensive, many new jobs could be created that do not require intensive training or education but instead rely on basic agricultural skills.

Strategically the plan evolves from current green spaces to an augumented green infrastructure

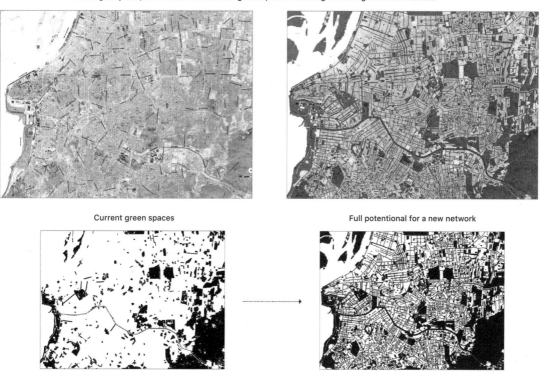

Current green spaces

Full potentional for a new network

Augmenting a network of productive urban green spaces over time, Porto Alegre, plan: Jacques Abelman

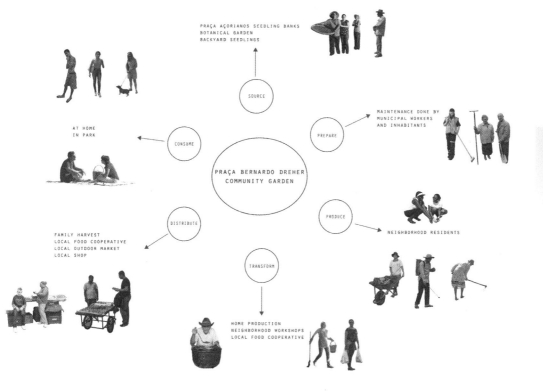

Thinking in assemblages of stakeholders, scheme: Jacques Abelman

Praça dos Açorianos: a Flagship Project for the Heart of the City

Praça dos Açorianos is the heart of the central administrative district in downtown Porto Alegre. Most public transportation networks take passengers by this plaza, whose centre features a monument to the first Azorean settlers of the city. A lot of manpower is required in such a central, public space. People as well as plants are carefully kept out of the plaza. Municipal workers keep the wide spaces of the pristine plaza constantly free of bushes or clumps of weeds or anything that might possibly create shelter for humans or other creatures. Some people take to sleeping in relatively unpoliced areas. At night these spaces become dangerous.

Cidades sem fome, as well as the Zero Hunger Project[2] relate to a governmental programme called the National Food and Nutritional Security Policy[3] concerning projects to combat hunger in cities across Brazil. In Porto Alegre, large and empty urban plazas could serve as the sites for urban orchards whose beauty and productivity, seen by all, would become a new badge of identity. Rows of native fruit trees would increase the beauty and leisure value of areas that were previously lawn or concrete, creating a new form of urban park as well as low-skilled jobs.

Conclusions

The practice of landscape architecture in this context moves from fieldwork and analysis to normative illustration of spatial change. As such it becomes a creative research endeavour that understands an urban context and makes a projection—through design—about best-practice scenarios. Large-scale urban and landscape analysis create a framework for establishing the structure and linkages of the network. The network relies and reacts to the ecological as well as human capacity found within it.

The principles of the emergent field of landscape democracy allow us to see urban space as a field of negotiation between people, places, and power. Within this field, finding the everyday practices that link people and place make it possible to augment and connect these practices into a larger strategy, based on dialogue, design, and the democratic ideal of inclusion.

2   J.F. Graziano da Silva, M.E. Del Grossi, and C.G. de França, *Fome Zero (Zero Hunger) Program* (Brasilia: Ministry of Agrarian Development, 2011), www.fao.org/3/a-i3023e.pdf (accessed 20-02-2018).

3   D. Chmielewska and D. Souza, *The Food Security Policy Context in Brazil* (Country Study; no. 22) (Brasilia: International Policy Centre for Inclusive Growth, 2011).

Marielle Dubbeling & Laura Bracalenti

ROSARIO: PARTICIPATORY DESIGN OF SPACES FOR MULTIFUNCTIONAL URBAN AGRICULTURE

Introduction

In Rosario, the third largest metropolis in Argentina, urban agriculture has been supported since the early nineties through government policies that were initially introduced through the National Institute of Agroecological Technologies (INTA), and from 2002 onwards through the city's *Programa de Agricultura Urbana* (PAU: Urban Agriculture Programme) as a response to the economic crisis in 2000. The purpose of this government policy was to combat poverty and simultaneously create more jobs. Unemployed people could sign up with the municipality, work in the gardens for at least 4 hours per day and earn 150 pesos (US$50) per month. The programme started with around 10,000 farmers/gardeners. A large number of people left the programme, as they found jobs in other sectors that were growing again after the crisis. Others joined and those that stayed expanded their urban agriculture activities into full-time jobs providing for their families. The programme grew from a focus on food cultivation for self-sufficiency to a focus on creating viable commercial channels for gardeners to make an adequate living.

Besides support for capacity building on farming techniques and the development of commercialization channels, the PAU has given a lot of attention to developing and valorizing the multiple functions of urban agriculture. First, from its start the PAU has had a strong focus on social inclusion and creating income and employment opportunities for poorer sections of the population that were most severely hit by the economic crisis. Also, after the Argentinian economy gradually recuperated the PAU continued to maintain a strong focus on building a social economy in Rosario. Secondly, it has developed a successful approach in making vacant and often unused public spaces, accessible for productive use in combination with a wide range of other social and ecological functions. This approach has turned the agro-ecological production spaces that were developed as part of the PAU into public spaces that not only serve production purposes but are also spaces of social encounter, training, and leisure and contribute to various ecological functions, such as biodiversity and adaptation to climate change.

1 G. Romero, *La participación en el diseño urbano y arquitectónico en la producción social del hábitat* (s.l.: UNAM, Facultad de Arquitectura, Programa de Maestría y Doctorado en Arquitectura y Urbanismo, 2004).

2 R. Pesci, *Del Titanic al Velero* (Buenos Aires: FLACAM Fundación CEPA, 2000).

Participatory Design of
Multifunctional Urban Agriculture

Participatory development and design of multifunctional spaces for urban agriculture has played an important role in the development of urban agriculture in Rosario. The concept of participatory design differs from traditional approaches to landscape design.[1] In a participatory design process, designs are made based on the inputs of and consensus between the clients (the users), landscape architects, and other involved actors (for example the Municipality). All this with the objective of making optimum use of and valorizing the contributions of each of these stakeholders in the design, management, and financing of the project.[2]

The participatory design of multifunctional spaces for urban agriculture was facilitated by an action-oriented project entitled *Making the Edible Landscape*, which ran from 2004 to 2006 and was coordinated by McGill University in Canada, the Urban Management Programme, and the RUAF Foundation. The main goal was to build collective strategies to facilitate the transition of traditional state-funded housing projects to 'productive neighbourhoods' that integrate urban agriculture in urban design, upgrading, and development, thus providing households with food-production and income-generating opportunities in addition to housing and basic services.

The areas selected for this project were the Molino Blanco and La Lagunita settlements. Situated at the southern fringe of the city limit, Molino Blanco is a neighbourhood that in 2004 held 798 families (3,500 people), of whom almost 30% were to be relocated to a new settlement as their houses were built on flooding areas or too close to roads. The settlement would then be regularized, giving not only titles to residents, but also providing them with the basic municipal services such as potable water, sewage, drainage, gas, electricity, paved roads, and footpaths. La Lagunita (Spanish for Lagoon) is located in the west of Rosario. It owes its name to the fact that the area becomes flooded after heavy rain. The area was first occupied over twenty years ago by families coming from the Chaco province, who basically settled on private land. Over the years, the original families brought their relatives from the provinces resulting in a very close-knit community. After 2001, a second wave of settlers (about 50 families) occupied state-owned land inside the settlement.

Parque Huerta Molino Blanco, Ciudad Rosario

Typology of Spaces
The Making the Edible Landscape project focused on the participatory design and implementation of the following types of spaces:

- *Garden parks*. Larger public green areas in which recreational, productive, educational, and commercial activities are developed. This required designs that focused on integrating playgrounds and areas for leisure, sports, and training activities with areas set aside for vegetable and fruit production as well as the production of medicinal and ornamental plants.
- *Productive squares*. Neighbourhood squares designed for recreational, productive, and possibly commercial activities, responding to the community needs for playgrounds, social meeting places, urban greening, and production.
- *Productive streets*. Streets designed for farming (including food trees) on available roadsides as well as for food selling and bartering. As such these streets become spaces for social interaction, without obstructing the normal traffic and pedestrian flow.

To date, as a result of this project and further activities of the PAU, an Urban System of Agro-ecological Spaces has been consolidated in Rosario, made up of various types of spaces, designed in function of the socio-spatial and functional requirements of different areas. The typologies currently used are: Reference Centres; Collective Gardens; Green corridors; Demonstration Gardens; Educational Gardens, Health Gardens (in hospitals and community health centres) and Garden Parks. A total of 25 of such spaces currently occupy a little more than 20 hectares distributed throughout the city.

The Participatory Design Process
The participatory design process in Rosario included the following activities:

1. Formation, preparation and capacity building of an interdisciplinary design team, formed by planners, architects, and urban agriculture.
2. Base-line studies, analysis of secondary and collection or primary information (field work, meetings with interest groups, and interviews with key-informants) on current and previous characteristics and land uses.
3. Preparation of materials (maps, graphical and visual materials, and models to share information on the site and facilitate a creative design process; videos and images on similar sites and possible designs to broaden the vision of the participants, and so on).
4. Implementation of a series of community design workshops in order to:

   - discuss with the users their needs, visions and aspirations associated to the sites;
   - broaden the vision of the participants regarding the possible forms of multifunctional land use of the site;
   - define the various (land use) components, their relations, and (physical) dimensions;
   - collectively construct design plans and models and discus management aspects of the area;
   - revise draft proto-typical site plans, program implementation activities and assign responsibilities.

5. Elaborating the site plans and sub-contracting the work.
6. Implementation of the project.
7. Monitoring and evaluation for internal learning, feedback, and improvement.
8. Systematizing the process and adjusting the mode of working.

Conclusions

The participatory design process required an intense dynamic of training and community workshops throughout the process. Landscape architects and designers had to learn to trust and work with the community and pay attention to community dynamics in order to ensure equal participation of various groups. This also meant that although a general methodology was followed in both settlements, the process had to be adapted to the specific characteristics of each situation. In La Lagunita, for example, where community members had no prior experience with urban agriculture, much more time had to be spent on explaining the concept and visiting existing urban agriculture areas than in Molino Blanco Sur. The initial plan for housing improvement in La Lagunita did not include urban agriculture activities, in contrast to that of Molino Blanco. Also, in Molino Blanco a community gardening organization already existed that allowed them to define common problems and seek solutions that bring improvements to all and to better organize themselves for participation in the design workshops. In La Lagunita no such community organization or platform existed and still had to be constructed. Potential conflict situations on desired uses did occur, and new values of open and green areas had to be promoted. This required extensive information, communication, consultation, reconciliation, and motivation.

Results of the participatory design processes include increased social acceptance and responsibility of the designed areas. In both cases, the community was and is responsible for the installation and maintenance of the gardens and other uses. This helped to strengthen the relations of the community with their own surroundings and provided it its own identity. On their turn inhabitants were stimulated to feel proud of their own environment.

Neighbourhood upgrading and housing development schemes are common measures taken by city councils and provide a good vehicle for incorporating urban agriculture into design and planning. New visions on sustainable urban development and urban greening should promote the planning and preservation of open spaces for natural habitats, active recreation, and multifunctional agriculture. Cities like Rosario illustrate the benefits of integrating food production in design and management of urban open spaces to improve food security and reduce malnutrition in cities, reduce poverty by enabling income generation, and improve the urban environment by making cities more habitable, while also providing for cultural, educational, and leisure activities.

The two participatory design experiences in La Lagunita and Molino Blanco Sur have served as examples and laboratories for the city of Rosario and other cities in the region. Involving the architects of Rosario and applying a similar participatory design process, two more garden parks were designed, in Villa María del Triunfo and Villa El Salvador-Lima, Peru, which integrate productive and recreational functions, and also small wastewater treatment plants for irrigation.

In addition to the design of a variety of intra-urban spaces, since 2015, Rosario municipality and surrounding towns are also protecting and re-organizing peri-urban production areas in the city-region's greenbelt. Aggregation of production is key to increasing local production. Responsible consumers and retailers support marketing and consumption of local products. Spatial design thus goes hand in hand with other strategies such as conversion to agro-ecological production, product control, and certification and direct marketing.

VIGO CITY REGION

Lola Domínguez García & Paul Swagemakers

CREATING EDIBLE LANDSCAPES THROUGH COMMONS LAND USE IN THE

Vigo

Introduction

Green areas in metropolitan regions are increasingly understood as landscapes that serve multiple purposes, and which, for those reasons, must also be protected. In the city region of Vigo (Galicia, Spain), green areas and buildings alternate, blurring the differences between the urban and the rural. The city region of Vigo is made up of 14 municipalities (approximately 479,256 inhabitants), and Vigo (about 300,000 inhabitants) is the largest urban municipality in Galicia in socio-economic terms as well in size. Located here are the largest European fishery seaport and an important car manufacturing industry, supplying jobs to about 10,000 employees in the city region. A major portion of the area consists of green infrastructure formed by public municipal parks, many scattered private plots in use for vegetable gardening and maize production, and mountain land locally known as Monte. In Galicia, the Monte is managed by public authorities (the state) and private owners, with part of it managed as common property. In this chapter we focus on these common-ly managed Monte areas.

Monte in Galicia

The Monte in Galicia consists of forest and scrubland. In the past, the Monte was a space for both farming activities (pasture, cereal production, and fertilizer provision) and mixed forestry and as such it played a crucial role in supplying inputs to sustain the resource base of family farming. There are different forms of ownership of the Monte in Galicia: public (45,000 hectares), private (1,385,690 hectares) and commons (608,728 hectares). Here, commons refers to land that is privately owned (as opposed to state ownership) but is managed by a group of neighbours of a specific parish. These managers have the right to make decisions about how the common land is used. These decisions are made in assemblies and must comply with the statutes of the Association of Commons, which are framed by legislation and based on century-long traditions. Characteristic of commons is that they are:

- inalienable, implying that owners can never sell their share, and neither a government nor any other authority can ignore this ownership;
- imprescriptible, meaning that owners never lose their rights to the land, except by expropriation for public needs (such as the construction of roads and hospitals, but also wind parks and mines);
- unseizable, inferring that the government or banks cannot confiscate land in cases of owner debt;
- indivisible, entailing that the land cannot be divided. It remains a commonly managed unit and people must decide together on its objectives and management.

Currently there are 2,800 Associations of Commons in Galicia, which manage about 608,000 hectares of Monte, or 25% of the total Galician territory. In the city region of Vigo about 33% of the Monte area, which equals 24,400 hectares, is managed by approximately 100 Associations of Commons. During the period of the Franco dictatorship (1939–1975), common property was lost due to an expropriation process. The Monte lost its multifunctional use during that time due to monocultural forestry policies, industrialization and specialization of farming, and migration from rural areas. Based on a law issued in 1968, property formally went back to the Associations of Commons but it took until the mid-1980s to check all property rights and prepare the paperwork to actually return ownership of the land to the Associations of Commons. However, this did not lead to a fundamental change in land use. Still, over the past two decades, some commons in the city region of Vigo are restoring the multifunctional use of the Monte through various projects. This can be seen as an important step in further developing the city region's attractiveness, promoting the protection of green areas and creating opportunities for income generation and employment. One of the most active commons in the area is the Association of Vincios. Over the past twenty years this association has carried out different projects to promote more sustainable uses of its common land, stressing the importance of recovering multifunctional land use and quality (food) products as well as biodiversity and leisure functions.

Creating Spatial Synergies through Common Land Use in Vincios

Vincios, with 2,000 inhabitants, is only ten minutes by car from the centre of Vigo. The Association of Commons in Vincios—hereafter referred to as the Vincios Commons—manages 678 hectares of which a significant portion (around 400 hectares) has been transformed, since the early 1990s, by implementing of a range of activities for biodiversity and landscape protection, food production, and raising cultural and social awareness among community members. The aim of the Vincios Commons is to rebuild the resource base that has been degraded through monoculture afforestation of Monte land in the past decades (Montalvo and Casaleiro, 2008). A side effect of monoculture forestry with eucalyptus trees is an increased risk of forest fires. When there is no good management or control after forest fires, Eucalyptus tree density increases, thereby further increasing the risk of forest fires. Moreover, the abandonment of traditional management practices makes scrubland with a high presence of Toxo *(Ulex europaeus)* and Xesta *(Cytisus scoparius)* grow uncontrollably, which is another reason for the higher incidence of fast spreading forest fires in the region. In order to break out of this negative cycle and improve the profitability of the commons, the Vincios Commons carries out multifunctional land-use projects that aim to recover natural spaces and traditional landscapes. Examples of implemented and planned projects are:

— extensive grazing of cattle to support local economic development and to control scrub naturally, as well as encourage natural beef production;
— mushroom cropping by mycorrhization of pines and oaks to recover soils and produce mushrooms;
— chestnut afforestation to increase biodiversity, produce high-quality wood, improve landscape, diminish forest-fire spreading, and establish chestnut production;
— sustainable afforestation with leafy

deciduous species to promote alternative models of sustainable forest production;
— biomass plant to produce compost from green waste (pruning, clearing out) in the Monte, reduce forest fire risk, and improve soil fertility.

These and other projects combine forestry, agriculture, stockbreeding, hunting and leisure while simultaneously preserving the natural, cultural, and historic assets of the area. With this strategy, the Vincios Commons aims to reduce the risk of forest fires and to maintain land productivity. To this end, biomass from the Monte area—from removing scrubland to clearing up plantations, and thinning and pruning of trees—has been used in a pilot project for compost production. Inspired by the private enterprise Abonos Lourido,[1] a pioneer in composting Toxo shrubs for high-quality organic fertilizer, the goal is to construct a biomass plant together with other Associations of Commons in the region. A pilot project as well as a socio-economic and technical study carried out from 1999 to 2001 showed positive socio-economic and environmental impacts. In 2009 a viability study confirmed these results. In 2013, the biomass plant project was approved by the local administration after overcoming various administrative problems.

Meanwhile, the Vincios Commons has implemented projects to improve soil fertility by combining reforestation with local varieties (eliminating Eucalyptus), using algae as fertilizer, creating pastures (for sheep, cows and horses) or producing its own compost at a smaller scale from available biomass. The community has realized, and also demonstrated, that the use of available biomass and the promotion of multifunctional land use provides opportunities for rebuilding and developing a food system grounded in proper management of the commons. Further expansion of the edible landscape, characterized by chestnut, mushroom, and beef production in combination with improving soil fertility, should bring opportunities to start new, productive

1   http://abonoslourido.com/es/.

Integration of urban and rural in Vigo, Galicia, photo: Saline Verhoeven

Chestnut afforestation, Vincios, Vigo, Galicia, photo: Saline Verhoeven

Grazing area, Vincios, Vigo, Galicia, photo: Saline Verhoeven

activities. In addition to environmental improvements, the Vincios Commons has achieved economic returns from selling wood and also from leasing out land for industrial uses. More importantly, the Vincios Commons has reinvested these returns in developing the above-mentioned projects and activities, as well as other activities from which the earnings directly return to the community. By law, entities that manage Monte land are obliged to reinvest at least 40% of their annual turnover in land management and improvement—a minimum that Vincios easily meets, with a reinvestment of 65% in 2012 (Domínguez García et al., 2014). Besides land-use projects (for which sometimes extra, external subsidy was found), Vincios supports activities that improve the quality of life in the community. They reinvested another 32% of their turnover in sports and cultural activities and in the school canteen. In the future, the biomass plant, in addition to fertilizing productive common land, may generate an additional cash flow from compost sales. At the same time, the new multifunctional land-use management and the use of green waste both reduce the risk of fire and its damage to the natural and aesthetic value of the area, and provide an opportunity for reconnecting green areas around the city with the food system in the city region.

Conclusions
————

Organizational forms like the Vincios Commons ensure that edible landscapes become core business and an anchor for the planning, design, and governance of cities that aim to preserve and create spaces for food production and ecosystem services. Societal needs occupy an increasingly prominent place in local policy on employment, health, social justice, and sustainability. This should be anchored in a legal framework that still needs to be better suited to city regions and to regional and national food policies. Support for this self-regulatory organizational form does not generate direct costs to local and/or regional governments and at the same time multifunctional land use is guaranteed. Private, individual initiatives would benefit most from training in ecological entrepreneurship by means of networks bringing together various stakeholders, including city region administrations.

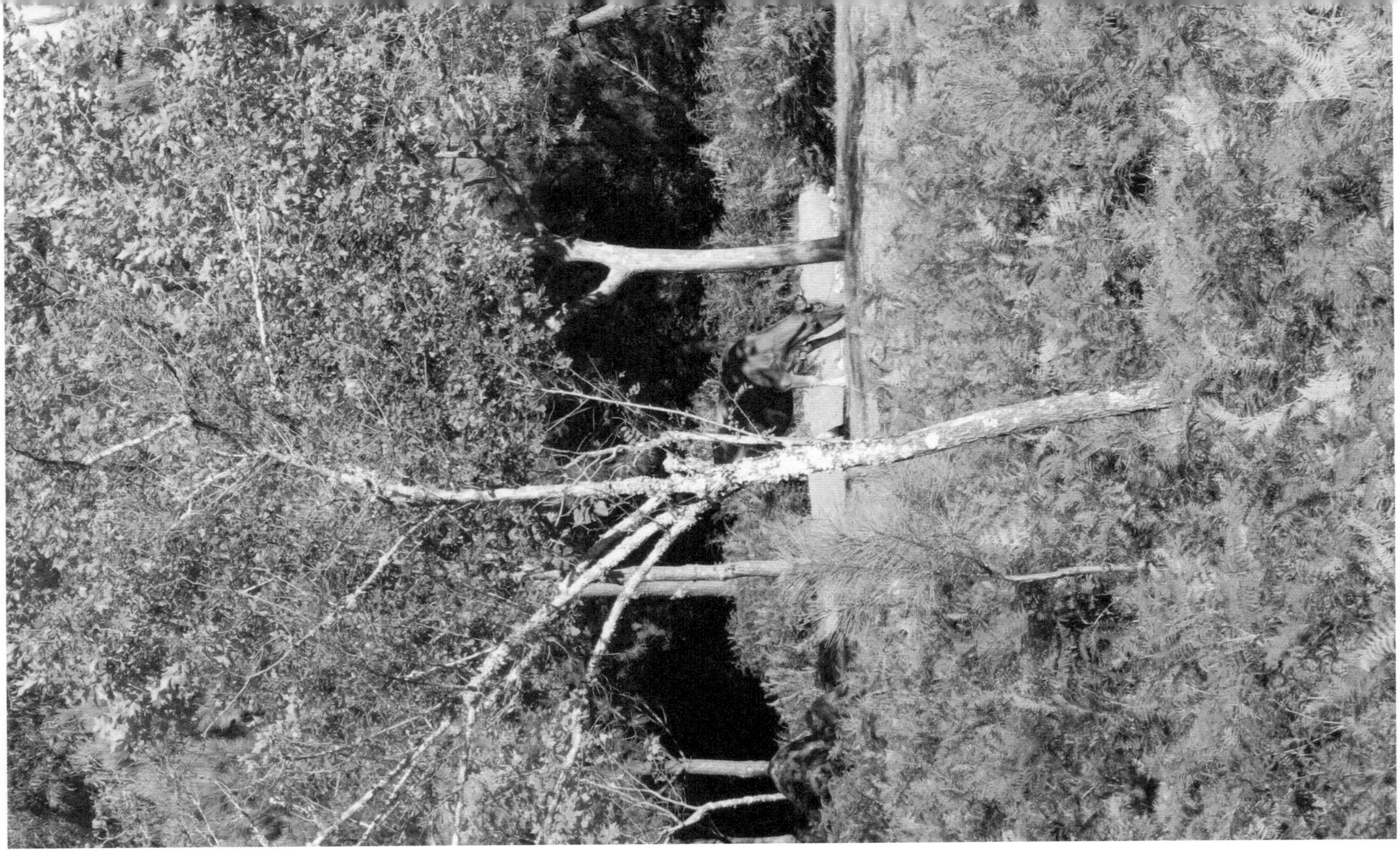

Grazing cattle, Vincios, Vigo, Galicia, photo: Saline Verhoeven

Johannes S.C. Wiskerke & Saline Verhoeven

FOOD UTOPIAS

1   www.hungrycitybook.
co.uk/blog/?page_id=17
(accessed 08-01-2018).

In the last chapter of her book *Hungry City*,
Carolyn Steel proposes *sitopia* as a new framework
for future food provisioning systems and for thinking about the relation between food and cities.
Sitopia is an amalgamation of two words: *sitos* and
topos. *Sitos* (σίτος) is the Greek word for wheat, or,
more in general, for food, while *topos* (τόπος) means
place. *Sitopia* thus means food-place. Carolyn Steel
argues that if places and our lives are shaped by
food, we may as well use food to shape our everyday
places and lives more positively.[1] This is an argu-
ment that we fully adhere to.

Somewhat surprisingly, Carolyn Steel also ex-
presses that she sees *sitopia* in opposition to utopia.
Utopia is derived from the Greek prefix *ou-* (οὐ),
meaning not, and the suffix *-iā* (-ία) is typical of
toponyms. Utopia thus literally means nowhere.
There is however a common misunderstanding that
utopia is derived from the prefix *eu-* (εὐ), which
means good. Utopia then literally translates as
'good place'. As a result, utopia is nowadays generally used to refer to a non-existent place or society
that is considered to be better than what currently
exists. Carolyn Steel reasons that utopianism aims
at perfection and is therefore not a realistic approach.

However, in this chapter and with our fifth
socio-spatial design principle—conceiving multiple food utopias—we argue that we urgently need
multiple utopian visions to address the contemporary food system challenges (see pp. 22ff.). Some
food utopias may be realistic, in the sense that they
represent current practices that are, however, not
seen or understood within prevailing scientific or
policy frameworks. Others may be non-existing
and idealistic. But we need both in order not be
constrained by contemporary mainstream thinking
and arguing. To envision what a better food future
could look like it is crucial to encourage out-of-the-
box thinking and to stimulate creativity. To do so
we need real utopian thinking and multiple future
imaginations. This may help to create food places
that are better than the ones that currently exist.
In this chapter we first discuss food utopian think-

ing within the social sciences, where the focus tends to be on real food utopias, i.e. the desirable food places and practices that already exist but that are often neglected in scientific research and policy-making. We then take this a step further with a plea for imaginary food utopias and argue that spatial design can play an important role in envisioning alternative and hopeful food futures. This is followed by a discussion about the role of food utopias in transformation processes towards other and better food futures. We will conclude this chapter with an introduction to the cases. Similar to the cases of the second socio-spatial design principle (linking scales), which all focused on Dar es Salaam, the cases illustrating this fifth socio-spatial design principle all focus on one city region, namely the Metropolitan Region of Amsterdam (MRA).

Food Utopias

All over the world we can find food systems and foodscapes that are overlooked, downplayed, marginalized and/or misunderstood by scientists and policymakers. This is largely due to the capitalocentric vision on food provisioning (and on economic activities in general) that tends to prevail in scientific and policy communities and discourses: 'Over the past thirty years, capitalist realism has successfully installed a "business ontology" in which it is simply obvious that everything in society, including healthcare and education, should be run as a business'.[2] Capitalocentrism thus refers to 'the dominant representation of all economic activities in terms of their relationship to capitalism'.[3] This representation tends to neglect or exclude a large variety of existing and emerging food provisioning practices, i.e. those that deviate from the capitalist mode.

The capitalocentric vision on food provisioning and other activities can be illustrated by means of the iceberg image. What is generally considered as 'the food economy' or the 'formal food system' (capitalist food businesses, food as a market commodity and wage labour for the production, processing, distribution, and sales of food) is only the visible part of the iceberg.[4] Below the surface we find a whole range of other activities by which food is produced and exchanged in ways that do not align with or that are contrary to capitalism. Examples are self-provisioning (e.g. home, allotment and community gardening), food sharing, hunting and gathering, community supported agriculture, and solidarity purchasing groups. These modes of food provisioning are not imaginary but real as they exist in many parts of the world, albeit that they are sometimes, though not always, small (in terms of amounts of food being produced, processed, exchanged, and eaten) compared to the formal capitalist mode. And many of these non-capitalist or alternative-to-capitalist modes of food provisioning are (potentially) capable of addressing contemporary food challenges in a more sustainable, inclusive, and just way compared to the dominant capitalist mode.[5]

Opening up or widening our imagination of possible food provisioning practices and foodscapes thus begins by considering what is already happening, in particular by paying attention to everything that belongs to the underwater part of the iceberg. Imagining what is or could be possible then comes down to exploring, supporting, and developing the ideals, practices, and promises that are already present. It means that food utopias are sought not in pure novelty but in that which is neglected and disproved by capitalocentric thinking. Hence, it is important to make real the possibilities that are already present, i.e. the real food utopias.[6]

While making visible the food practices 'below the surface' and imagining the kind of food futures resulting from fully exploiting the potentials of these food practices is an important step, we propose that utopian thinking also requires us to go beyond what is real, yet invisible, marginalized, and/or downplayed. In other words, in addition to real food utopias we also need to construct and design imaginary food utopias: desirable food futures that are not constrained by contemporary states of affairs (such as technical artefacts, property rights, legislation). Imaginary food utopias are means to express the food futures we would like to see become real and can help us to ask ourselves what it takes to make them real.

Utopian thinking, in terms of both real and imaginary food utopias, can help to open up an ontological space to think in terms of possible food futures, thereby expanding our ideas and beliefs of what is desirable and considered to be possible.[7]

W. Fisher, *Capitalist Realism: Is There No Alternative?* (Hants: Zero Books, 2009), p. 9.
www.communityeconomies.org/home/key-ideas (accessed 05-02-2018)
Ibid.
M.C.A. Wegerif, *Feeding Dar es Salaam: A Symbiotic Food System Perspective*, PhD thesis (Wageningen: Wageningen University, 2017); P.V. Stock, M. Carolan, and C. Rosin, *Food Utopias: Reimagining Citizenship, Ethics and Community* (Abingdon: Routledge, 2015); A. Hill, 'A Helping Hand and Many Green Thumbs: Local Government, Citizens and The Growth Of A Community-based Food Economy', *Local Environment* 16, no. 6 (2011), pp. 539–553; J. Cameron and R. Gordon, 'Building Sustainable and Ethical Food Futures through Economic Diversity: Options for a Mid-sized City', paper presented at the Policy Workshop on The Future of Australia's Mid-Sized Cities, 28 & 29 September 2010 (Bendigo: Latrobe University, 2010).
A. Brower, 'Agri-food Activism and the Imagination of the Possible', *New Zealand Sociology* 28, no. 4 (2013), pp. 90–92.
Stock et al., *Food Utopias.*
www.architonic.com/en/story/simon-keane-cowell-this-man-is-seeing-things-carlo-ratti/7001830 (accessed 05-02-2018).

Spatial design is essentially the visualization of utopian thinking. It makes a potential future visible and thus shows a possible reality that is different from the present. Most of the designs presented, explained, and discussed in previous chapters in this book obviously are food utopias. And many are hybrids of real and imaginary food utopias. Take for example Anna Fink's design proposal for the unused multi-storey market building in Dar es Salaam (pp. 99ff.). The building is there (best understood as a real dystopia) and so are the many well-functioning people's markets (real utopias). The everyday practices and routines that shape these real utopias are used as a source of inspiration for transforming a dystopian building into a utopian one. Another example is Jacques Abelman's vision for a productive city (pp. 187ff.). It is a utopian image but based on a combination of existing urban food growing practices, urban typologies, and native agroforestry species and a creative visualization of what food growing spaces could become and of what an entire city could look like if it was transformed into a continuous productive urban landscape. While these two and many other examples in this book envision a potential desirable future, only one food utopia is proposed.

To provoke debate and explore possible food futures it is important to design a variety of future options, a diversity of food utopias. This aligns with the vision of architect Carlo Ratti that the role of the designer 'is not to provide the solution; it is to provide different possibilities for the future'.[8] These different possibilities can be real food utopias, imaginary food utopias, or combinations thereof. Different utopian images, visualized through design, can play an important role in academic, policy, and societal debates about the future of our food provisioning systems. What kind of food system do we want and need in the light of contemporary and anticipated food system challenges? Thinking and debating about the future of food is, of course, not something new. Scientists, governments, companies, NGOs, and international organizations regularly undertake foresight studies[9] to explore the future, or different futures, in a structured way. This is done in different ways:[10]

1. Through trend extrapolation, which is based on the assumption that no major changes will occur and that everything develops along a trajectory from past to future. Trend extrapolation focuses on what will (most likely) happen and thus predicts one future.
2. By developing strategic scenarios, which implies exploring different possible futures by anticipating and predicting important (technological, societal, environmental, economic, and/or political) changes or exploring different options. Strategic scenarios thus envision what could happen under different conditions or assumptions.
3. By developing normative scenarios, which comes down to imagining different desirable futures (utopias) by asking what should happen. Normative scenarios are often combined with backcasting, i.e. the development and implementation of the strategies and pathways that are needed to achieve those utopias.

Our fifth socio-spatial design principle refers primarily to the third type of foresight study, although it can also be used in developing strategic scenarios by visualizing what could happen. The main message is to envision different futures and to be creative in designing desirable food futures. Creativity may be inspired by real utopias as well as by completely out-of-the-box imaginations. With this we also aim to contribute to filling one of the gaps in foresight studies, namely that methods based on creativity are currently under-exploited in exploring and envisioning possible or desirable futures.[11]

Introducing the Case of the Metropolitan Region of Amsterdam

The fifth socio-spatial design principle has been applied to the Metropolitan Region of Amsterdam (MRA). Towards this end three different utopian scenarios for growing food in the MRA have been developed to explore and visualize the implications for the use of space and spatial quality:

1. Urban agriculture. Food production within the city, using vacant lots and public spaces for food production as well as growing food on (rooftops) and in buildings.
2. Multifunctional agriculture. Food production in combination with other activities and functions, such as sports, leisure, education, health care and nature, and transforming all areas now used for nature and recreation into productive areas while maintaining the nature or recreation function.
3. Sustainable industrial agriculture. High-tech forms of food production in fields, greenhouses, and buildings in areas currently used for agricultural production, with specific attention to environmental sustainability and animal welfare.

The starting point for these three scenarios was the question: What if the MRA has to be fed from within a 25-kilometre radius from the city centre? And from this main question several sub-questions followed:

— Is it possible to produce enough food within this area for all its 2.4 million inhabitants?
— If needed, how can additional food production space be realized?
— Which kind of food products could or should be produced where?
— What will the foodscape look like in each utopian scenario?

K. Cuhls, 'From Forecasting to Foresight Processes: New Participative Foresight Activities in Germany', *Journal of Forecasting* 22 (2003), pp. 93–111.
P. Vergragt and J. Quist, 'Backcasting for Sustainability: Introduction to the Special Issue', *Technological Forecasting & Social Change* 78 (2011), pp. 747–755.
R. Popper, 'How Are Foresight Methods Selected?', *Foresight* 10, no. 6 (2008), pp. 62–89.
www.mtdls.nl/en (accessed 13-02-2018).
www.la4sale.nl/ (accessed 13-02-2018).
www.vpxdg.nl/ (accessed 13-02-2018).

To answer these questions, we collaborated with a group of students of the Amsterdam Academy of Architecture and three design firms. Our research and design process consisted of two main steps. The first step was to understand the spatial needs to produce food for all the inhabitants of the MRA. This was calculated on the basis of current consumption levels per capita and of current yields realized by means of conventional agricultural production systems in the Netherlands. Additionally, we also explored the impact of different diets on spatial needs. The main results of this first step are presented and discussed in 'Redesigning the Foodscape of the Metropolitan Region of Amsterdam' (pp. 219ff.), together with a short spatial food history of the MRA.

The second step was to design three different utopian foodscapes for the MRA as a means to envision what could be produced, how and where, and what kind of spatial quality that would bring. These designs were developed by three design firms in collaboration with the group of students, each firm being responsible for one of the utopian scenarios: MTD Landscape architects & Urban designers[12] for the urban agriculture scenario, LA4SALE[13] for the multifunctional agriculture scenario, and Van Paridon X De Groot[14] for the sustainable industrial agriculture scenario. The scenarios and preliminary designs were discussed twice with a group of experts in the fields of agricultural production, urban agriculture, land use planning, regional development, health and nutrition, and business models in the agrifood sector. The final utopian foodscapes were presented and discussed at a public event at the Amsterdam Academy of Architecture and the feedback from this event was used to finalize the three utopian foodscape scenario reports. All three reports were very rich in imaginations of the future but because of a limit on the number of available pages only part of this richness could be included in the three chapters dedicated to the different utopian foodscape scenarios: urban agriculture (pp. 235ff.), multifunctional agriculture (pp. 249ff.) and sustainable industrial agriculture (pp. 261ff.). A comparison of these three chapters shows that the different utopian food-scapes result in very different spatial qualities for the MRA.

For the development of the different utopian scenarios for the MRA, which serves as an illustration of the fifth socio-spatial design principle, we have also built on and incorporated, where possible, the other four design principles:

— The MRA case in general, and more specifically the multifunctional agriculture and sustainable industrial agriculture scenarios are examples of *adopting a city region perspective* by focusing on urban-rural food production and consumption relations in geographical proximity. The scenarios indicate that nowadays it is difficult or even impossible for the MRA to be self-sufficient in food provisioning, although a lot can be achieved through an industrial approach if a relation with the sea (thus going beyond the 25-kilometre boundary) is established for the production of animal feed. A common proposition in all three scenarios is *no more unproductive space*. Hence, in all three scenarios the available space for the production of food is increased by making unproductive spaces productive. In all three scenarios the waterscape is integrated in the food production system, as a supplier of protein for direct human consumption or as a supplier of animal feed.
— The second principle of *linking scales* also features in all three scenarios. Mainly by developing agricultural production typologies at the level of building, farm or field, which are then scaled up to larger spatial areas. Finally, a map with the proposed locations of different production typologies is made at the level of the city (urban agriculture scenario) or the city region.
— The principle of *connecting flows* has been important in the development of all three scenarios, albeit in different forms. For the urban agri-

culture scenario, a catalogue of circular urban production systems has been developed as basis for envisioning the possibilities for urban food growing. Some of these typologies are similar—but on a smaller scale—to the circular production systems proposed in the sustainable industrial agriculture scenario. The connection of flows in the multifunctional scenario is much more based on circularity found in nature, resulting in mixed (i.e. combining plant and animal production) farming systems and permaculture as agricultural production typologies.
— *Enhancing spatial diversity and synergies* forms the basis of the multifunctional agriculture scenario. It illustrates under what circumstances spaces for food production can be intertwined with other functions such as leisure, recreation, education, and health care. But the other two scenarios too show how the (urban) foodscape can be enjoyed as part of an attractive living environment and can contribute to climate change adaptation and mitigation. The different scenarios also show that intensification of the food production in the region can result in a more diversified landscape and more biodiverse foodscape.

Saline Verhoeven & Johannes S.C. Wiskerke

REDESIGNING THE FOODSCAPE OF THE METROPOLITAN REGION OF AMSTERDAM

FOOD

The Historical Relation between Amsterdam and Its Surrounding Countryside

The landscape surrounding Amsterdam historically supplied the city with food. Farmers provided urban residents with dairy products, meat, fruits, and vegetables.[1] Milk and fruit were produced closest to the city or in orchards and vegetable gardens within the city. Cheese was made at a range too far away from the city to transport fresh milk and grain was grown even further away. The sea close by provided fish. For centuries herring was an important component of the Dutch diet. Being rich in calories, vitamins, and micronutrients, herring has a high nutritional value. But it also had a high economic value: in the 17th century the herring fishery sector constituted almost 10% of the Gross National Product.[2]

The food provisioning link between the city of Amsterdam and its rural hinterland and sea is still visible today when looking at the *Stelling van Amsterdam*, the 135 km long circular defence line around the city that has been on UNESCO's world heritage list since 1996. It is 135 km long and was built between 1880 and 1914 around the city of Amsterdam, with a radius of 15 to 20 km. It was deliberately designed to include enough rural area to feed the city's one million inhabitants for half a year during a possible siege.

Being located close to the sea also meant that the city was very well connected. By transporting goods via water to and from Amsterdam international trade was relatively easy and cheap. Speculation with cheese, seed breeding, and seed potatoes turned Amsterdam into an international centre for trade and finance. Ever since the Late Middle Ages the landscape was cultivated, to fight against the threat of water from the large lakes around Amsterdam and to make the land productive. New water management technologies transformed the wet peat lands and lakes into farmland. The most famous and biggest example of this is the polder De Beemster, another UNESCO world heritage site. Its land-scape plan with a grid of canals and allotments was designed according to the then prevailing geometric ideal of beauty. Not only the technical innovation but also the pure geometry was admired internationally.[3]

The desire to control the inaccessible peat lands led to the implementation of a sophisticated water management system. Controlled by an advanced structure of canals, ditches, dams, dykes, sluices, and windmills this water system became the most important means of transport.[4] It provided a regional infrastructure of waterways and roads on dykes connecting the rural landscape with the urban environment, thus creating the Dutch water city. Produce from the farmlands was transported to the city via water. In Amsterdam the canals were used to transport and sell agricultural products on floating markets, like the ones in the Prinsengracht, which became the most important traffic artery of the city in the 17th century.

The urban investment in reclaiming land for agriculture purposes created new landscapes around the city. These landscapes were discovered by rich Amsterdam residents, as an escape from the crowded and polluted cities during the summer. This actually started within the city in what is now known as the Plantage (plantation), home to the botanical gardens and Artis zoo. It was an attempt to bring the rural landscape into the city, by transforming peatland within the city into gardens, thereby creating a leisure area for the bourgeoisie.[5] It was a mixture of private and public gardens, formal tree lanes, and herbal gardens with medicinal plants; a place for people to leisurely stroll around. At that time too this was considered to be important for people's health.[6]

1 T. Bakker, *Amsterdamse markten, door de eeuwen heen gevolgd door de stad*, www.theobakker.net/pdf/markten.pdf (accessed 18-12-2017).

2 http://hollandsenieuwe.tumblr.com (accessed 22-12-2017).

3 M. Glaudemans, *Amsterdams Arcadia: De ontdekking van het achterland* (Nijmegen: SUN, 2000), p. 130.

4 C. van der Hoeven and Louwe, *Amsterdam als stedelijk bouwwerk: E morfologische analys* (Nijmegen: SUN, 1985) p. 41.

5 Glaudemans, *Amsterdams Arcadia*, p. 74.

6 Ibid., p. 80.

Average diet per day of one person in Amsterdam, image: van Paridon x de Groot landschapsarchitecten

Chocolate
13g/day

Coffee
11g/day

Non-alcoholic drinks
1,715g/day

Cookies, cake and biscuits
46g/day

Alcoholic drinks
236g/day

Sugar, sweets
49g/day

Legumes
3g/day

Greases
24g/day

Bread and cereals
219g/day

Fish, shell-fish, crustacean
8g/day

Eggs
11g/day

Dairy
391g/day

Meat and meat products
120g/day

Vegetables
100g/day

Potatoes, tubers
96g/day

Fruit
98g/day

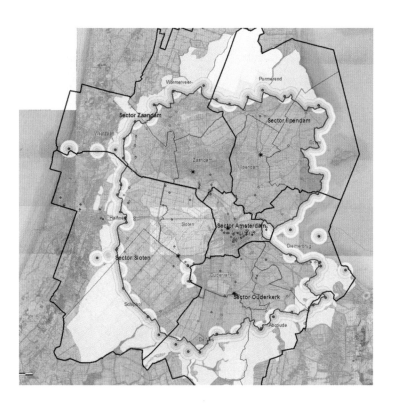

Stelling van Amsterdam, Defence Line of Amsterdam

Outside the city of Amsterdam but within a range of about 20 km around the city centre mostly entrepreneurs and merchants living in the city developed estates and built villas.[7] First they created pleasure gardens, orchards, and vegetable gardens and (later) agricultural estates. Forests served as domains for hunting. The 20-km range meant that the city was always close by. When looking at the city from the countryside the church towers of Amsterdam could still be seen and the city was easy to reach, only 5 to 7 hours by *trekschuit* (a canalboat pulled by horses).

The network of waterways for boats transporting goods and people is still in place, as are the historical peat lands with meadows and cows close to the city. This type of Dutch landscape is rare in other countries in Northwestern Europe, so its international significance is great.[8] Although this historical landscape still exists today, the food provisioning relationship between Amsterdam and its rural context has largely disappeared. Especially after World War II, agricultural development in the Netherlands was geared towards specialization, mechanization of the labour process, intensification of production and scale enlargement.[9] As a result, the Netherlands became one of the world's biggest exporters of agricultural products. But it also became more dependent on importing some of the ingredients of the average Dutch diet. This is illustrated by the fact that nowadays the ingredients of the average meal consumed in Amsterdam travel 33,000 kilometres.[10]

7   Ibid., p. 72.
8   www.clo.nl/indicatoren/ nl1034-internatio- nale-betekenis-van-ned- erlandse-landschappen (accessed 18-12-2017).
9   J. L. van Zanden, *The Economic History of the Netherlands 1914–1995: A Small Open Economy in the 'Long' Twentieth Century*, Vol. 1 (Oxford: Routledge, 2005).
10 De Boer et al., 2011.

School garden, Amsterdam, photo: Saline Verhoeven

Food Utopias / Redesigning
the Foodscape of the Metropolitan Region of Amsterdam

School garden, Amsterdam, photo: Saline Verhoeven

The Current Food System: The Relation between Food Consumption and Required Agricultural Production Area

Today the Metropolitan Region of Amsterdam (MRA) is a fast-growing, internationally competing metropolis. Around 2.4 million people, 14% of the total population of the Netherlands, live within the MRA. Each year 17 million people visit the city and its surroundings. As mentioned in the previous chapter we raised the following question: What if those 2.4 million inhabitants had to be fed from within a 25 km radius from the city centre? Would that be possible and what might it look like?

Re-thinking the food system of the Amsterdam Metropolitan Area began with an analysis of the current food system in terms of food consumption levels and land use needs for agricultural production to meet consumption demands. As a starting point we took the contemporary average Dutch diet, based on the results of the national consumption survey carried out by the National Institute for Public Health and the Environment.[11] Projecting this on the 2.4 million inhabitants of the MRA, we were able to calculate the amounts of various food items (e.g. potatoes, cheese, beef, eggs, green leafy vegetables, and so on) that are consumed annually within the MRA. By linking this to agricultural yields of these food items, based on data collected by Wageningen UR,[12] we were able to estimate how much agricultural land is needed to produce the food items for the average diet of the 2.4 million inhabitants of the MRA.

[11] www.rivm.nl/en/ Topics/D/Dutch_National_Food_Consumption_Survey (accessed 12-01-2018).

[12] www.wur.nl/nl/show/ KWIN-AGV-2015. htm for arable crops; www.wur.nl/nl/show/ Handboek-Kwantitatieve-Informatie-Veehouderij-KWIN.htm for livestock; www.wur.n nieuws/Kwantitatieve formatie-voor-de-Gla tuinbouw-KWIN-2012 htm for greenhouse horticulture.

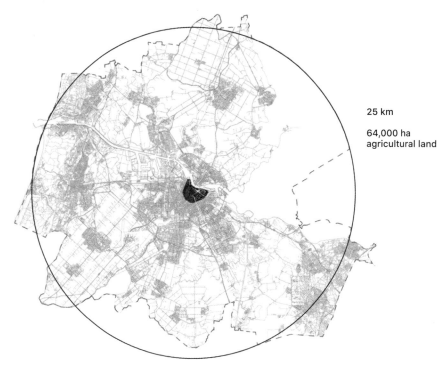

25 km

64,000 ha
agricultural land

Metropolitan region Amsterdam

2015 — 2,100,000 people
2040 — 2,400,000 people

1 Person

Metropolitan region Amsterdam, image: van Paridon x de Groot landschapsarchitecten

Average
consumption

Eggs (3,708 ha)

Sugar, sweets (531 ha)
Potatoes, tubers (1,813 ha)

Fats
(5,272
ha)

Vegetables (1,220 ha)
Legumes (386 ha)

Fish, shell-fish,
crustacean
(1,490 ha)

Fruit (3,055 ha)

Dairy (24,778 ha)

Grain and cereals
(10,088 ha)

Available agricultural
land (64,000 ha)

Agricultural land
needed (226,000)

28%

Meat and meat
products (173,355 ha)

Produced in NL, it does not yet fit...

1,000 m²/year/person – 226,000 ha in 2040

The healthy diet
a lot more legumes,
vegetables, fruit,
fish, etc.

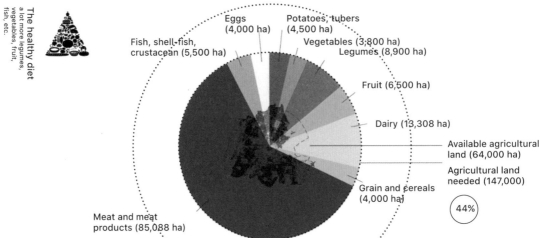

Eggs
(4,000 ha)

Potatoes, tubers
(4,500 ha)

Fish, shell-fish,
crustacean (5,500 ha)

Vegetables (3,800 ha)
Legumes (8,900 ha)

Fruit (6,500 ha)

Dairy (13,308 ha)

Available agricultural
land (64,000 ha)

Agricultural land
needed (147,000)

44%

Grain and cereals
(4,000 ha)

Meat and meat
products (85,088 ha)

Adapting food pattern helps, but is not enough...

The healthy diet

Food Utopias / Redesigning
the Foodscape of the Metropolitan Region of Amsterdam

Classical
vegetarian

VEGETARIAN
FOOD

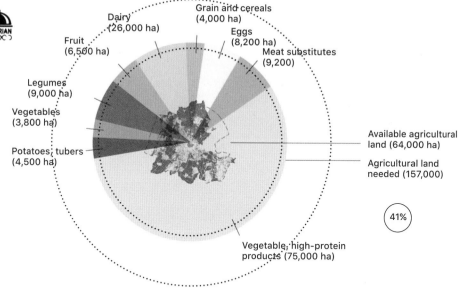

Dairy
(26,000 ha)

Grain and cereals
(4,000 ha)

Eggs
(8,200 ha)

Meat substitutes
(9,200)

Fruit
(6,500 ha)

Legumes
(9,000 ha)

Vegetables
(3,800 ha)

Potatoes, tubers
(4,500 ha)

Available agricultural
land (64,000 ha)

Agricultural land
needed (157,000)

41%

Vegetable, high-protein
products (75,000 ha)

Adapting food pattern helps, but is not enough...

Classical vegetarian food

Amsterdam

Space needed for food production for the Amsterdam region per year, image: van Paridon x de Groot landschapsarchitecten

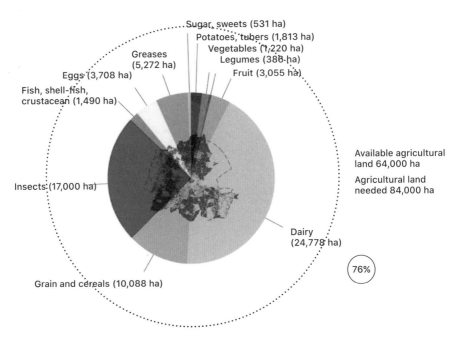

Vegan

Grain and cereals
(4,000 ha)

Fruit
(6,500 ha)

Meat substitutes, nuts
(10,000 ha)

Legumes
(9,000 ha)

Vegetables
(3,800 ha)

Potatoes, tubers
(4,500 ha)

Available agricultural
land (64,000 ha)

Agricultural land
needed (170,000)

Soy milk
(23,000 ha)

38%

Vegetable high-protein
products (82,000 ha)

Adapting food pattern helps, but is not enough...

Vegan

Insects

Average
consumption

Sugar, sweets (531 ha)

Potatoes, tubers (1,813 ha)

Vegetables (1,220 ha)

Legumes (388 ha)

Fruit (3,055 ha)

Greases
(5,272 ha)

Eggs (3,708 ha)

Fish, shell-fish,
crustacean (1,490 ha)

Available agricultural
land 64,000 ha

Agricultural land
needed 84,000 ha

Insects (17,000 ha)

Dairy
(24,778 ha)

76%

Grain and cereals (10,088 ha)

Adapting food pattern helps, but is not enough...

Insects instead of meat (based on average consumption)

Food Utopias / Redesigning
the Foodscape of the Metropolitan Region of Amsterdam

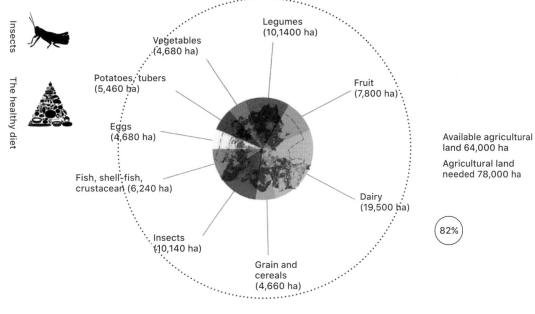

Insects

The healthy diet

Legumes
(10,1400 ha)

Vegetables
(4,680 ha)

Potatoes, tubers
(5,460 ha)

Fruit
(7,800 ha)

Eggs
(4,680 ha)

Fish, shell-fish,
crustacean (6,240 ha)

Dairy
(19,500 ha)

Insects
(10,140 ha)

Grain and
cereals
(4,660 ha)

Available agricultural
land 64,000 ha

Agricultural land
needed 78,000 ha

82%

Adapting food pattern helps, but is not enough...

Insects instead of meat (based on the healthy diet)

Effect of change of diet on space needed for production; Image: van Paridon x de Groot landschapsarchitecten

How Much Space Do the
Inhabitants of the MRA Consume?
Our baseline calculations show that
226,000 hectares (560,000 acres) of
agricultural land is needed to feed all
inhabitants of the MRA. The size of agricultural land available within the MRA
is 64,000 ha (160,000 acres), meaning
that with the current average diet only
28% of the MRA population can be fed
from within the metropolitan region.
It is important to emphasize that this
does not reflect current practices, as a
substantial amount of our food and of
the feed and fodder needed for the production of animal proteins (eggs, dairy,
meat) is produced abroad. In particular
the production of meat (red in the dia-
grams) takes up a lot of space, but the
intensity of the production per hectare
and the space needed per kilogramme
of meat varies significantly per country.[13] In Brazil, 420 m² of land is required
for the production of 1 kilo of beef; in
Ireland approximately 60 m²; and in the
Netherlands just under 15 m² of land.
This implies that at present much more
agricultural land is used globally to feed
the MRA inhabitants than the 226,000
ha needed if all animal protein (thus
including all feed and fodder) would be
produced in the Netherlands.

What is the Impact of
Changing Diets?
Next we questioned the impact of
dietary change on the consumption of
agricultural space and took the following diets into consideration:

1. The 'healthy' diet: the diet recommended by the Health Council and
   the Dutch Centre for Nutrition;
2. The vegetarian diet: a vegetarian
   version of the average current diet;
3. The vegan diet: a vegan version of
   the average current diet;
4. The insect diet: a version of the
   average current diet in which all
   pork, beef and chicken meat is
   replaced by insect protein;
5. The 'healthy' insect diet: a combination of diets 1 and 4.

The figures show that a change in
diet notably helps to reduce the
amount of production space needed.
However, meat replacements and
vegetable proteins, such as nuts,
legumes, and soy products, also take
up quite a bit of production space.
So, changing to a classical vegetarian
diet (with eggs, milk, and cheese) or a
vegan diet will not sufficiently reduce
the demand for production space. Even
if everyone in the area followed the
recommended diet and also started to
eat insects for protein, instead of meat,
the MRA would not be entirely self-
sufficient.

13 H. Blonk, *Milieueffecten
van Nederlandse con-
sumptie van eiwitrijke
producten: gevolgen van
vervanging van dierlijke
eiwitten anno 2008* (s.l.:
Blonk Milieu Advies,
2008), http://library.wur.
nl/WebQuery/wurpubs/
fulltext/117665 (ac-
cessed 20-02-2018).

Food Utopias / Redesigning
the Foodscape of the Metropolitan Region of Amsterdam

Country house Boschrijk in the Beemster, Holland, photo: Ton van der Wal

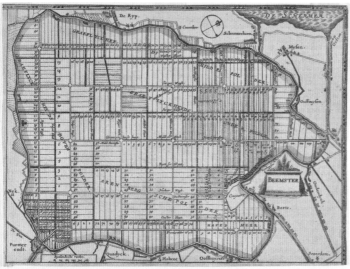

Plan for the agricultural polder the Beemster, Holland

Translating different diets into spatial needs does make the spatial demand for feeding the MRA concrete and tangible. It demonstrates that change of diet is one of the solutions, but it will not be enough to produce enough food within the MRA to feed all its inhabitants.

Numbers show that in order to feed the MRA from within its region, we must look at agricultural production differently: either we need to increase yields per hectare or we should find ways to create more productive space. If and how this can be done and what that implies for the qualities and characteristics of the MRA foodscape will be explored in the following three chapters.

Niké van Keulen, Minke Mulder & Chloé Charreton

MRA UTOPIA 1: URBAN AGRICULTURE

FOOD UTOPIAS

'Urban agriculture is agriculture in and bordering a city, which interacts with local urban conditions and produces, processes and distributes food for the urban market.'[1]

Introduction

Food is part of the daily routine of urban residents. Every day they have to buy, prepare, and eat food; food that is usually produced in rural areas, often far away from where it is bought and eaten. Hence, food production is generally not part of the daily life of people who live in cities. Urban agriculture differs from rural agriculture because of its geographical and relational proximity to urban markets. Therefore, it makes food production part of the everyday urban experience. Because of the urban pressure on space, it is important to incorporate functions and qualities associated with urban green in the development of urban agriculture. Productive green roofs, green walls, and green spaces can, for example, contribute to the adaptation to and mitigation of climate change in the built environment and provide new opportunities for the productive re-use of urban wastes. This chapter explores the spatial and visual impacts of implementing various forms of food production within the urban fabric of the city of Amsterdam.

The main question that inspired our exploration of the first utopian vision for Amsterdam is: How to design a typology of urban agriculture production systems that contributes to the spatial quality of the city and is integrated into the urban fabric of Amsterdam, and what might this look like? The type of urban agriculture production systems that enable most synergies with other urban functions and qualities are circular production systems. As designers our strength is to envision what new forms of urban foodscapes could look like. As previous research[2] has shown, it is impossible to feed all urban inhabitants with food produced within the city borders. Therefore, our exploration is not aimed at creating the self-sufficient city. Rather, the focus is on strengthening the spatial quality of the city by making food production an integral part of urban life. However, at the end of this chapter we do provide a general calculation of the urban yield at city level to visualize the productive potential of urban agriculture in Amsterdam.

1 P. de Graaf, *Ruimte voor stadslandbouw in Rotterdam* (Rotterdam: Stimuleringsfonds voor Architectuur/Vereniging Eetbaar Rotterdam, 2011) www.pauldegraaf.eu/downloads/RvSL/RvSL_PdeGraaf0&O-2011.pdf (accessed 20-02-2018).

2 M. Mulder and C. Oude Aarninkhof, *Stadslandbouwdoos* (Den Haag: Atelier Rijksbouwmeester, 2014), https://issuu.com/claire_oa/docs/stadslandbouwdoos_lr (accessed 20-02-2018).

3 *Southeast False Creek Urban Agriculture Strategy* (Vancouver: Holland Barrs Planning Group, 2002), www.scribd.com/document/34476007/Urban-Agriculture-Strategy (accessed 20-02-2018).

The study and design of urban agriculture often focuses solely on food production within a city. The potential for addressing issues of spatial quality and sustainability is likely to be greatly enhanced by also examining other aspects of the food system on a structural level. Such as how and where food is processed, and how it is distributed. In addition, there may be synergies that result from integrating food production with opportunities for processing and distributing food.[3]

Creating Hubs in Transport and Distribution

At the scale of the city, transport networks and distribution nodes structure the foodscape of Amsterdam. Integrating transport, distribution, and production at every scale level of the city and city region is an important condition for developing urban agriculture. In the design for Amsterdam a coherent food transport network is proposed, including main roads, canals, and railway stations that reconnect the largest productive spaces to densely populated consumption areas. The existing mobility networks, from regional roads, railroads, and waterways to intensive neighbourhood cycling networks provide possibilities for sustainable transport. Using modalities such as electric cars, boats via main water transport lines, bicycles via separate fast bicycle lanes, or tram transport.

On the scale of neighbourhoods, centres where consumers and producers are closely linked structure the local foodscape. These are the spots where the local and city scale meet, as hubs in the food system. Those nodes combine transport and distribution and connect them to places for processing food, warehousing, and consumption. Places with a social quality and relation to food, such as social restaurants, streets with many restaurants and bars, food markets, canteens, offices, urban incubators, schools, and health institutions. Urban renewal programs can integrate food production related to these hubs. Together the transport network and the food hubs form the productive structure of Amsterdam.

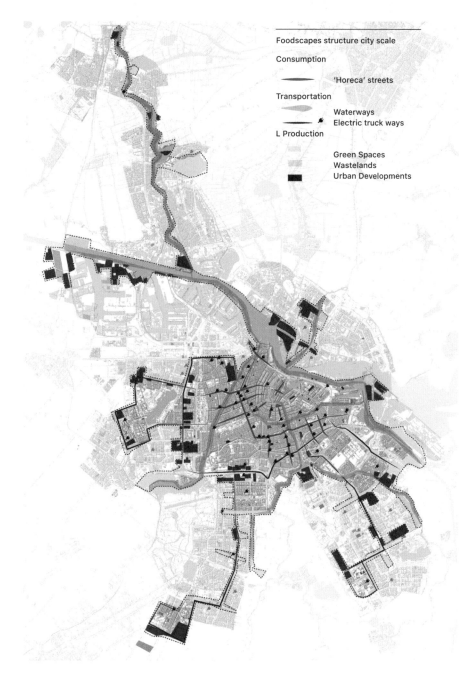

Foodscapes structure city scale

Consumption

—————— 'Horeca' streets

Transportation

—————— Waterways
—————— Electric truck ways

L Production

Green Spaces
Wastelands
Urban Developments

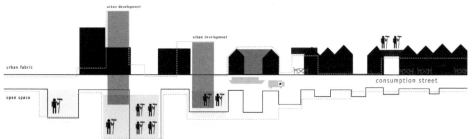

urban development

urban development

urban fabric

consumption street

open space

Amsterdam

Structure on a city scale, scheme: MTD Landscape Architects

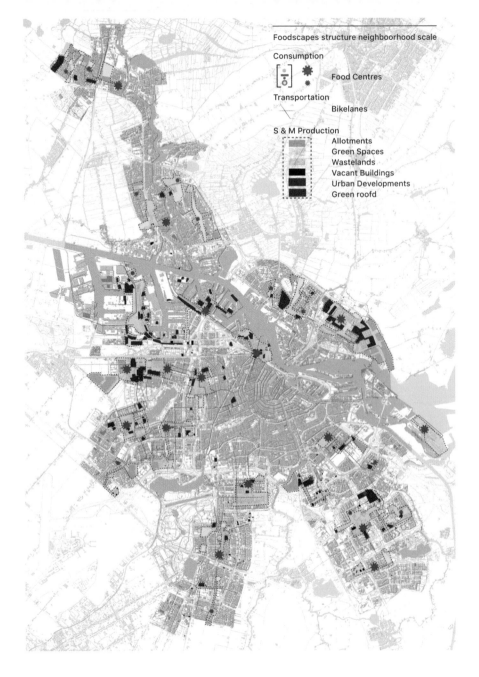

Foodscapes structure neighboorhood scale

Consumption

Food Centres

Transportation

Bikelanes

S & M Production

Allotments
Green Spaces
Wastelands
Vacant Buildings
Urban Developments
Green roofd

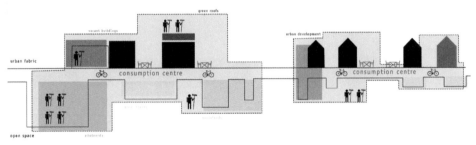

Structure on a neighbourhood scale, scheme: MTD Landscape Architects

Circular Systems in Urban Agriculture

Planning for sustainable development essentially comes down to dealing with the flows of food, water, oxygen and CO_2 energy, and waste. Cities and the people in it are both consumers and suppliers of nutrients and other indispensable resources for agriculture. Urban food production is economically interesting if it fits the following criteria:[4] an excellent quality of produce which justifies a higher price, a high yield per m^2; optimal use of (cheap) space to avoid competition with other urban functions; implementable in existing green spaces with a social or recreational function; and use of waste as a resource and closing of nutrient cycles. Circular production systems are in line with those criteria, because they use space efficiently, the different crops and animals supplement each other and use each other's waste as resource. Hence, the challenge lies in circular thinking: connecting flows and closing cycles at different levels of scale, from small (neighbourhood), to medium (city) and large (city region).

For the purpose of our exploration we have developed a catalogue of different typologies of circular production systems, fitting the urban fabric at different scale levels. Urban farming can take place in various urban locations: outdoor in public spaces, outdoor on rooftops, and indoor with sunlight, with artificial light (LED), or without light. Suitable spaces have medium maintenance intensity and not too high cultural, historical, or nature values, such as allotments, public green, small leftover green spaces in the urban fabric, wasteland, vacant buildings, planned urban development, and green roofs. In every circular system, there is a combination of vegetables and/or fruit production with animal protein production, in order to a) have the most healthy and varied diet; b) think about sustainable food production in the way that crops supplement each other and use each other's waste as nutrients; c) use space efficiently; and d) add a green spatial quality. Potential forms of urban farming are horticulture (vegetables and fruits), poultry farm-ing, pig farming, mushrooms growing, hydroponics (vegetables), aquaponics (fish and green leafy vegetables), and honeybee keeping.

Transforming existing leftover spaces can help to increase levels of urban food production. Walls and blind façades, smaller patches of green and the sides of roads can be incorporated into the urban food production system. For example, by planting nut trees and flowering fruit trees along roads and growing duckweed in smaller water bodies. This will make green structures also beneficial as providers of food. Communities or entrepreneurs can be made responsible for the picking of the ripe fruits. Neighbourhood harvest festivals can be celebrated with home-made pies and sweet cherries. Falling fruit doesn't have to be a nuisance if harvesting is organized and, maybe, even celebrated.

4 De Graaf, *Ruimte voor stadslandbouw in Rotterdam*.

CIRCULAR PRODUCTION

outdoor
public space

outdoor
rooftop

SMALL

max.
2ha

small scale individual production
volunteers
closed community
strong social connection
short availability (less than 5 years)

productivity rating
80% in allotment gardens
80% in vacant lands
40% in new housing developments
80% on rooftops

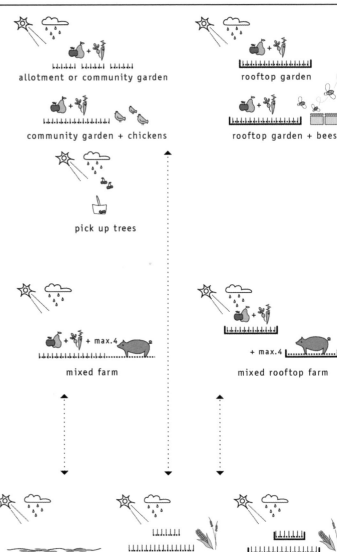

allotment or community garden

rooftop garden

community garden + chickens

rooftop garden + bees

pick up trees

MEDIUM

min.
2ha

community production
entrepeneur and volunteers
open and mixed community
strong social connection
medium availability (between 5-10 years)

productivity rating
80% in vacant land
40% in existing public green
80% on rooftop
20% in indoor of vacant buildings

+ max.4

mixed farm

+ max.4

mixed rooftop farm

LARGE

min.
2ha

duckweed farm

cereals | maïs
farm

cereals | maïs
rooftop farm

plots diveded over the borough as
one maintenance system
entrepeneur
weak social connection
link with mixed farm
long availability (more than 10 years)

productivity rating
80% in vacant lans
80% in existing public green / roofs

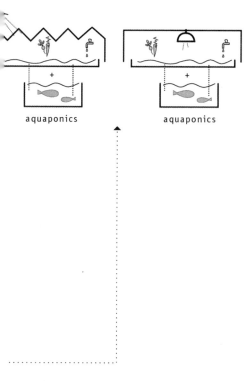

indoor
sunlight

indoor
artificial light

hydroponics

hydroponics

mushrooms

aquaponics

aquaponics

Testing on Neighbourhood and City Scale

To get an idea of the amount and the kind of food that can be produced in the urban setting, we calculated the expected yield in three pilot areas . In this calculation the production system that fits the typology of the urban spaces best, and enhances its identity, is applied. Results were extrapolated and projected, leading to the Amsterdam productive landscape and Amsterdam agglomeration productive structure.

Calculations show that the population of the Amsterdam region can be supplied with enough vegetables and fruits from within its city borders. The production of mushrooms diversifies this category of food. Particularly aquaponics is a very efficient system, producing twice as much as needed to cater for the diet of the population of Amsterdam. On the other hand, pig and poultry farms do not produce enough food to feed all inhabitants. However, yields still appear generous and more accurate data should be collected.

Amsterdam agglomeration production

To each typology of urban spaces, the production of the circular system which reveals the most the identity of the space is calculated. On one hand, almost all of them produce vegetables and fruits. So, more than the population of Amsterdam is supplied with vegetables. Furthermore, the production of mushrooms diversifies this category of food. Particularly, aquaponic is a very efficient system, producing twice as much as the diet of the population of Amsterdam. On the other hand, pigs and poultry farms do not produce enough. However, yields seem generous and other datas would permit to precise them.

Production

Allotments	Vegatables
Green Spaces	Poultry Farming
Wastelands	Pig Farming
Vacant Buildings	Mushrooms
Urban Developments	Hydroponics
Green Roofs	Honey Bees

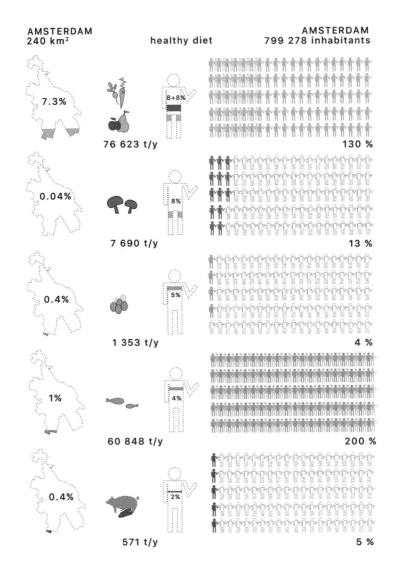

AMSTERDAM
240 km²

healthy diet

AMSTERDAM
799 278 inhabitants

7.3% — 3+8% — 76 623 t/y — 130 %

0.04% — 8% — 7 690 t/y — 13 %

0.4% — 5% — 1 353 t/y — 4 %

1% — 4% — 60 848 t/y — 200 %

0.4% — 2% — 571 t/y — 5 %

Estimated yield from urban agriculture related to demand, scheme: MTD Landscape Architects

Potential productive areas in the city

Conclusions

Agriculture and horticulture are key in a circular economy, both as supplier and user. Circular production systems combine nutrient cycles and increase the variety of urban produce. Circular systems, either indoor or outdoor, multifunctional gardens, roofs, and green structures that can mix with the public realm and enrich the open space system are the way to go for creating beautiful sustainable foodscapes. They contribute to greening the city and add more varied green to the city. This makes the city attractive and will have a positive impact on the city's infiltration and retention capacity of rainwater as well as its capacity to reduce the urban heat island effect. By developing and implementing a logistical system in accordance with the use of public space by city residents, a high-quality built environment is created that invites to be outside and to spend more time moving around in a green environment. Finally, urban agriculture is a form of food production that participates in the rhythms and practices of the urban population, diminishing the distance between producer and consumer.[5] Urban agriculture adds to the 'porosity of the city',[6] which refers to ecological permeability, accessibility, and hydrological safety.

5 P. Viganò and B. Secchi, *Antwerp, Territory of a New Modernity* (Nijmegen: Sun Uitgeverij, 2001).

6 B. Secchi and P. Viganò, *La Ville poreuse* (Geneva: Edition Metis-Presses, 2011).

Vegetable gardens and production of cereals on rooftop of warehouses, image: MTD Landscape Architects

Marieke Timmermans, Pepijn Godefroy, Kim Kool, Floris Grondman & Claire Callander

MRA UTOPIA 2: MULTI-FUNCTIONAL AGRICULTURE

The starting point of the second utopian vision – multifunctional agriculture – for the Metropolitan Region of Amsterdam (MRA) is to make better use of the available space for food production purposes. This can be realized by increasing levels of production; not by increasing the use of external inputs such as nutrients, water, and energy, but by replacing conventional agricultural systems (monocultures) with 'new' circular production systems (polycultures) such as agroforestry, forest gardening, sylvopasture, and permaculture. Another approach is using all available agricultural land for food production (rather than for the production of flowers, or starch for industrial use), by transforming non-productive forest, nature, and recreational areas into food production areas (while maintaining their nature or recreation function) and by using inland water, lakes, and the sea for food production.

The motto of the multifunctional agriculture utopia is to produce locally what can be produced locally, obtain from further away what cannot be produced locally, and eat what's in season. Producing more food locally is also a means to restore the spatial and social proximity relations between food production and consumption that have become disconnected in the process of agricultural modernization, industrialization and globalization (see also pp. 17ff.). The incentive behind this utopian vision is therefore to involve consumers more effectively as participants in the food production and processing process. The idea is to create new food communities, by establishing a network of *food hubs* where inhabitants of the MRA can not only see and buy produce, but also participate in growing, processing, and preparing food.

Towards a Multifunctional Foodscape

The questions that informed our utopian designs were:

— How can we fully dedicate the landscape around Amsterdam to food production?
— How can MRA inhabitants be involved in food provisioning activities?
— What will the landscape look like?
— What will it deliver in terms of food products?

We have explored and visualized this for several locations in the MRA and in this chapter we present a few examples.

Enlarge Production Possibilities
Better land use

Mono

Expand

Double

Involved system

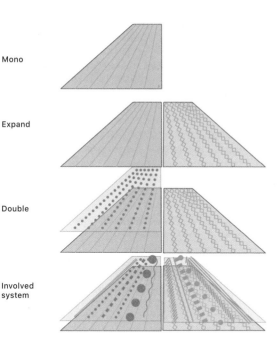

Healthy Efficient Diet
New Production

Innovative products
innovative systems

-Bulk products: Northern polders
mono production system
patatoes, onion, cabbage,
fish, wheat, quinoa, Lupine,
soy.......

-Bulk products: Middle polders
double production system
nuts, insects, seaweed, chicken, mussels, mushrooms,
apples, pears, rye, ...

-Luxury products   Forests, dunes, innerdune-
involved production systems   land, around the city
Tomatoes, berries, game,
herbs, cherry, cow, dairy,
pork, courgette, melon

Enlarging proudction possibilities, image: Landscape Architects for Sale

Nature for Nurture

Nowadays we hardly use the potential of our nature and recreation areas to feed ourselves. Take the dunes and forests between Castricum and Beverwijk, for instance, only half an hour by car and one hour by public transport from the centre of Amsterdam. The food production potential of this kind of landscape is high but is not utilized at all at present. Introducing pigs like the Bonte Bentheimer in the forest during the season would turn the tons of acorns that fall from the trees every year into a tasteful source of protein and provide a nice piece of free-range pork. Pigs are natural foragers. They enjoy rooting and they fertilize the soil. In turn, this would allow different plant and mushroom species to grow in the forest. As a result, more mushrooms can be collected in the fall. Ponds and flowering meadows will be created, attracting wildlife that can be hunted in the open season. Beehives with bees collecting nectar and pollen from the flowering fields provide honey. Additional planting of edible species such as blueberries, blackberries, and buckthorn can produce fruit. During the rest of the year, herds of sheep and goats can keep the meadows and heath open, and produce meat and milk at the same time.

Nature remains nature but provides food at the same time. And recreation areas are still meant for recreation but also provide a lot more meaningful food experiences. The free-range pig is not a wild boar and can be safely fondled by children. Guided by a professional, anyone can search for edible mushrooms and berries. And if that is not exciting enough, you can start hunting. Under guidance and trained by the hunting association, anyone over 16 with a 'my-first-gun' can begin to hunt pheasants or hares, and from the age of 18 deer. With agro-hunting and agro-gathering recreation becomes involvement in food production.

The soil of a forest is a delicate ecosystem. Implementation of food production within the forest ecosystem needs to be carefully considered. The crux is a sophisticated management system of strategic planting and a sophisticated system of animals and people in the right places in the right time. In that way the forest can generate a maximum yield of food products in a sustainable way. Visitor's centres new style can be the starting point for food collections and hunting excursions. After the walk everyone takes home the picking or spoil of the day. Or you buy some from a hunter who had more time or luck that day.

FAZANT   PATRIJS   WILD KONIJN   HERT   REE   WILD ZWIJN   HAAS

Food Hubs for Fun

Part of the land around Amsterdam is extensively used for recreational purposes and nature conservation, such as the peat meadows south of Weesp or the monofunctional recreational areas such as Spaarnwoude. Our statement is to make outdoor leisure activities and hobbies food-productive. This will add more than 13,500 hectares to the MRA foodscape and will help to address the urban demand for allotment gardens. Being close to Amsterdam with many helping hands available, these places are suitable for more intensive permaculture gardens.

Food hubs are the centres where materials and tools are stored, knowledge and experiences are shared, and coffee (imported) and tea (own grown mint or verbena tea) are served. In adjacent gardens the whole assortment of Dutch vegetables and herbs are produced in an interrelated system. Fields surrounding the gardens are planted with lupines. As a leguminous it is good for the soil, it can serve as feed for grazing (goat) herds, and as an alternative source of flour. The holistic resource management of meadows, where the abundance and diversity of natural systems is being introduced into large-scale permaculture systems,[1] allows for quite a high number of livestock. They provide a substantial source of meat, dairy, and manure to fertilize the gardens. Chickens can be kept together with the goats. They deliver eggs and meat and help to improve the soil.

The food hub is the alternative to one's own vegetable garden, but at the same time it is the community centre, the day-care, the gym, village café (increasingly missing in many places), the village supermarket, and a place for events. A network of food hubs in the MRA can be seen as a modern defence line of Amsterdam (see pp. 219ff.). It can help the MRA inhabitants to defend themselves against the threats of modern times: loneliness, overweight, and malnutrition.

1   www.permades.nl/
allan-savory/ (accessed
20-02-2018).

Care for Crops

A slightly different version of the more recreational food hub is the care hub, where post-hospital and revalidation care is combined with professional food production. Instead of an institutional garden to wander around in, the clients (and their visitors) actively participate in the production of food. *Care farm* becomes *farm care*. Being outside a lot, moving more, and eating healthy; it can all contribute to the vitality and recovery of patients.

Fish for Phosphates
The landscape around Amsterdam
is originally very wet. It takes a lot
of energy to dry the polders (former
lakes) and peat lands to make agriculture possible, while creating sub-
optimal conditions for dairy farming.
Maintaining low groundwater levels to
enable agriculture also leads to growing problems like land subsidence and
consequently CO_2 emission. Likewise,
salinization is becoming problematic
for agricultural production. Hence, we
propose to flip the water-land ratio in
favour of the first and combine different forms of food production in circular
systems. Hydroponic and aquaponic
systems could provide fish and shell-
fish, fed with algae and seaweeds from
the North Sea farms, the protein rich
larvae of the black soldier fly, and waste
from other food production processes such as bread mills. This could be
combined with floating horticulture of
green leafy vegetables on the water
(fresh or brackish).[2] The hubs could be
very obvious starting points for boat
trips ending with home cooked fish or
an algae burger.

2   M. Gijsbertsen, 'Wierin-
germeer heeft primeur
in Europa: Eerste
kwekerij van Chinese
wolhandkrab', *Noord-
hollands Dagblad*, 23
september 2017.

Water Structure

*Structure linked
by production
water gardens and
recreational routes*

Fish for phosphates, image: Landscape Architects for Sale

Amsterdam

Conclusion

The area for food production can be expanded by using all available agricultural land for food production, by making nature reserves and recreation areas food productive, and by using the sea and inland waters for the production of food and feed. This multifunctional utopian foodscape is composed of a mixture of these different production systems, of which the productive capacity in the MRA is yet unknown. We can show what kind of food items can be produced, but not how much. Besides food, the multifunctional foodscape creates social benefits. The examples show that food production can be combined with other societal functions and objectives such as education, employment, care, and health. As a result, the landscape itself is regenerated and becomes richer, livelier, and more varied. The map shows the different food production systems that could fit within the 25-km radius around Amsterdam. This gives an insight into the foodscape of the future on a larger scale and of the spatial quality that comes with it.

Foodtypologies

 Free Agroforestry

 Professional mixed mono production

 Communual Permaculture / forest farming

 Agrisilviculture

 Natural conditions wildlife

 Forest Paleoculture Hunting & gathering

 Dune Paleoculture Hunting & gathering

25KM

Matchmaking between landscape and food production typologies, image: Landscape Architects for Sale

Ruut van Paridon, Karen de Groot & Antoine Fourrier

MRA UTOPIA 3: SUSTAINABLE INDUSTRIAL AGRICULTURE

Amsterdam

1 www.wur.nl/en/Expertise-Services/Research-Institutes/Environmental-Research/Projects/Metropolitan-Food-Clusters-and-Agroparks.htm (accessed 04-01-2018).

Feeding all inhabitants of the MRA from within the MRA requires a combined effort of changing diets (see also p. 232) and intensifying agricultural production. This can be done by combining different technological innovations to create sustainable farming methods that are capable of increasing yields per hectare but depend less on external inputs such as nutrients, water, and energy. Developing more circular systems based on industrial ecology could be a way forward. In recent years new systems such as agroparks and metropolitan food clusters have been developed.[1] Although these systems seem to have certain benefits in terms of resource-use efficiency and reduced transport of animals, they tend to be seen as technocratic failures incapable of enhancing social proximity between production and consumption (see also chapter 2). We think that agroparks and similar industrial food production systems will lack societal support, in particular in the MRA.

Hence, the question guiding this third utopian vision is what kind of sustainable industrial mode of food production would be feasible and socially acceptable. Starting point of our utopian vision is the potential of the different agricultural landscapes in the MRA, such as the polders, the horticulture areas, and the peatland meadows. For each agrarian landscape we have explored how—by using new and innovative production techniques—the production can be intensified, while reducing the environmental impact and use of external resources and enhancing animal welfare, and what the consequences are for the landscape and its future spatial quality.

Redesigning the Agricultural Landscapes of the MRA

The Polders

The polders, with their fertile sea clay soils, are very suitable for the production of vegetables, potatoes, cereals, legumes, beans, roots, and tubers. And the polders are very suitable for the implementation of precision farming, an innovative food production technique using GPS, ICT, remote sensing, and drones to adapt production methods to the specific local circumstances of soil type, groundwater level, and available nutrients. The expectation is that these new technologies can increase production by 10 to 15 per cent. The production of the crops will also be much more sustainable, by saving on water, pesticides, nutrients, and fossil energy.

With precision farming differences in subsoil are better utilized. Sowing is no longer organized per field but can be optimized per square metre. A seed drill can sow more or less seed, depending on the circumstances, but can also combine different seeds. This creates opportunities to shift from monocultures on large plots to polycultures: a combination of multiple crops, mutually beneficial, to create a better microclimate and to provide effective disease and pest control. On a large scale this is still virtually undiscovered, but the first tests with precision farming with 'agricultural printers' open up the thinking about the relation between landscape, agriculture, and digitalization.

As agriculture becomes more digital, the scale of the agricultural landscape will probably increase further. But at the same time, a greater variation in crops will result in more diversity on the small scale. Multi-cropping, intercropping, companion planting, and beneficial weeds will refine and enrich the image of the landscape and the biodiversity of the large arable farmlands.

Horticulture Areas

Climate-controlled greenhouses offer many options for intensifying the food production. In the greenhouse industry cutting edge agricultural innovations and developments increase production per square metre while saving energy and water, optimizing the use of available nutrients and lowering the use of pesticides. Applying new systems such as the multilayer cultivation systems using LED-lights, hydroponics, and aquaponics enhances the efficient use of water and nutrients. With these new production methods yields can multiply up to 4 times compared to conventional greenhouses. Stacked in layers, production per hectare can increase even further.

Growing greens, vegetables, and fruits requires the input of nutrients. A shift towards a more regional production of food asks for sustainable use of available resources and the closing of nutrient cycles. The sewage treatment plants of Amsterdam-West and Schiphol City can be a source of nutrients as they can produce pure struvite crystals by mining phosphate and nitrate from (human) wastewater. The port area of Amsterdam can supply residual CO_2 from the industry.

To intensify horticulture, a landscape framework is designed, linked to the city's green structure, in which new, contemporary greenhouse complexes can be developed. Via public routes through the greenhouses people can access these fascinating, high-tech production places. Stairs take visitors to the different levels and in a central market produce from the complex and the nearby allotments can be purchased.

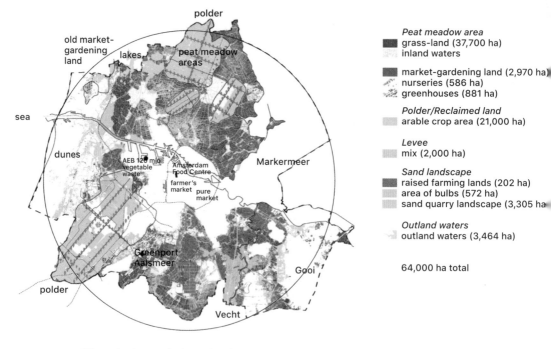

Different landscapes in the region, image: van Paridon x de Groot landschapsarchitecten

The Polders

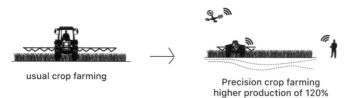

usual crop farming

Precision crop farming
higher production of 120%

Precision crop farming, 100% ecological
higher production of 115%

Hightec polyculture
higher production of 150%

Crop farming higher production
result of 115 to 150%

Turbo agriculture in polders, image: van Paridon x de Groot landschapsarchitecten

Usual market-gardening

vegetables

In greenhouses
higher production of 15%

vegetables

LED/vegetables

Two layers
higher production of 200%

vertical vegetables

LED/vegetables

Aquaponic/fish

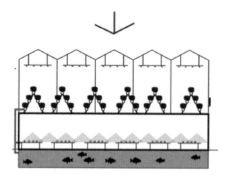

More layers/rotation
Higher production of 400%

Prototype horticulture, image: van Paridon x de Groot landschapsarchitecten

Animal friendly dairy farming, image: van Paridon x de Groot landschapsarchitecten

Peatlands

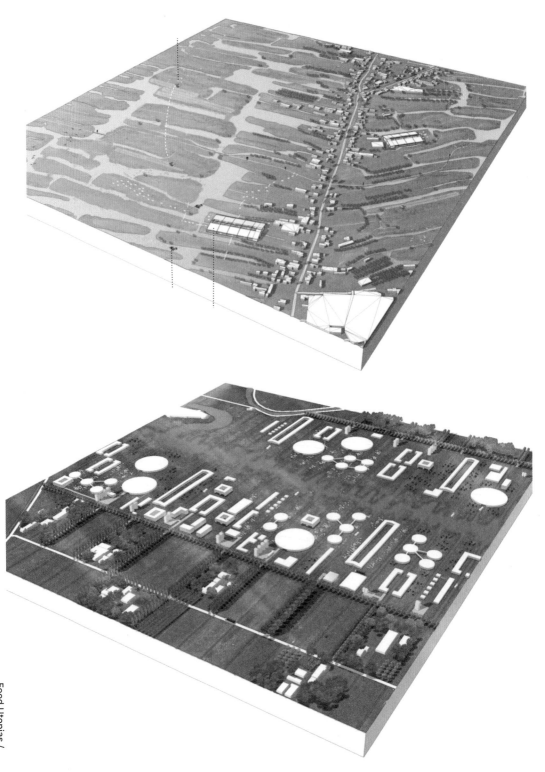

Meat production in open air stables, image: van Paridon x de Groot landschapsarchitecten

Horticultural clusters, image: van Paridon x de Groot landschapsarchitecten

Peatlands

The biggest challenge is to produce enough animal protein in the MRA. Even with a shift towards a healthy diet (see p. 232) the MRA will need to accommodate 29,000 beef cattle, 400,000 pigs, 16 million chickens, 690,000 laying hens and 23,000 dairy cows to provide its inhabitants with meat, dairy products, and eggs. Based on current production methods at least 85,000 hectares of agricultural land are needed for the production of animal protein. However, after deducting the area of the polders and the greenhouses, only 38,000 hectares remains. Meat and dairy production must therefore be at least twice as intensive as today to feed the region.

Research[2] shows that the living space for the animals actually forms a small percentage of the total space used. Most space is needed for feed and fodder. In our utopian vision we propose to radically increase the living space of animals. This also means finding ways to intensify the production of fodder crops or shift towards other sources for animal feed.

There is insufficient grassland and cropland in the region to feed all the 23,000 cows needed to provide the MRA with dairy products. Duckweed can be an alternative source of protein. For the supply of 23,000 dairy cows, an area of 16,500 ha is required where duckweed can be harvested in the wild. This corresponds to 60% of the open water in the peat land areas.

Duckweed and Azolla production offer opportunities for the future of the peat lands around Amsterdam. Water levels in peat-grasslands can rise again, the on-going subsidence can be stopped and CO_2 emissions can be eliminated. The peatland meadows can become more extensive, with a greater bio-diversity of flowering grasses and herbs or turn into marshland with reed and willow. The raw material coming from the wetlands can be used in the stables for the animals to lie on. The use of sturdy manure on grasslands serves meadow birds and is a good fertilizer for horticulture. Also, the wild flower grass, reed and willow wood can be a good addition to the protein-rich diet of duckweed, which will make the cows healthier. Farming in the water-rich peat-grasslands will adapt to the landscape with space for animals to walk outside freely, closer to the farm and with fodder production in the more natural lands and waters further away.

The polder Ronde Venen could be a future centre for meat production. It is located close enough to the new intensive horticulture/glass clusters to set up compact nutrient cycles. The development of the meat production area can be combined with raising the groundwater level and creating more open water in the area, which will benefit the surrounding nature areas. The animals can partially be fed with the duckweed that is harvested nearby and brought to the stables directly via the waterways. Additional fodder can come from organic waste from the nearby flower auction of Aalsmeer or from new seaweed farms in the North Sea. Via the river Amstel boats transport the fodder to a small harbour in the Ronde Venen, where it is transhipped to light electric vessels that boat to the stables. Small on-site slaughterhouses will be built, to avoid unnecessary transport of animals.

2   H. Blonk et al., *Milieu-effecten van Neder-landse consumptie van eiwitrijke producten: Gevolgen van vervang-ing van dierlijke eiwitten anno 2008* (s.l.: Blonk Milieu Advies, 2018) http://library.wur.nl/WebQuery/wurpubs/fulltext/117665 (accessed 20-02-2018).

Horticultural clusters in the polder, image: van Paridon x de Groot landschapsarchitecten

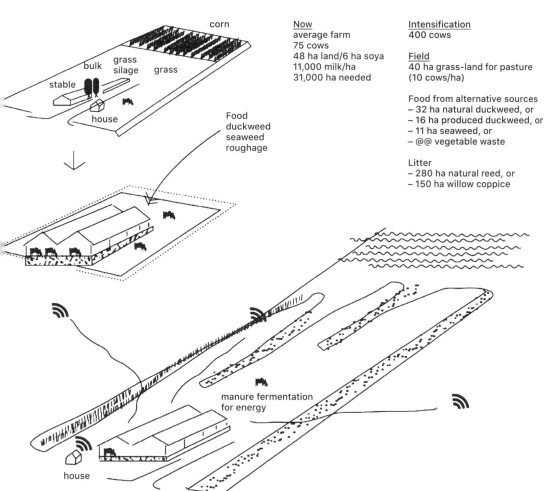

hydroponic

multi-layered grocery

led grocery

fish

public visit

free-range stables

CO2

fertilizers

Prototype dairy farming, image: van Paridon x de Groot landschapsarchitecten

corn

grass silage

bulk

grass

stable

house

Food
duckweed
seaweed
roughage

Now
average farm
75 cows
48 ha land/6 ha soya
11,000 milk/ha
31,000 ha needed

Intensification
400 cows

Field
40 ha grass-land for pasture
(10 cows/ha)

Food from alternative sources
– 32 ha natural duckweed, or
– 16 ha produced duckweed, or
– 11 ha seaweed, or
– @@ vegetable waste

Litter
– 280 ha natural reed, or
– 150 ha willow coppice

manure fermentation
for energy

house

Underwater Vertical
Seaweed Farms

Research has shown that duckweed is such an effective source of protein that all animals in the MRA could be fed from the region. But to reduce the pressure on the water and the natural landscape and to maintain sufficient variation in feed and fodder other durable sources of protein are also needed. Experimental farms[3] show that cultivating and harvesting seaweed is thirty times as productive as grassland. The seaweed grows on ropes in frames that hang in the sea. The first tests show promising results: 6,000 hectares of seabed can supply all the necessary protein for the region.

On the map, about 6,000 ha of seabed is created under the offshore wind farms that are being developed in the North Sea. The windmills can serve as anchors for the seaweed frames. The seaweed farms can mine phosphates and other fertilizers from the sea, thus closing nutrient cycles on a larger scale. The wind and seaweed farms, not accessible for fishing boats, can form artificial reefs, creating new living areas for (shell)fish, crabs, mussels, cod, lobsters, porpoises, and so on.[4] Could the wind farms or seaweed farms also be a place to go? An offshore attraction, where you go for a dive and eat a seaweed burger?

farm

sea weed

3   W.A. Brandenburg, *Sustainable Farming at Sea: To Secure Food, Feed, Green Chemistry and Energy* (Wageningen, 26 January 2016), www.wur.nl/nl/activiteit/The-Future-of-Our-Seas-Sustainable-Farming-at-Sea.htm (accessed 20-02-2018).

4   H.J. Lindeboom, *Waarom zijn kabeljauwen zo dol op windmolens?* (Wageningen UR, Wageningen, 2015).

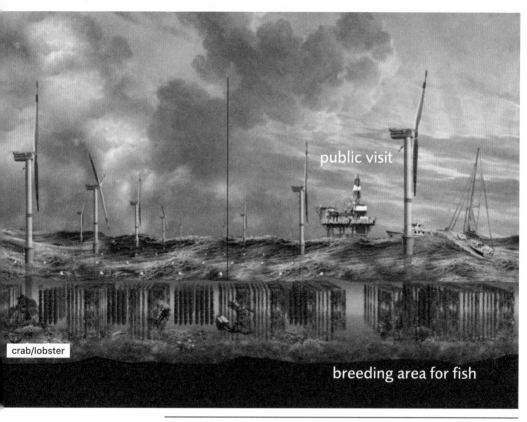

Sea farm, image: van Paridon x de Groot landschapsarchitecten

Conclusions

If the inhabitants of the MRA adhere to the healthy diet it should be possible to feed the MRA in this utopian vision. By spatially clustering agricultural production and intensifying it by making use of new technologies, production levels per hectare can increase significantly. Key to this is a different way of feeding animals by incorporating waterscapes (sea and inland water) as feed production areas into the MRA foodscape. This will enlarge the living space of animals, while creating space for other forms of land use, such as nature and recreation.

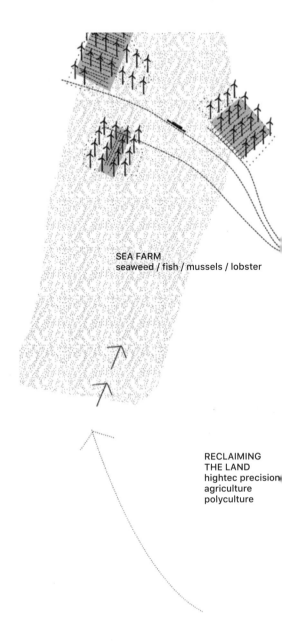

SEA FARM
seaweed / fish / mussels / lobster

RECLAIMING
THE LAND
hightec precision
agriculture
polyculture

laying hens in the orchard

dairy farming in natural peat area

glass clusters
vegetables/fish

meat cluster pigs
meat cows
meat poultry

Johannes S.C. Wiskerke & Saline Verhoeven

SOCIO-SPATIAL DESIGN

Food provisioning has not been a key focus of spatial design and planning in the past decades. And if it was addressed, it was mainly limited to spatial design and planning of either agricultural production areas in the countryside or food outlets and allotment gardens in urban areas. One of the main reasons for this lack of interest in food provisioning by designers and planners has to do with the historically grown dichotomy between urban and rural policy, with food being equated to agriculture and thus belonging to the rural policy and planning domain.[1] Another reason is that food provisioning has increasingly become a private sector responsibility, in particular since the government began to withdraw from regulating food markets and food prices in the 1980s. Concomitantly, food provisioning became less of a public issue and responsibility and this may explain why there was no real need to look at food provisioning from a design and planning perspective. The more so since food provisioning actors (farmers, food processors, retailers, buyers) often operate in different geographical areas. A third reason is that the multifunctionality of food provisioning was, and still is, often not seen and understood by policymakers, researchers, and planners.[2] With the multifunctionality of food provisioning we refer to the fact that food provisioning is not only about the production, processing, distribution, selling and buying, preparing, and eating of food (i.e. the different food provisioning practices that make up the food supply chain) but also about food-related issues such as health, employment, education, biodiversity, climate change, waste, and social inequality (see also pp. 17ff.). These interlinkages were well understood by the municipalities of Belo Horizonte (see pp. 75ff.) and Rosario (see pp. 193ff.) and a group of people that established the Toronto Food Policy Council.[3]

The first time, in recent decades, that the multifunctionality of food was explicitly addressed by planners was around the turn of the century when Pothukuchi and Kaufman published two papers in which they convincingly argued why food could no longer remain a stranger to the (urban) planning field.[4] A few years later this led to the establishment of a Food Systems Planning Interest Group within

1   K. Pothukuchi and J.L. Kaufman, 'Placing the Food System on the Urban Agenda: The Role Of Municipal Institutions in Food Systems Planning', *Agriculture and Human Values* 16, no. 2 (1999), pp. 213–224.

2   K. Pothukuchi and J.L. Kaufman, 'The Food System: A Stranger to The Planning Field', *Journal of the American Planning Association* 66, no. 2 (2000), pp. 113–124; K. Morgan, 'Nourishing the City: The Rise of the Urban Food Question in the Global North', *Urban Studies* 52, no. 8 (2015), pp. 1379–1394.

3   A. Blay-Palmer, 'The Canadian Pioneer: The Genesis of Urban Food Policy in Toronto', *International Planning Studies* 14, no. 4 (2009), pp. 401–416.

4   Pothukuchi and Kaufman, 'Placing the Food System on the Urban Agenda'; Pothukuchi and Kaufman, 'The Food System'.

the American Planning Association (APA).[5] Again a few years after that, in 2009, the Association of European Schools of Planning (AESOP) followed with the foundation of the Sustainable Food Planning Thematic Group and an annual Sustainable Food Planning Conference.[6] This annual conference attracts scientists and professionals from a variety of disciplines, backgrounds, and geographical contexts (also from outside Europe). This is also reflected in the wide variety of contributions to the book Sustainable Food Planning: Evolving Theory and Practice,[7] which is based on papers presented at the second conference, hosted by the School of Architecture and Design of Brighton University. This established a clear link with the spatial design field and ever since architects, urbanists, and landscape architects have been active contributors to the AESOP Sustainable Food Planning Group, in addition to planners, geographers, sociologists, anthropologists, and economists. Until now the growing interest in food in the field of spatial design and planning agenda tends to focus on designs for urban agriculture at different levels of scale, ranging from vertical farms to continuous productive landscapes.[8] Although this book also includes quite a few urban agriculture cases, our aim has been to take it a step further by providing guidelines to designers, planners, researchers, and professionals with other disciplinary backgrounds for designing and developing sustainable and regenerative foodscapes that encompass the entire range of food provisioning practices while also addressing the multifunctionality of food. In other words, with this book we intend to encourage designers and other professionals and academics to see contemporary challenges through a food lens and to use food (and food provisioning practices) as an entry point for spatial design to address these challenges. Towards this end we have proposed five socio-spatial design principles for sustainable and regenerative foodscapes.

5   https://apafig.word-press.com/ (accessed 21-02-2018).
6   https://aesopsfp.word-press.com/ (accessed 21-02-2018).
7   A. Viljoen and J.S.C. Wiskerke, *Sustainable Food Planning: Evolving Theory and Practice* (Wageningen: Wageningen Academic Publishers, 2012).
8   A. Viljoen and K. Bohn, *Second Nature Urban Agriculture: Designing Productive Cities* (Oxford: Routledge, 2014).

9   www.fao.org/in-action/
    food-for-cities-pro-
    gramme/approach-old/
    crfs/en/ (accessed 21-
    02-2018).
10 M.C.A. Wegerif and
    J.S.C. Wiskerke, 'Ex-
    ploring the Staple Food-
    scape of Dar es Salaam',
    Sustainability 9, no. 6
    (2017), 1081 (https://
    doi.org/10.3390/
    su9061081).

These five principles are meant to enable research-ers and professionals to explore the socio-spatial dynamics and relations of food provisioning. In addition, they are intended to provide guidelines to cope with the complexity of food provisioning dy-namics and challenges by indicating which relations and connections to take into account: urban-rural, scales, flows, functions, and present-futures. And, finally, they provide starting points to visualize data and translate these into the use of space and into spatial qualities. In this section we briefly reflect on what we consider to be the added value of these five principles to the socio-spatial exploration, visualiza-tion, and imagination of food provisioning.

Principle 1:
What Is the Added Value of City
Region Food System Thinking?

The first principle has been illustrated with the cases of Bristol, New York City, Ede, and Belo Horizonte, mainly to highlight the importance of taking urban-rural relations into consideration when exploring and designing systems of food provisioning. As mentioned in 'City-Region Per-spective' (pp. 39ff.), this aligns with the emergence of city region food systems (CRFS) approaches, which aim 'to foster the development of resilient and sustainable food systems within urban cen-tres, peri-urban and rural areas surrounding cit-ies by strengthening rural-urban linkages'.[9] The CRFS perspective has not only featured in the four aforementioned cases that served to illustrate this principle but also in 'Logistics and the City' (pp. 127ff.) about Dar es Salaam's food logistics and in several chapters about the Metropolitan Region of Amsterdam. At present, in many CRFS approaches geographical proximity thinking seems to domi-nate:[10] Can cities or metropolitan regions be fed from within the city region and/or how can this be achieved? This geographical proximity think-ing, which can also be understood as a normative approach based on the assumption that there is an inherent advantage to localizing food provisioning, clearly featured in the Metropolitan Region Amsterdam cases. With our first socio-spatial design principle we aim to broaden the scope of CRFS thinking and approaches by adding explorative-analytical and imaginative approaches. The explorative-analytical perspective follows from relational thinking and can be used to explore, analyse, and visualize the spatiality of food provisioning practices and their relations. This can help to shed light on how and from where food is procured and what this means in terms of the sustainability, vulnerability, and resilience of the food provisioning systems. The cases of Bristol, New York City, and Belo Horizonte are clear examples of such an explorative-analytical perspective. The imaginative perspective follows from utopian thinking and can be used to imagine and visualize what the spatiality of food practices and their relations could look like, and, through such an approach, explore what this would mean in terms of sustainability, vulnerability, and resilience as well as spatial quality. This has been explicitly addressed in the different food utopias for the Metropolitan Region of Amsterdam.

Principle 2:
Why Is a Multi-Scalar Perspective
on Foodscapes Necessary?

In 'The Spatiality of Food Provisioning' (pp. 17ff.), as well as in the introduction to the second socio-spatial design principle ('Linking Scales', pp. 83ff.), we stated that foodscapes can be defined at different levels of scale, ranging from the macro (e.g. the global food system) to the micro (e.g. the socio-spatial organization of food storage, cooking and eating at home). We subsequently argued that these different foodscape scales are nested. For example, what and how people eat at home is likely to be influenced by the kind of food outlets (e.g. fresh food markets, grocery stores, convenience stores, supermarkets, and fast food establishments) and their accessibility by different modes of transport. This implies that designing or redesigning foodscapes requires an integrated approach in which the different levels are addressed together to realize a working whole. In Dar es Salaam (see pp. 83ff.) food markets and street shops (*dukas*) play a crucial role in meeting the food needs of the urban poor. In a city that is rapidly growing in population size and spatially expanding and at the same time is increasingly prone to flooding, it is, from a food and nutrition security point of view, important that markets remain accessible during and after heavy rainfalls (see pp. 109ff.), that neighbourhoods are protected from flooding (see pp. 119ff.) and that the metropolitan region has an infrastructure capable of supplying the markets and *dukas* with food (see pp. 127ff.). Illustrating the significance of linking scales is not limited to the Dar es Salaam case, but also featured in many of the other examples. Many of the urban or city region food policies involve interventions, transformations and developments at different levels of scale. In Belo Horizonte (pp. 75ff.), for example, this ranges from creating space for urban agriculture to having a proper spatial distribution of subsidized food markets throughout the city and to giving peri-urban family farmers direct access to food markets. But the cases used to illustrate the third principle—connecting flows—also show that circularity can and has to be achieved at different levels of scale. The chapter about the green tides of Brittany (pp. 165ff.) is an interesting example of the link between different scales. On the one hand it shows how a regional foodscape is affected by an agricultural system that becomes part of a globalized food system: the global sourcing of animal feed leads to a surplus of nutrients in the region which, due to leaching of nitrogen, subsequently contributes to the green tide. On the other hand, a series of local and mutually supporting interventions are needed to change the regional foodscape. A final case worth mentioning here is the one about urban agroforestry in Porto Alegre (pp. 187ff.), which shows that a productive green infrastructure at city level begins with the identification, design, and development of urban agriculture typologies at square, street, park, and neighbourhood level. In many of these examples the double role of spatial design comes to the fore: Exploring and visualizing how different levels are connected and interact (analysis) and exploring and visualizing how different levels of scale could or should be redesigned and reconnected and what that yields in terms of spatial quality (imagination).

Principle 3:
What Is the Added Value of a
Circular Economy Perspective?

281

The depletion and scarcity of resources that are
fundamental to food provisioning (nutrients, water,
soil), the dependency of food provisioning systems
(including waste collection and processing) on fossil
fuels and the (anticipated) effects of climate change
on food provisioning, create a sense of urgency to
say farewell to linear thinking and embrace circular economy approaches. As connecting flows
and closing cycles is a multi-level challenge, spatial
designers (in collaboration with other professionals) can make visible how flows can be connected
at different levels. In this book we have presented
examples of circularity at different levels of scale,
starting with the NIOO-KNAW building (pp.
145ff.) as a prime example of designing a building,
and its surroundings, that is largely and if legally
possible would be entirely based on the concept of
circularity. This not only implied a design challenge
for the flows of water and energy but also for the
construction materials being used. At the other side
of the scalar spectrum the 'Green tides of Brittany'
(pp. 165ff.) featured as an example of a regional
landscape approach, which consisted of small-scale
interventions within a regional landscape strategy encompassing agriculture, cities, and the sea.
Additionally, this book includes several examples of
creating circularity in food production by designing different modes of permaculture, such as food
forest Vlaardingen (pp. 181ff.), urban agroforestry
in Porto Alegre (pp. 187ff.) and multifunctional
agriculture in the Metropolitan Region of Amsterdam (pp. 249ff.). Vigo's edible landscapes (pp.
201ff.) are another example of circular economy,
also due to the role that some of the associations of
commons play or want to play in recycling organic
waste.

The principle of connecting flows and closing
cycles tends to be confined to flows such as those
of nutrients, water, and energy. However, equally
important for designers is to have an eye for socio-economic relations and how spatial interventions impact on social networks and reciprocity
relations. One example of that is Belo Horizonte

(pp. 75ff.) where the challenges of combatting urban food insecurity and poverty alleviation of family farmers have been addressed simultaneously, for example by creating opportunities for farmers to deliver products to school feeding programmes or by creating market spaces for family farmers in the city to directly sell their produce. Another example are the *dukas* in Dar es Salaam (pp. 83ff.). They fulfil a crucial role in providing access to food close to where people live, but a *duka* is more than a street shop where food can be bought. It's a place where people can get food on credit, where refrigerator space can be used to store food and where people gather and meet. If, for some odd reason, these *dukas* were to be replaced by supermarkets, it would not only limit access to food but also break down social relations.

11 C. Folke, 'Resilience: The Emergence of a Perspective for Social-Ecological Systems Analyses', *Global Environmental Change* 16, no. 3 (2006), pp. 253–267.

Principle 4:
What Can Spatial Design Contribute
to Spatial Diversity and Synergies?

In the introduction to the fourth socio-spatial design principle we argued that enhancing and celebrating diversity is key to building resilience in food provisioning systems.[11] Here diversity does not only relate to (agro)biodiversity and genetic diversity in food crops and animal breeds, but also to diversity of spatial functions. The cases of food forest Vlaardingen (pp. 181ff.), urban agroforestry in Porto Alegre (pp. 187ff.) and multifunctional agriculture in the Metropolitan Region of Amsterdam (pp. 249ff.) are all examples of designing biodiverse food production systems based on the principles of natural ecosystems, and capable of increasing ecological and spatial diversity. But there are also other diversities that can be addressed through spatial design. An important one being the diversity of food provisioning spaces in cities. This includes space for urban agriculture, which was, for example, the focus of the urban agriculture scenario for the Metropolitan Region of Amsterdam (pp. 235ff.), but also maintaining or enlarging the diversity of different food outlets, such as street shops and people's markets in Dar es Salaam (pp. 83ff.) and the subsidized food markets in Belo Horizonte (pp. 75ff.). Another important contribution of spatial design lies in supporting the transformation from monofunctional to multifunctional foodscapes, in particular in the light of food and water-energy-environment-waste-climate change-social inequality-health nexus. Visualizing these and other functions as different layers that are or could be addressed through spatial (re)design is a powerful way of making spatial synergies visible.

Principle 5:
What Is the Contribution of Spatial
Design to Utopian Thinking?

The urgency to address the food-related challenges that we introduced in 'The Spatiality of Food Provisioning' (pp. 17ff.) calls for creative thinking about the future. To quote Albert Einstein: 'We can't solve problems by using the same kind of thinking we used when we created them.' In the introduction to the fifth socio-spatial design principle we stated that neo-liberal capitalism has been the dominant model of food system development in the past decades and that many of today's food system problems and failures can be attributed to that dominant development mode.[12] This means that solving problems requires us to move away from what J.K. Gibson-Graham call 'capitalocentric' thinking, or 'the dominant representation of all economic activities in terms of their relationship to capitalism'.[13] We argued that this representation tends to neglect or exclude the large variety of existing and emerging food provisioning practices that deviate from the capitalist mode of food provisioning. Utopian thinking thus begins by exploring, supporting, and developing the practices and systems that are already present, yet neglected and rejected by capitalocentric thinking. We refer to these practices and systems as real utopias.[14] In this book a wide variety of real utopias have been presented and discussed, such as Belo Horizonte's food policy (pp. 75ff.), the NIOO-KNAW building (pp. 145ff.), the zero-waste strategy of San Francisco (pp. 159ff.), the Urban Agriculture Programme in Rosario (pp. 193ff.) and the edible landscapes of the metropolitan area of Vigo (pp. 201ff.). These real utopias can serve as inspiration and building blocks for spatial transformations elsewhere. This is where real and

12 P.V. Stock, M. Carolan, and C. Rosin, *Food Utopias: Reimagining Citizenship, Ethics and Community* (Abingdon: Routledge, 2015).
13 www.communityeconomies.org/home/key-ideas (accessed 05-02-2018).
14 A. Brower, 'Agri-food Activism and the Imagination of the Possible'. *New Zealand Sociology*, 28, no. 4 (2013), pp. 90–92.

imaginative utopias meet and where spatial design can play an important role by visualizing what the future of a particular space could look like. And this book is full of these kinds of imaginations: the metamorphosis of the White Elephant in Dar es Salaam (pp. 99ff.), the revival of the Mokattam Ridge (pp. 151ff.), ending the green tides of Brittany (pp. 165ff.) and cultivating the city of Porto Alegre (pp. 187ff.). All these cases have in common that only one food utopia is designed. To provoke debate and explore the pros and cons of different possible and imaginative food futures, we argued in 'Food Utopias' (pp. 211ff.) that it is important to design a variety of future options, i.e. a diversity of food utopias. To repeat the words of Carlo Ratti, this also requires a different way of working for designers as their role 'is not to provide the solution; it is to provide different possibilities for the future'.[15] The three food utopias for the Metropolitan Region of Amsterdam are an expression of this.

15 www.architonic.com/
en/story/simon-keane-
cowell-this-man-is-
seeing-things-car-
lo-ratti/7001830
(accessed 05-02-2018).

By Way of Conclusion

In and with this book we have attempted to make clear that food provisioning is an important societal issue and that the magnitude of food-related problems requires urgent action. We have also aimed to make clear that food is an interesting and challenging lens for spatial design, in particular as food is an integrative field because of its multifunctionality. Food is, as we have emphasized several times, not only about production, processing, distribution, and consumption but also about the links with domains such as energy, biodiversity, climate change, health, and waste. Designers have the skills to integrate and visualize the relations between these different domains, thereby making visible the spatial qualities of different sets of relations. This can be done by being the creative artist who develops food utopias but also by being the facilitator of a spatial transformation process, as we have seen in the case of Rosario. In collaboration with other experts, designers can, in these more participatory and interactive processes, create and consider alternative futures and propose strategies and images that my help to resolve conflicting interest of different stakeholders.

Especially when it comes to food, it is important in design processes to see and understand the social practices and cultural patterns that shape food provisioning. As Anna Fink, who undertook the challenge of transforming the empty Machinga Complex based on well-functioning people's markets in Dar es Salaam, wrote:

> At the beginning of my journey, the markets seemed like an organized chaos of work, rest and trade. After a week observations and reflection, these actions slowly became habits and finally rituals of people, who together form a place. What started as an experience of oversaturation and a blurry image became a network of relationships formed by traders. And finally these relationships appeared in space and revealed an internal logic that organically formed itself.

With this book we invite designers, planners, policymakers, academics, and professionals to act. We encourage them to see contemporary challenges through a food lens and to use food and food provisioning practices as an entry point for spatial design to address these challenges. We invite them to create change through spatial design in such a way that it supports the regeneration of our food systems and their social and physical environments, in other words, in such a way that it enables our foodscapes to flourish.

Contributors

Editors and Authors

Johannes (Han) Wiskerke (born 1967) holds a MSc in Agronomy and a PhD in Rural Sociology. Since 2004 he is chair of the Rural Sociology Group and Professor of Rural Sociology at Wageningen University (NL). From 2013 to 2016 he was also Professor of Foodscapes (part time position) at the Academy of Architecture of the Amsterdam University of the Arts. His research interests include sustainable food networks, rural-urban relations and synergies, food policy and planning, and sustainable rural and regional development. Recent projects include 'Urbanising in Place: Building the Food-Water-Energy Nexus from Below (2018–2021; http://urbanisinginplace.org/); 'Rural-Urban Outlooks: Unlocking Synergies' (2017–2021; www.rural-urban. eu); and 'Towards Sustainable Modes of Urban and Peri-Urban Food Provisioning' (2012–2015; www.supurbfood.eu). Together with the British architect Andre Viljoen he published the book *Sustainable Food Planning: Evolving Theory and Practice*, in 2012.

Saline Verhoeven (born 1968) is a landscape architect, tutor and speaker, trained at the Wageningen University and Technical University Delft. She currently works for Landschap Noord-Holland, an NGO for nature and landscape development, and teaches at the Academies of Architecture in Amsterdam and Tilburg (NL). In 2010 she won first prize in the competition 'Public space as a motor for transformation', with an innovative approach that integrated process and design. As a follow-up to this she was invited as expert in placemaking in Fukuoka, Japan. After being part of the management team of Bureau B + B urbanism and landscape architecture she shifted her focus to the landscape and the regional scale with S-coop, at the Van Eesteren chair at TU Delft and in the Foodscapes research group at the Amsterdam Academy of Architecture. Recently the work of the Van Eesteren chair was published in the book *IJsselmeergebied, een ruimtelijk perspectief* (IJsselmeer, a spatial perspective), 2018.

Jacques Abelman is Assistant Professor of Landscape Architecture at the University of Oregon. His work envisions sustainable and equitable urban futures through the lens of landscape. His research weaves spatial design, food systems, and social justice questions into the fabric of public space and infrastructure. He is active in Europe, South America, and the United States.

Laura Bracalenti is an architect, specialized in bio-environmental design. She studied Human Environmental Systems, Urban Planning, City and Environment. She is a researcher of the Research Council of the National University of Rosario, and a member of Center of Studies of the Human Environment (CEAH) of the Faculty of Architecture, Planning and Design of Rosario, Argentina.

Claire Callander (born 1994) is a recent graduate in Landscape Architecture from Edinburgh College of Art and has worked in practices in the UK and Europe. Her most recent projects have focused on Intercultural Gardens and the capacity for green space to help integrate refugee communities in the UK. Callander lives and works in London.

Joy Carey lives in Bristol (UK) and works with cities on food system change as an independent Sustainable Food Systems consultant. Joy works internationally with the RUAF Foundation and the Food and Agriculture Organization of the United Nations (FAO). She has published extensively on urban sustainability and also wrote a short film, *Local Food Roots*, 2013 (co-produced with Sprout Films).

Chloé Charreton (born 1985) is a landscape engineer and urban designer who works as a project leader at Passagers des Villes, in Lyon, France. From 2015 to 2018 she worked at marco.broekman urbanism research and architecture on projects including: FlexTest Roc, Amsterdam and Atelier Rotterdam-International Architecture Biennale Rotterdam (IABR) 2016. Chloé Charreton lives and works in Lyon, France.

Maxime Cloarec (born 1989), landscape architect, has been working at MDP, Michel Desvigne Paysagiste, since 2015 and has since then taken on the role of project director. Maxime has a particular interest in large scale strategy and its implementation through site-specific design interventions.

Nevin Cohen is a professor at the CUNY School of Public Health and Research Director of its Urban Food Policy Institute. Current research examines the food-water-energy nexus of urban agriculture and food access policies. Cohen lives in New York City.

Maria Dolores (Lola) Domínguez García (born 1971) holds a PhD from Wageningen University (NL) and is Assistant Professor at the Department of Applied Economics, Public Economics and Political Economy at the Complutense University of Madrid. Her transdisciplinary research approach includes agroecology, sociology, and economics, which she applies to the fields of agricultural economics and urban and rural development.

Marielle Dubbeling is the Director of the RUAF Foundation-Global Partnership on Sustainable Urban Agriculture and Food Systems, based in the Netherlands. Marielle's work focuses on supporting cities and subnational governments around the world in designing, implementing and monitoring multi-stakeholder urban and peri-urban agriculture and urban food systems projects, programmes, and policies.

Anna Maria Fink (born 1987) is a landscape architect who received her Master's degree at the Academy of Architecture Amsterdam and is currently working as a designer at Bureau B+B. Her research focuses on the relationship between people and place. Anna explores new landscape narratives through on-site work and printed matter.

Antoine Fourrier is a landscape architect. He graduated from the Academy of Architecture, Amsterdam, after studying at the School of Nature and Landscape Architecture (ENSP, Blois, FR). Since 2015, he has been working on urban visions and the design of inspiring public spaces, at REDscape. Antoine has worked on several heritage sites, including UNESCO and national monuments. In 2016, he worked on the Foodscape research with van Paridon x de Groot.

Pepijn Godefroy (born 1974) is a landscape architect who graduated with distinction from the University of Wageningen in 1998. In 2000, he co-founded la4sale and, together with Marieke Timmermans, is a partner at Erfgoed BV, a cooperation of architects and builders for the development of 'non-parasitic housing' in the landscape.

Paul de Graaf (born 1972) is a researcher, designer and initiator. He explores possibilities for designing the human habitat as a sustainable socio-ecological system, both independently and in self-initiated networks such as the Rotterdam Forest Garden Network. He has realised several food forests; his recent projects include 'Food Forestry in the Delta Landscape' and 'Engaging Urban Food Initiatives in Planning'.

Floris Grondman (born 1986) is a landscape architect who studied at the School of Arts, Utrecht and the Academy of Architecture, Amsterdam. His work focuses on creating adaptive landscapes through the use of innovative adaptations in response to contemporary issues. Floris currently works as a designer of public space for the municipality of Amsterdam.

Karen de Groot (born 1972) is a landscape architect and strategic designer, researching and working on urban and rural planning. She studied at the Academy of Architecture, Amsterdam and graduated together with Ruut van Paridon on the project 'Knooperven'. Together with Van Paridon she set up the design office van Paridon x de Groot landschapsarchitecten in 2007.

David Habets (born 1988) is a physicist and aspiring landscape architect who studied at the Academy of Architecture, Amsterdam. He worked as freelancer for TNO, the AMC and has been intensively involved in projects at RAAAF. His work investigates inter-scalar societal issues through spatial research, animation and architectural prototypes.

Daniel Keech (born 1967) is a senior researcher at the CCRI, University of Gloucestershire (UK). His current research interests include food and cultural geography. Keech lives in Somerset (UK).

Niké van Keulen is a landscape architect who studied at LU Wageningen (NL). She works as an associate at MTD Landscape Architects. Niké teaches at the Academies of Architecture in Amsterdam and Tilburg and has been a member of the committees for enforcing regulations regarding the external appearance of buildings in Almere and The Hague.

Kim Kool (born 1989) is a landscape architect, graduated in 2017 at the Academy of Architecture Amsterdam. In her work she uses the history and heritage of specific sites to connect people with the landscape. Kim Kool lives and works in Amsterdam.

Tim Kort (born 1987) is a landscape architect who graduated from the Academy of Architecture Amsterdam and is currently working at Bureau B+B. Tim graduated with a project that concerned the development of the peat area of Amstelland into a sustainable landscape suitable for agriculture, business and leisure. He presented this project at the Landscape Triennale and the IABR/International Architecture Biennale Rotterdam.

Jerryt Krombeen (born 1988) studied urbanism at the Academy of Architecture Amsterdam and now works as senior urban designer for the municipality of Amsterdam, as independent designer for jerryt.nl and is also a tutor at the Academy of Architecture in Amsterdam. Krombeen lives in The Hague.

Minke Mulder (born 1983) is a landscape architect MSc from Wageningen University (NL) and graduated in 2008 with a research-by-design on 'Productive Urban Landscapes: urban agriculture in post-industrial cities' (with Claire Oude Aarninkhof). Mulder has worked at MTD Landscape Architects from 2008 until 2015. Since 2015, Minke designs and details public (green) spaces at AG FREIRAUM in Freiburg im Breisgau (DE).

Ruut van Paridon (born 1970) is a landscape architect and studied at the Academy of Architecture in Amsterdam. Together with Karen de Groot he is the owner of the design office van Paridon x de Groot landschapsarchitecten. The office works on issues concerning landscape, agriculture, nature, water, sustainable energy, and climate change.

Matthew Reed (born 1970) is a sociologist who studied at the University of the West of England (Bristol) and is currently a Reader at the Countryside and Community Research Institute of the University of Gloucestershire. His work has focused on how food and technology can lead to broader social changes, a focus that has taken him from rural areas to coastal ones and now into the city.

Cecilia Rocha is a researcher at the Centre for Studies in Food Security at Ryerson University, Toronto (CA). She is the author of a number of papers and reports on food policy and programmes in Brazil, and is a member of the International Panel of Experts on Sustainable Food Systems (IPES-Food).

Lara Sibbing (born 1990) is passionate about food governance. She is a food policy advisor for the municipality of Ede (NL), which is a pioneer in local food system governance. She combines her work with her PhD research at the Public Administration and Policy group of Wageningen University. Her research focuses on the emergence of local food governance in the Netherlands.

Paul Swagemakers (born 1974) is a rural sociologist, holding a PhD in Social Sciences from Wageningen University (NL). As a researcher at the Department of Applied Economics at the University of Vigo (Spain) his interest is in urban-rural linkages, especially in farming in relation to rural development and (urban) food systems.

Marieke Timmermans (born 1956) is a landscape architect who graduated with first class honours from the Academy of Architecture Amsterdam in 1994. She co-founded la4sale in 2000, a network office for strategic and innovative research and design in the rural and urban field. From 2009–2014 she was also head of the Department of Landscape Architecture at the Academy of Architecture.

Louise E.M. Vet (born 1954) is director of the Netherlands Institute of Ecology (NIOO-KNAW) and professor in Evolutionary Ecology at Wageningen University. Vet is devoted to stimulating positive interactions between ecology and economy. She was the driving force behind NIOO's prize-winning sustainable laboratory and office complex for which she received the 2012 Golden Pyramid state prize.

Mark van Vilsteren (born 1988) is a landscape architect. He studied at the Academy of Architecture in Amsterdam (MSc), at the University of Copenhagen, and at Van Hall Larenstein in Velp (BSc). His work focuses on how particular landscapes influence and improve the livelihood of their inhabitants.

Marc Wegerif is a postdoctoral fellow researching food and land rights with the Human Economy Programme, University of Pretoria (SA). His Doctorate from Wageningen University focused on the food provisioning system of Dar es Salaam (TZ). Marc has worked on development and human rights issues in a range of organizations for 30 years.

Colophon

Editors and authors:
  Johannes S.C. Wiskerke,
  Saline Verhoeven
Contributions: Jacques Abelman,
  Laura Bracalenti, Claire
  Callander, Joy Carey, Chloé
  Charreton, Maxim Cloarec,
  Nevin Cohen, Lola Domínguez
  García, Marielle Dubbeling,
  Anna Maria Fink, Antoine
  Fourrier, Pepijn Godefroy, Paul
  de Graaf, Floris Grondman,
  Karen de Groot, David Habets,
  Daniel Keech, Niké van
  Keulen, Kim Kool, Tim Kort,
  Jerryt Krombeen, Madeleine
  Maaskant, Minke Mulder, Ruut
  van Paridon, Matthew Reed,
  Cecilia Rocha, Lara Sibbing,
  Paul Swagemakers, Marieke
  Timmermans, Louise E.M. Vet,
  Mark van Vilsteren, Marc C.A.
  Wegerif
Translation and copy-editing:
  Leo Reijnen
Proofreading: Els Brinkman
Index: Elke Stevens

Graphic design: Hans
  Gremmen
Typefaces: SFPro Text, Plantin
Paper inside: Munken Print
  White 100 g, 1.5
Paper cover: Starline
  Creamback, 250 g
Lithography: Mariska Bijl,
  Wilco Art Books
Printing: Bariet Ten Brink,
  Meppel
Co-publisher: Academy of
  Architecture, Amsterdam
Publisher: Pia Pol & Astrid
  Vorstermans, Valiz, Amsterdam

International distribution
BE/NL/LU: Centraal Boekhuis,
  www.centraal.boekhuis.nl
GB/IE: Anagram Books,
  www.anagrambooks.com
Europe/Asia: Idea Books,
  www.ideabooks.nl
USA: D.A.P.,
  www.artbook.com
Australia: Perimeter Books,
  www.perimeterbooks.com
Individual orders:
  www.valiz.nl; info@valiz.nl

This publication was made
possible through the generous
support of the Creative
Industries Fund NL.

**creative
industries
fund NL**

Academy of Architecture
Amsterdam University of the Arts

ISBN 978 94 92095 38 1
NUR 900, 648, 906
Printed and bound in the EU